THE COMPLETE GREEK TRAGEDIES

VOLUME II

SOPHOCLES

THE COMPLETE GREEK TRAGEDIES

Edited by David Grene and Richmond Lattimore

VOLUME II

SOPHOCLES

THE  UNIVERSITY OF CHICAGO PRESS
CHICAGO AND LONDON

Collector's Edition
Standard Book Number: 226-30772-7

The University of Chicago Press, Chicago 60637
The University of Chicago Press, Ltd., London

Oedipus the King
© 1942 by The University of Chicago

Oedipus at Colonus
© 1941 by Harcourt, Brace and Company

Antigone
© 1954 by The University of Chicago

Ajax, The Women of Trachis, Electra, Philoctetes
© 1957 by The University of Chicago

All rights reserved
Volume II published 1959. Third impression 1969
Printed in the United States of America

CONTENTS

INTRODUCTION

"The Theban Plays" by Sophocles

Tʜɪs series of plays, *Oedipus the King, Oedipus at Colonus,* and *Antigone,* was written over a wide interval of years. The dating is only approximate, for reliable evidence is lacking; but the *Antigone* was produced in 441 B.C. when Sophocles was probably fifty-four, and *Oedipus the King* some fourteen or fifteen years later. *Oedipus at Colonus* was apparently produced the year after its author's death at the age of ninety in 405 B.C. Thus, although the three plays are concerned with the same legend, they were not conceived and executed at the same time and with a single purpose, as is the case with Aeschylus' *Oresteia.* We can here see how a story teased the imagination of Sophocles until it found its final expression. We can see the degrees of variation in treatment he gave the myth each time he handled it. And perhaps we can come to some notion of what the myths meant to Sophocles as raw material for the theater.

The internal dramatic dates of the three plays do not agree with the order of their composition. As far as the legend is concerned, the story runs in sequence: *Oedipus the King, Oedipus at Colonus, Antigone.* But Sophocles wrote them in the order: *Antigone, Oedipus the King, Oedipus at Colonus.* In view of this and the long interval between the composition of the individual plays, we would expect some inconsistencies between the three versions. And there are fairly serious inconsistencies—in facts, for instance. At the conclusion of *Oedipus the King,* Creon is in undisputed authority after the removal of Oedipus. Though he appeals to him to look after his daughters, Oedipus refrains from asking Creon to do anything for his sons, who, he says, will be all right on their own (*OK* 1460). It is Creon who will succeed Oedipus in Thebes, and there is no question of any legitimate claim of Oedipus' descendants (*OK* 1418). But in *Antigone*, Creon tells the chorus that he has favorably observed their loyalty first to Oedipus and then to his sons, and so has hope of their devotion to himself. In *Oedipus at Colonus*—the last of the three plays he wrote—Sophocles makes one of his very few clumsy efforts to patch the discrepancies together. In *Oedipus at Colonus* (ll. 367 ff.), Ismene says that *at first* the two sons were willing to leave the throne to Creon in view of their fatal family heritage, but after a while they decided to take over the monarchy and the quarrel was only between themselves as to who should succeed. At this point Creon has vanished out of the picture altogether! Again, the responsibility for the decision to expel Oedipus from Thebes and keep him out rests, in *Oedipus the King,* entirely with Creon, who announces that he will consult Apollo in the matter. In *Oedipus at Colonus* his sons' guilt in condemning their father to exile is one of the bitterest counts in Oedipus' indictment of them (*OC* 1360 ff.). These are important differences. We do not know anything really certain about the manner of publication of the plays after their production. We know even less about Sophocles' treatment of his own scripts. Maybe he simply did not bother to keep them after he saw them as far as the stage, though that seems unlikely. Or it is possible and likelier that Sophocles, as he wrote the last play in extreme old age and in what seems to be the characteristic self-absorption of the last years of his life, cared little about whether *Oedipus at Colonus* exactly tallied, in its presentation, with the stories he had written thirty-seven and twenty-two years earlier.

Let us for the moment disregard the details of the story and concentrate on what would seem to be the central theme of the first two plays in order of composition. And here we find something very curious. Most critics have felt the significance of the *Antigone* to lie in the opposition of Creon and Antigone and all that this opposition represents. It is thus a play about something quite different from *Oedipus the King.* And yet what a remarkable similarity there is in the dilemma of Creon in *Antigone* and Oedipus himself in the first Oedipus play. In both of them a king has taken a decision which is disobeyed or questioned by his subjects. In both, the ruler misconstrues the role of the rebel and his own as a sovereign. In both, he has a crucial encounter with the priest Teiresias, who warns him that the forces of religion are against him. In both, he charges that the priest has been suborned. There the resemblance ends; for, after abusing the old prophet, Creon is overcome with fear of his authority and, too late, tries to undo his mistake. In *Oedipus the King* the king defies all assaults upon his decision until the deadly self-knowledge which starts to work in him has accomplished its course and he is convicted out of his own mouth.

Usually, as we know, the *Antigone* is interpreted entirely as the conflict between Creon and Antigone. It has often been regarded as the classical statement of the struggle between the law of the individual conscience and the central power of the state. Unquestionably, these issues are inherent in the play. Unquestionably, even, Sophocles would understand the modern way of seeing his play, for the issue of the opposition of the individual and the state was sufficiently present to his mind to make this significant for him. But can the parallelism between the position of Oedipus in the one play and Creon in the other be quite irrelevant to the interpretation of the two? And is it not very striking that such a large share of the *Antigone* should be devoted to the conclusion of the conflict, as far as Creon is concerned, and to the destruction of his human happiness?

What I would suggest is this: that Sophocles had at the time of writing the first play (in 442 B.C.) a theme in mind which centered in the Theban trilogy. One might express it by saying that it is the story of a ruler who makes a mistaken decision, though in good faith, and who then finds himself opposed in a fashion which he misunderstands and which induces him to persist in his mistake. This story is later on going to be that of a man who breaks divine law without realizing that he is doing so, and whose destruction is then brought about by the voice of the divine law in society. Between the *Antigone* and *Oedipus the King,* the theme has developed further, for in the latter play Sophocles is showing how the ruler who breaks the divine law may, for all he can see and understand, be entirely innocent, but nonetheless his guilt is an objective fact. In the third play, *Oedipus at Colonus,* this issue reaches its final statement. The old Oedipus is admittedly a kind of monster. Wherever he comes, people shrink from him. Yet his guilt carries with it some sort of innocence on which God will set his seal. For the old man is both cursed and blessed. The god gives him an extraordinary end, and the last place of his mortal habitation is blessed forever.

What this interpretation would mean, if correct, is that Sophocles started to write about the Theban legend, the story of Oedipus and his children, without having fully understood what he wanted to say about it. He may have been, and probably was, drawn, unknown to himself, to the dramatization of this particular legend because in it lay the material of the greatest theme of his later artistic life. But first he tried his hand at it in the opposition of Creon and Antigone. However, even while he did this, the character of Creon and his role in the play were shaping what was to be the decisive turn in the story he was going to write—the Oedipus saga.

Thus there is a certain elasticity in the entire treatment of myth. The author will accent a certain character at one time to suit a play and change the accent to suit another. Or he may even discover the same theme in a different myth. This is suggested by a short comparison of the *Philoctetes* and *Oedipus at Colonus,* both written in the last few years of Sophocles' life. The figure of Philoctetes, though occurring in a totally different legend from Oedipus, is a twin child with Oedipus in Sophocles' dramatic imagination. In both these plays, the *Philoctetes* and *Oedipus at Colonus,* the hero is a man whose value is inextricably coupled with his offensive quality. Philoctetes is the archer whose bow will overcome Troy. He is also the creature whose stinking infested wound moves everyone to disgust who has to do with him. Oedipus is accursed in the sight of all men; he had committed the two crimes, parricide and incest, which rendered him an outcast in any human society. But he is also the one to whom, at his end, God will give the marks of his favor, and the place where he is last seen on earth will be lucky and blessed. This combination of the evil and the good is too marked, in these two plays, to be accidental. It is surely the idea which inspired the old Sophocles for his two last plays. There is, however, an important further development of the theme in the *Oedipus at Colonus.* For there in Oedipus' mind the rational innocence—the fact that he had committed the offenses unknowingly—is, for him at least, important in God's final justification of him. Sophocles is declaring that the sin of Oedipus is real; that the consequences in the form of the loneliness, neglect, and suffering of the years of wandering are inevitable; but that the will and the consciousness are also some measure of man's sin—and when the sinner sinned necessarily and unwittingly, his suffering can be compensation enough for his guilt. He may at the end be blessed and a blessing. This is not the same doctrine as that of Aeschylus, when he asserts that through suffering comes wisdom. Nor is it the Christian doctrine of a man purified by suffering as by fire. Oedipus in his contact with Creon, in his interview with Polyneices shows himself as bitter, sudden in anger, and implacable as ever. He is indeed a monstrous old man. But at the last, he is, in a measure, *vindicated*. Yet in *Philoctetes* the theme of the union of the offensive and the beneficial, which in *Oedipus at Colonus* becomes the curse and the blessing, is seen without the addition of conscious innocence and unconscious guilt. Can we say that Sophocles finally felt that the consciousness of innocence in Oedipus is the balancing factor in the story? That in this sense *Oedipus at Colonus* is the further step beyond *Philoctetes* in the clarification of the dramatic subject which occupied the very old author? Or that the consciousness of innocence when linked with objective guilt is only the human shield against the cruelty of the irrational—that Oedipus is meaningful in his combination of guilt and innocence as a manifestation of God and of destiny and that his explanation of his conscious innocence is only the poor human inadequate explanation? Everyone will answer this according to his own choice. But, clearly, the theme of Philoctetes and the theme of the old Oedipus are connected.

If an analysis such as this has importance, it is to show the relation of Sophocles to the raw material of his plays—the myth. It is to show the maturing of a theme in Sophocles' mind and his successive treatments of it in the same and different legends. In the Oedipus story it is a certain fundamental situation which becomes significant for Sophocles, and the characters are altered to suit the story. Creon in the first, Oedipus in the second, are examples of the same sort of dilemma, even though the dilemma of Creon in the *Antigone* is incidental to the main emphasis of the play, which is on Antigone. But the dilemma was to be much more fruitful for Sophocles as a writer and thinker than the plain issue between Antigone and Creon. The dilemma resolves itself in the last play at the end of Sophocles' life into the dramatic statement of a principle, of the union of the blessed and the cursed, of the just and the unjust, and sometimes (not always) of the consciously innocent and the unconsciously guilty. The fact that Sophocles could in two successive treatments of the play fifteen years apart switch the parts of Creon and Oedipus indicates that neither the moral color of the characters nor even their identity was absolutely fixed in his mind. The same conclusion is borne out by the great similarity between the *Philoctetes* and the *Oedipus at Colonus*. Sophocles in his last days was incessantly thinking of the man who is blessed and cursed. For the theater he became once the lame castaway Philoctetes, who yet, in virtue of his archery, is to be the conqueror of Troy; in the next play he is Oedipus, who sinned against the order of human society but is still to be the blessing of Athens and the patron saint of Colonus. It is the theme and not the man that matters. Consequently, it is the kernel of the legend, as he saw it for the moment, that is sacred for Sophocles, not the identification of all the characters in a certain relation to one another. True, he has treated the Oedipus story three times in his life, which means that the Oedipus story had a certain fascination for him—that somehow hidden in it he knew there was what he wanted to say. But he did not have to think of the whole story and the interdependence of its characters when he made his changes each time. One stage of the theme borne by the hero is given to a character in a totally different myth. The sequence is Creon, Oedipus, Philoctetes, Oedipus. It may seem absurd to link Creon, the obvious form of tyrant (as conceived by the Athenians), and Philoctetes. But it is the progression we should notice. The tyrant who with true and good intentions orders what is wrong, morally and religiously, is crudely represented in Creon; he is much more subtly represented in Oedipus himself in the next play. But the similarity of the situation and the nature of the opposition to him proves how generically the character is conceived. You can switch the labels, and Creon becomes Oedipus. But if the character is generic, the situation is deepening. We are beginning to understand *why* a certain sort of tyrant may be a tyrant and in a shadowy way how conscious and unconscious guilt are related. In the *Philoctetes* and *Oedipus at Colonus* the situation is being seen in its last stages. We are no longer concerned with how Philoctetes came to sin or how Oedipus is the author of his own ruin. But only how does it feel to be an object both of disgust and of fear to your fellows, while you yourself are simultaneously aware of the injustice of your treatment and at last, in *Oedipus at Colonus,* of the objective proofs of God's favor.

For Sophocles the myth was the treatment of the generic aspect of human dilemmas. What he made of the myth in his plays was neither history nor the kind of dramatic creation represented by *Hamlet* or *Macbeth.* Not history, for in no sense is the uniqueness of the event or the uniqueness of the character important; not drama in the Shakespearean sense, because Sophocles' figures do not have, as Shakespeare's do, the timeless and complete reality in themselves. Behind the figure of Oedipus or Creon stands the tyrant of the legend; and behind the tyrant of the legend, the meaning of all despotic authority. Behind the old Oedipus is the beggar and wanderer of the legend, and behind him the mysterious human combination of opposites—opposites in meaning and in fact. And so the character may fluctuate or the names may vary. It is the theme, the generic side of tragedy, which is important; it is there that the emphasis of the play rests.

DAVID GRENE

UNIVERSITY OF CHICAGO

OEDIPUS
THE
KING

Translated by

DAVID GRENE

CHARACTERS

Oedipus, King of Thebes

Jocasta, His Wife

Creon, His Brother-in-Law

Teiresias, an Old Blind Prophet

A Priest

First Messenger

Second Messenger

A Herdsman

A Chorus of Old Men of Thebes

OEDIPUS THE KING

Scene: *In front of the palace of Oedipus at Thebes. To the right of the stage near the altar stands the Priest with a crowd of children. Oedipus emerges from the central door.*

Oedipus

    Children, young sons and daughters of old Cadmus,
    why do you sit here with your suppliant crowns?
    The town is heavy with a mingled burden
    of sounds and smells, of groans and hymns and incense;   5
    I did not think it fit that I should hear
    of this from messengers but came myself,—
    I Oedipus whom all men call the Great.

                                  (*He turns to the Priest.*)

    You're old and they are young; come, speak for them.
    What do you fear or want, that you sit here   10
    suppliant? Indeed I'm willing to give all
    that you may need; I would be very hard
    should I not pity suppliants like these.

Priest

    O ruler of my country, Oedipus,
    you see our company around the altar;   15
    you see our ages; some of us, like these,
    who cannot yet fly far, and some of us
    heavy with age; these children are the chosen
    among the young, and I the priest of Zeus.
    Within the market place sit others crowned   20
    with suppliant garlands, at the double shrine
    of Pallas and the temple where Ismenus
    gives oracles by fire. King, you yourself
    have seen our city reeling like a wreck
    already; it can scarcely lift its prow
    out of the depths, out of the bloody surf.

A blight is on the fruitful plants of the earth,   25
A blight is on the cattle in the fields,
a blight is on our women that no children
are born to them; a God that carries fire,
a deadly pestilence, is on our town,
strikes us and spares not, and the house of Cadmus
is emptied of its people while black Death
grows rich in groaning and in lamentation.   30
We have not come as suppliants to this altar
because we thought of you as of a God,
but rather judging you the first of men
in all the chances of this life and when
we mortals have to do with more than man.
You came and by your coming saved our city,   35
freed us from tribute which we paid of old
to the Sphinx, cruel singer. This you did
in virtue of no knowledge we could give you,
in virtue of no teaching; it was God
that aided you, men say, and you are held
with God's assistance to have saved our lives.
Now Oedipus, Greatest in all men's eyes,   40
here falling at your feet we all entreat you,
find us some strength for rescue.
Perhaps you'll hear a wise word from some God,
perhaps you will learn something from a man
(for I have seen that for the skilled of practice
the outcome of their counsels live the most).   45
Noblest of men, go, and raise up our city,
go,—and give heed. For now this land of ours
calls you its savior since you saved it once.
So, let us never speak about your reign
as of a time when first our feet were set
secure on high, but later fell to ruin.   50
Raise up our city, save it and raise it up.
Once you have brought us luck with happy omen;
be no less now in fortune.

If you will rule this land, as now you rule it,
better to rule it full of men than empty.   55
For neither tower nor ship is anything
when empty, and none live in it together.

Oedipus

I pity you, children. You have come full of longing,
but I have known the story before you told it
only too well. I know you are all sick,
yet there is not one of you, sick though you are,   60
that is as sick as I myself.
Your several sorrows each have single scope
and touch but one of you. My spirit groans
for city and myself and you at once.
You have not roused me like a man from sleep;   65
know that I have given many tears to this,
gone many ways wandering in thought,
but as I thought I found only one remedy
and that I took. I sent Menoeceus' son
Creon, Jocasta's brother, to Apollo,   70
to his Pythian temple,
that he might learn there by what act or word
I could save this city. As I count the days,
it vexes me what ails him; he is gone
far longer than he needed for the journey.   75
But when he comes, then, may I prove a villain,
if I shall not do all the God commands.

Priest

Thanks for your gracious words. Your servants here
signal that Creon is this moment coming.

Oedipus

His face is bright. O holy Lord Apollo,   80
grant that his news too may be bright for us
and bring us safety.

Priest

    It is happy news,
    I think, for else his head would not be crowned
    with sprigs of fruitful laurel.

Oedipus

                We will know soon,
    he's within hail. Lord Creon, my good brother,   85
    what is the word you bring us from the God?

                                  (Creon enters.)

Creon

    A good word,—for things hard to bear themselves
    if in the final issue all is well
    I count complete good fortune.

Oedipus

                What do you mean?
    What you have said so far
    leaves me uncertain whether to trust or fear.   90

Creon

    If you will hear my news before these others
    I am ready to speak, or else to go within.

Oedipus

    Speak it to all;
    the grief I bear, I bear it more for these
    than for my own heart.

Creon

                I will tell you, then,   95
    what I heard from the God.
    King Phoebus in plain words commanded us
    to drive out a pollution from our land,
    pollution grown ingrained within the land;
    drive it out, said the God, not cherish it,
    till it's past cure.

Oedipus

                What is the rite
    of purification? How shall it be done?

Creon

By banishing a man, or expiation   100
of blood by blood, since it is murder guilt
which holds our city in this destroying storm.

Oedipus

Who is this man whose fate the God pronounces?

Creon

My Lord, before you piloted the state
we had a king called Laius.

Oedipus

I know of him by hearsay. I have not seen him.   105

Creon

The God commanded clearly: let some one
punish with force this dead man's murderers.

Oedipus

Where are they in the world? Where would a trace
of this old crime be found? It would be hard
to guess where.

Creon

                              The clue is in this land;   110
that which is sought is found;
the unheeded thing escapes:
so said the God.

Oedipus

                              Was it at home,
or in the country that death came upon him,
or in another country travelling?

Creon

He went, he said himself, upon an embassy,
but never returned when he set out from home.   115

Oedipus

Was there no messenger, no fellow traveller
who knew what happened? Such a one might tell
something of use.

Creon

> They were all killed save one. He fled in terror
> and he could tell us nothing in clear terms
> of what he knew, nothing, but one thing only.

Oedipus

> What was it?   120
> If we could even find a slim beginning
> in which to hope, we might discover much.

Creon

> This man said that the robbers they encountered
> were many and the hands that did the murder
> were many; it was no man's single power.

Oedipus

> How could a robber dare a deed like this
> were he not helped with money from the city,
> money and treachery?   125

Creon

>   That indeed was thought.
> But Laius was dead and in our trouble
> there was none to help.

Oedipus

> What trouble was so great to hinder you
> inquiring out the murder of your king?

Creon

> The riddling Sphinx induced us to neglect   130
> mysterious crimes and rather seek solution
> of troubles at our feet.

Oedipus

> I will bring this to light again. King Phoebus
> fittingly took this care about the dead,
> and you too fittingly.
> And justly you will see in me an ally,   135
> a champion of my country and the God.
> For when I drive pollution from the land

I will not serve a distant friend's advantage,
but act in my own interest. Whoever
he was that killed the king may readily
wish to dispatch me with his murderous hand;   140
so helping the dead king I help myself.

Come, children, take your suppliant boughs and go;
up from the altars now. Call the assembly
and let it meet upon the understanding
that I'll do everything. God will decide   145
whether we prosper or remain in sorrow.

Priest

Rise, children—it was this we came to seek,
which of himself the king now offers us.
May Phoebus who gave us the oracle
come to our rescue and stay the plague.   150

               (*Exeunt all but the Chorus.*)

Chorus

  Strophe

What is the sweet spoken word of God from the shrine of Pytho
    rich in gold
that has come to glorious Thebes?
I am stretched on the rack of doubt, and terror and trembling
    hold
my heart, O Delian Healer, and I worship full of fears
for what doom you will bring to pass, new or renewed in the   155
    revolving years.
Speak to me, immortal voice,
child of golden Hope.

  Antistrophe

First I call on you, Athene, deathless daughter of Zeus,
and Artemis, Earth Upholder,   160
who sits in the midst of the market place in the throne which
    men call Fame,
and Phoebus, the Far Shooter, three averters of Fate,

come to us now, if ever before, when ruin rushed upon the state,   165
you drove destruction's flame away
out of our land.

Strophe
Our sorrows defy number;
all the ship's timbers are rotten;
taking of thought is no spear for the driving away of the plague.   170
There are no growing children in this famous land;
there are no women bearing the pangs of childbirth.
You may see them one with another, like birds swift on the
   wing,   175
quicker than fire unmastered,
speeding away to the coast of the Western God.

Antistrophe
In the unnumbered deaths
of its people the city dies;
those children that are born lie dead on the naked earth
unpitied, spreading contagion of death; and grey haired mothers
   and wives
everywhere stand at the altar's edge, suppliant, moaning;   182–85
the hymn to the healing God rings out but with it the wailing
   voices are blended.
From these our sufferings grant us, O golden Daughter of Zeus,
glad-faced deliverance.

Strophe
There is no clash of brazen shields but our fight is with the War
   God,
a War God ringed with the cries of men, a savage God who burns   191
   us;
grant that he turn in racing course backwards out of our country's bounds
to the great palace of Amphitrite or where the waves of the   195
   Thracian sea
deny the stranger safe anchorage.
Whatsoever escapes the night

at last the light of day revisits;
so smite the War God, Father Zeus,
beneath your thunderbolt,
for you are the Lord of the lightning, the lightning that
    carries fire.   200

Antistrophe
And your unconquered arrow shafts, winged by the golden
    corded bow,
Lycean King, I beg to be at our side for help;   205
and the gleaming torches of Artemis with which she scours the
    Lycean hills,
and I call on the God with the turban of gold, who gave his name
    to this country of ours,   210
the Bacchic God with the wind flushed face,
Evian One, who travel
with the Maenad company,
combat the God that burns us
with your torch of pine;
for the God that is our enemy is a God unhonoured among the   215
    Gods.
                                      (*Oedipus returns.*)

Oedipus
For what you ask me—if you will hear my words,
and hearing welcome them and fight the plague,
you will find strength and lightening of your load.

Hark to me; what I say to you, I say
as one that is a stranger to the story
as stranger to the deed. For I would not   220
be far upon the track if I alone
were tracing it without a clue. But now,
since after all was finished, I became
a citizen among you, citizens—
now I proclaim to all the men of Thebes:
who so among you knows the murderer   225
by whose hand Laius, son of Labdacus,

died—I command him to tell everything
to me,—yes, though he fears himself to take the blame
on his own head; for bitter punishment
he shall have none, but leave this land unharmed.
Or if he knows the murderer, another,   230
a foreigner, still let him speak the truth.
For I will pay him and be grateful, too.
But if you shall keep silence, if perhaps
some one of you, to shield a guilty friend,
or for his own sake shall reject my words—
hear what I shall do then: 235
I forbid that man, whoever he be, my land,
my land where I hold sovereignty and throne;
and I forbid any to welcome him
or cry him greeting or make him a sharer   240
in sacrifice or offering to the Gods,
or give him water for his hands to wash.
I command all to drive him from their homes,
since he is our pollution, as the oracle
of Pytho's God proclaimed him now to me.
So I stand forth a champion of the God
and of the man who died.   245
Upon the murderer I invoke this curse—
whether he is one man and all unknown,
or one of many—may he wear out his life
in misery to miserable doom!
If with my knowledge he lives at my hearth   250
I pray that I myself may feel my curse.
On you I lay my charge to fulfill all this
for me, for the God, and for this land of ours
destroyed and blighted, by the God forsaken.

Even were this no matter of God's ordinance   255
it would not fit you so to leave it lie,
unpurified, since a good man is dead
and one that was a king. Search it out.

Since I am now the holder of his office,
and have his bed and wife that once was his, 260
and had his line not been unfortunate
we would have common children—(fortune leaped
upon his head)—because of all these things,
I fight in his defence as for my father,
and I shall try all means to take the murderer 265
of Laius the son of Labdacus
the son of Polydorus and before him
of Cadmus and before him of Agenor.
Those who do not obey me, may the Gods
grant no crops springing from the ground they plough 270
nor children to their women! May a fate
like this, or one still worse than this consume them!
For you whom these words please, the other Thebans,
may Justice as your ally and all the Gods
live with you, blessing you now and for ever! 275

Chorus

As you have held me to my oath, I speak:
I neither killed the king nor can declare
the killer; but since Phoebus set the quest
it is his part to tell who the man is.

Oedipus

Right; but to put compulsion on the Gods 280
against their will—no man can do that.

Chorus

May I then say what I think second best?

Oedipus

If there's a third best, too, spare not to tell it.

Chorus

I know that what the Lord Teiresias
sees, is most often what the Lord Apollo 285
sees. If you should inquire of this from him
you might find out most clearly.

Oedipus

Even in this my actions have not been sluggard.
On Creon's word I have sent two messengers
and why the prophet is not here already
I have been wondering.

Chorus

His skill apart   290
there is besides only an old faint story.

Oedipus

What is it?
I look at every story.

Chorus

It was said
that he was killed by certain wayfarers.

Oedipus

I heard that, too, but no one saw the killer.

Chorus

Yet if he has a share of fear at all,
his courage will not stand firm, hearing your curse.   295

Oedipus

The man who in the doing did not shrink
will fear no word.

Chorus

Here comes his prosecutor:
led by your men the godly prophet comes
in whom alone of mankind truth is native.

(Enter Teiresias, led by a little boy.)

Oedipus

Teiresias, you are versed in everything,   300
things teachable and things not to be spoken,
things of the heaven and earth-creeping things.
You have no eyes but in your mind you know
with what a plague our city is afflicted.
My lord, in you alone we find a champion,

in you alone one that can rescue us.
Perhaps you have not heard the messengers,   305
but Phoebus sent in answer to our sending
an oracle declaring that our freedom
from this disease would only come when we
should learn the names of those who killed King Laius,
and kill them or expel from our country.
Do not begrudge us oracles from birds,   310
or any other way of prophecy
within your skill; save yourself and the city,
save me; redeem the debt of our pollution
that lies on us because of this dead man.
We are in your hands; pains are most nobly taken
to help another when you have means and power.   315

Teiresias
Alas, how terrible is wisdom when
it brings no profit to the man that's wise!
This I knew well, but had forgotten it,
else I would not have come here.

Oedipus
                  What is this?
How sad you are now you have come!

Teiresias
               Let me
go home. It will be easiest for us both   320
to bear our several destinies to the end
if you will follow my advice.

Oedipus
              You'd rob us
of this your gift of prophecy? You talk
as one who had no care for law nor love
for Thebes who reared you.

Teiresias
Yes, but I see that even your own words
miss the mark; therefore I must fear for mine.   325

Oedipus

For God's sake if you know of anything,
do not turn from us; all of us kneel to you,
all of us here, your suppliants.

Teiresias

All of you here know nothing. I will not
bring to the light of day my troubles, mine—
rather than call them yours.

Oedipus

What do you mean?
You know of something but refuse to speak.   330
Would you betray us and destroy the city?

Teiresias

I will not bring this pain upon us both,
neither on you nor on myself. Why is it
you question me and waste your labour? I
will tell you nothing.

Oedipus

You would provoke a stone! Tell us, you villain,   335
tell us, and do not stand there quietly
unmoved and balking at the issue.

Teiresias

You blame my temper but you do not see
your own that lives within you; it is me
you chide.

Oedipus

Who would not feel his temper rise
at words like these with which you shame our city?   340

Teiresias

Of themselves things will come, although I hide them
and breathe no word of them.

Oedipus

Since they will come
tell them to me.

Teiresias
                              I will say nothing further.
   Against this answer let your temper rage
   as wildly as you will.

Oedipus
                              Indeed I am   345
   so angry I shall not hold back a jot
   of what I think. For I would have you know
   I think you were complotter of the deed
   and doer of the deed save in so far
   as for the actual killing. Had you had eyes
   I would have said alone you murdered him.

Teiresias
   Yes? Then I warn you faithfully to keep   350
   the letter of your proclamation and
   from this day forth to speak no word of greeting
   to these nor me; you are the land's pollution.

Oedipus
   How shamelessly you started up this taunt!
   How do you think you will escape?   355

Teiresias
                              I have.
   I have escaped; the truth is what I cherish
   and that's my strength.

Oedipus
                              And who has taught you truth?
   Not your profession surely!

Teiresias
                              You have taught me,
   for you have made me speak against my will.

Oedipus
   Speak what? Tell me again that I may learn it better.

Teiresias
   Did you not understand before or would you
   provoke me into speaking?   360

Oedipus
                    I did not grasp it,
    not so to call it known. Say it again.

Teiresias
    I say you are the murderer of the king
    whose murderer you seek.

Oedipus
                    Not twice you shall
    say calumnies like this and stay unpunished.

Teiresias
    Shall I say more to tempt your anger more?

Oedipus
    As much as you desire; it will be said   365
    in vain.

Teiresias
                    I say that with those you love best
    you live in foulest shame unconsciously
    and do not see where you are in calamity.

Oedipus
    Do you imagine you can always talk
    like this, and live to laugh at it hereafter?

Teiresias
    Yes, if the truth has anything of strength.

Oedipus
    It has, but not for you; it has no strength   370
    for you because you are blind in mind and ears
    as well as in your eyes.

Teiresias
                    You are a poor wretch
    to taunt me with the very insults which
    every one soon will heap upon yourself.

Oedipus
    Your life is one long night so that you cannot
    hurt me or any other who sees the light.   375

Teiresias
> It is not fate that I should be your ruin,
> Apollo is enough; it is his care
> to work this out.

Oedipus
>   Was this your own design
>   or Creon's?

Teiresias
>   Creon is no hurt to you,
>   but you are to yourself.

Oedipus
> Wealth, sovereignty and skill outmatching skill   380
> for the contrivance of an envied life!
> Great store of jealousy fill your treasury chests,
> if my friend Creon, friend from the first and loyal,   385
> thus secretly attacks me, secretly
> desires to drive me out and secretly
> suborns this juggling, trick devising quack,
> this wily beggar who has only eyes
> for his own gains, but blindness in his skill.
> For, tell me, where have you seen clear, Teiresias,   390
> with your prophetic eyes? When the dark singer,
> the sphinx, was in your country, did you speak
> word of deliverance to its citizens?
> And yet the riddle's answer was not the province
> of a chance comer. It was a prophet's task
> and plainly you had no such gift of prophecy   395
> from birds nor otherwise from any God
> to glean a word of knowledge. But I came,
> Oedipus, who knew nothing, and I stopped her.
> I solved the riddle by my wit alone.
> Mine was no knowledge got from birds. And now
> you would expel me,
> because you think that you will find a place   400
> by Creon's throne. I think you will be sorry,

both you and your accomplice, for your plot
to drive me out. And did I not regard you
as an old man, some suffering would have taught you
that what was in your heart was treason.

Chorus

We look at this man's words and yours, my king,
and we find both have spoken them in anger.   405
We need no angry words but only thought
how we may best hit the God's meaning for us.

Teiresias

If you are king, at least I have the right
no less to speak in my defence against you.
Of that much I am master. I am no slave   410
of yours, but Loxias', and so I shall not
enroll myself with Creon for my patron.
Since you have taunted me with being blind,
here is my word for you.
You have your eyes but see not where you are
in sin, nor where you live, nor whom you live with.
Do you know who your parents are? Unknowing   415
you are an enemy to kith and kin
in death, beneath the earth, and in this life.
A deadly footed, double striking curse,
from father and mother both, shall drive you forth
out of this land, with darkness on your eyes,
that now have such straight vision. Shall there be
a place will not be harbour to your cries,   420
a corner of Cithaeron will not ring
in echo to your cries, soon, soon,—
when you shall learn the secret of your marriage,
which steered you to a haven in this house,—
haven no haven, after lucky voyage?
And of the multitude of other evils
establishing a grim equality
between you and your children, you know nothing.   425

So, muddy with contempt my words and Creon's!
Misery shall grind no man as it will you.

Oedipus

Is it endurable that I should hear
such words from him? Go and a curse go with you!   430
Quick, home with you! Out of my house at once!

Teiresias

I would not have come either had you not called me.

Oedipus

I did not know then you would talk like a fool—
or it would have been long before I called you.

Teiresias

I am a fool then, as it seems to you—   435
but to the parents who have bred you, wise.

Oedipus

What parents? Stop! Who are they of all the world?

Teiresias

This day will show your birth and will destroy you.

Oedipus

How needlessly your riddles darken everything.

Teiresias

But it's in riddle answering you are strongest.   440

Oedipus

Yes. Taunt me where you will find me great.

Teiresias

It is this very luck that has destroyed you.

Oedipus

I do not care, if it has saved this city.

Teiresias

Well, I will go. Come, boy, lead me away.

Oedipus

Yes, lead him off. So long as you are here,   445

you'll be a stumbling block and a vexation;
once gone, you will not trouble me again.

Teiresias

I have said
what I came here to say not fearing your
countenance: there is no way you can hurt me.
I tell you, king, this man, this murderer
(whom you have long declared you are in search of,
indicting him in threatening proclamation   450
as murderer of Laius)—he is here.
In name he is a stranger among citizens
but soon he will be shown to be a citizen
true native Theban, and he'll have no joy
of the discovery: blindness for sight
and beggary for riches his exchange,   455
he shall go journeying to a foreign country
tapping his way before him with a stick.
He shall be proved father and brother both
to his own children in his house; to her
that gave him birth, a son and husband both;
a fellow sower in his father's bed
with that same father that he murdered.
Go within, reckon that out, and if you find me   460
mistaken, say I have no skill in prophecy.

(*Exeunt separately Teiresias and Oedipus.*)

Chorus

Strophe
Who is the man proclaimed
by Delphi's prophetic rock
as the bloody handed murderer,   465
the doer of deeds that none dare name?
Now is the time for him to run
with a stronger foot
than Pegasus
for the child of Zeus leaps in arms upon him   470
with fire and the lightning bolt,

and terribly close on his heels
are the Fates that never miss.

Antistrophe
Lately from snowy Parnassus
clearly the voice flashed forth,
bidding each Theban track him down,   475
the unknown murderer.
In the savage forests he lurks and in
the caverns like
the mountain bull.
He is sad and lonely, and lonely his feet
that carry him far from the navel of earth;   480
but its prophecies, ever living,
flutter around his head.

Strophe
The augur has spread confusion,
terrible confusion;
I do not approve what was said   485
nor can I deny it.
I do not know what to say;
I am in a flutter of foreboding;
I never heard in the present
nor past of a quarrel between   490
the sons of Labdacus and Polybus,
that I might bring as proof
in attacking the popular fame
of Oedipus, seeking
to take vengeance for undiscovered
death in the line of Labdacus.   495

Antistrophe
Truly Zeus and Apollo are wise
and in human things all knowing;
but amongst men there is no   500
distinct judgment, between the prophet
and me—which of us is right.

One man may pass another in wisdom
but I would never agree
with those that find fault with the king
till I should see the word
proved right beyond doubt. For once
in visible form the Sphinx
came on him and all of us
saw his wisdom and in that test
he saved the city. So he will not be condemned by my mind.   512

(*Enter Creon.*)

Creon

Citizens, I have come because I heard
deadly words spread about me, that the king
accuses me. I cannot take that from him.
If he believes that in these present troubles   515
he has been wronged by me in word or deed
I do not want to live on with the burden
of such a scandal on me. The report   520
injures me doubly and most vitally—
for I'll be called a traitor to my city
and traitor also to my friends and you.

Chorus

Perhaps it was a sudden gust of anger
that forced that insult from him, and no judgment.

Creon

But did he say that it was in compliance   525
with schemes of mine that the seer told him lies?

Chorus

Yes, he said that, but why, I do not know.

Creon

Were his eyes straight in his head? Was his mind right
when he accused me in this fashion?

Chorus

I do not know; I have no eyes to see   530
what princes do. Here comes the king himself.

(*Enter Oedipus.*)

Oedipus

You, sir, how is it you come here? Have you so much
brazen-faced daring that you venture in
my house although you are proved manifestly
the murderer of that man, and though you tried,
openly, highway robbery of my crown?   535
For God's sake, tell me what you saw in me,
what cowardice or what stupidity,
that made you lay a plot like this against me?
Did you imagine I should not observe
the crafty scheme that stole upon me or   540
seeing it, take no means to counter it?
Was it not stupid of you to make the attempt,
to try to hunt down royal power without
the people at your back or friends? For only
with the people at your back or money can
the hunt end in the capture of a crown.

Creon

Do you know what you're doing? Will you listen
to words to answer yours, and then pass judgment?

Oedipus

You're quick to speak, but I am slow to grasp you,   545
for I have found you dangerous,—and my foe.

Creon

First of all hear what I shall say to that.

Oedipus

At least don't tell me that you are not guilty.

Creon

If you think obstinacy without wisdom
a valuable possession, you are wrong.   550

Oedipus

And you are wrong if you believe that one,
a criminal, will not be punished only
because he is my kinsman.

Creon

                          This is but just—
  but tell me, then, of what offense I'm guilty?

Oedipus

  Did you or did you not urge me to send   555
  to this prophetic mumbler?

Creon

                          I did indeed,
  and I shall stand by what I told you.

Oedipus

  How long ago is it since Laius. . . .

Creon

  What about Laius? I don't understand.

Oedipus

  Vanished—died—was murdered?   560

Creon

                          It is long,
  a long, long time to reckon.

Oedipus

                          Was this prophet
  in the profession then?

Creon

                          He was, and honoured
  as highly as he is today.

Oedipus

  At that time did he say a word about me?

Creon

  Never, at least when I was near him.   565

Oedipus

  You never made a search for the dead man?

Creon

  We searched, indeed, but never learned of anything.

Oedipus

  Why did our wise old friend not say this then?

Creon

I don't know; and when I know nothing, I
usually hold my tongue.

Oedipus

You know this much,   570

and can declare this much if you are loyal.

Creon

What is it? If I know, I'll not deny it.

Oedipus

That he would not have said that I killed Laius
had he not met you first.

Creon

You know yourself

whether he said this, but I demand that I   575

should hear as much from you as you from me.

Oedipus

Then hear,—I'll not be proved a murderer.

Creon

Well, then. You're married to my sister.

Oedipus

Yes,

that I am not disposed to deny.

Creon

You rule

this country giving her an equal share
in the government?

Oedipus

Yes, everything she wants   580

she has from me.

Creon

And I, as thirdsman to you,

am rated as the equal of you two?

Oedipus

Yes, and it's there you've proved yourself false friend.

Creon

Not if you will reflect on it as I do.
Consider, first, if you think any one
would choose to rule and fear rather than rule 585
and sleep untroubled by a fear if power
were equal in both cases. I, at least,
I was not born with such a frantic yearning
to be a king—but to do what kings do.
And so it is with every one who has learned
wisdom and self-control. As it stands now,
the prizes are all mine—and without fear. 590
But if I were the king myself, I must
do much that went against the grain.
How should despotic rule seem sweeter to me
than painless power and an assured authority?
I am not so besotted yet that I
want other honours than those that come with profit. 595
Now every man's my pleasure; every man greets me;
now those who are your suitors fawn on me,—
success for them depends upon my favour.
Why should I let all this go to win that?
My mind would not be traitor if it's wise; 600
I am no treason lover, of my nature,
nor would I ever dare to join a plot.
Prove what I say. Go to the oracle
at Pytho and inquire about the answers,
if they are as I told you. For the rest, 605
if you discover I laid any plot
together with the seer, kill me, I say,
not only by your vote but by my own.
But do not charge me on obscure opinion
without some proof to back it. It's not just
lightly to count your knaves as honest men, 610
nor honest men as knaves. To throw away
an honest friend is, as it were, to throw
your life away, which a man loves the best.

In time you will know all with certainty;
time is the only test of honest men,
one day is space enough to know a rogue.   615

Chorus

His words are wise, king, if one fears to fall.
Those who are quick of temper are not safe.

Oedipus

When he that plots against me secretly
moves quickly, I must quickly counterplot.
If I wait taking no decisive measure   620
his business will be done, and mine be spoiled.

Creon

What do you want to do then? Banish me?

Oedipus

No, certainly; kill you, not banish you.[1]

Creon

I do not think that you've your wits about you.   626

Oedipus

For my own interests, yes.

Creon
                              But for mine, too,
you should think equally.

Oedipus
                              You are a rogue.

Creon

Suppose you do not understand?

Oedipus
                              But yet
I must be ruler.

1. Two lines omitted here owing to the confusion in the dialogue consequent on
the loss of a third line. The lines as they stand in Jebb's edition (1902) are:
Oed.: That you may show what manner of thing is envy.
Creon: You speak as one that will not yield or trust.
[Oed. lost line.]

Creon

> Not if you rule badly.

Oedipus

O, city, city!

Creon

> I too have some share   630
in the city; it is not yours alone.

Chorus

Stop, my lords! Here—and in the nick of time
I see Jocasta coming from the house;
with her help lay the quarrel that now stirs you.

> *(Enter Jocasta.)*

Jocasta

For shame! Why have you raised this foolish squabbling
brawl? Are you not ashamed to air your private   635
griefs when the country's sick? Go in, you, Oedipus,
and you, too, Creon, into the house. Don't magnify
your nothing troubles.

Creon

> Sister, Oedipus,
your husband, thinks he has the right to do
terrible wrongs—he has but to choose between   640
two terrors: banishing or killing me.

Oedipus

He's right, Jocasta; for I find him plotting
with knavish tricks against my person.

Creon

That God may never bless me! May I die
accursed, if I have been guilty of   645
one tittle of the charge you bring against me!

Jocasta

I beg you, Oedipus, trust him in this,
spare him for the sake of this his oath to God,
for my sake, and the sake of those who stand here.

Chorus

Be gracious, be merciful,   649
we beg of you.

Oedipus

In what would you have me yield?

Chorus

He has been no silly child in the past.
He is strong in his oath now.
Spare him.

Oedipus

Do you know what you ask?

Chorus

Yes.

Oedipus

Tell me then.

Chorus

He has been your friend before all men's eyes; do not cast him   656
away dishonoured on an obscure conjecture.

Oedipus

I would have you know that this request of yours
really requests my death or banishment.

Chorus

May the Sun God, king of Gods, forbid! May I die without God's   660
blessing, without friends' help, if I had any such thought. But my
spirit is broken by my unhappiness for my wasting country; and   665
this would but add troubles amongst ourselves to the other
troubles.

Oedipus

Well, let him go then—if I must die ten times for it,   669
or be sent out dishonoured into exile.
It is your lips that prayed for him I pitied,
not his; wherever he is, I shall hate him.

Creon

I see you sulk in yielding and you're dangerous
when you are out of temper; natures like yours
are justly heaviest for themselves to bear.   675

Oedipus

Leave me alone! Take yourself off, I tell you.

Creon

I'll go, you have not known me, but they have,
and they have known my innocence.

                                                    (*Exit.*)

Chorus

Won't you take him inside, lady?

Jocasta

Yes, when I've found out what was the matter.   680

Chorus

There was some misconceived suspicion of a story, and on the
other side the sting of injustice.

Jocasta

So, on both sides?

Chorus

Yes.

Jocasta

What was the story?

Chorus

I think it best, in the interests of the country, to leave it where   685
it ended.

Oedipus

You see where you have ended, straight of judgment
although you are, by softening my anger.

Chorus

Sir, I have said before and I say again—be sure that I would have   689
been proved a madman, bankrupt in sane council, if I should put
you away, you who steered the country I love safely when she

was crazed with troubles. God grant that now, too, you may   695
prove a fortunate guide for us.

Jocasta
Tell me, my lord, I beg of you, what was it
that roused your anger so?

Oedipus
                Yes, I will tell you.   700
I honour you more than I honour them.
It was Creon and the plots he laid against me.

Jocasta
Tell me—if you can clearly tell the quarrel—

Oedipus
             Creon says
that I'm the murderer of Laius.

Jocasta
Of his own knowledge or on information?

Oedipus
He sent this rascal prophet to me, since   705
he keeps his own mouth clean of any guilt.

Jocasta
Do not concern yourself about this matter;
listen to me and learn that human beings
have no part in the craft of prophecy.
Of that I'll show you a short proof.   710
There was an oracle once that came to Laius,—
I will not say that it was Phoebus' own,
but it was from his servants—and it told him
that it was fate that he should die a victim
at the hands of his own son, a son to be born
of Laius and me. But, see now, he,
the king, was killed by foreign highway robbers   715
at a place where three roads meet—so goes the story;
and for the son—before three days were out
after his birth King Laius pierced his ankles

and by the hands of others cast him forth
upon a pathless hillside. So Apollo   720
failed to fulfill his oracle to the son,
that he should kill his father, and to Laius
also proved false in that the thing he feared,
death at his son's hands, never came to pass.
So clear in this case were the oracles,
so clear and false. Give them no heed, I say;
what God discovers need of, easily
he shows to us himself.   725

Oedipus

O dear Jocasta,
as I hear this from you, there comes upon me
a wandering of the soul—I could run mad.

Jocasta

What trouble is it, that you turn again
and speak like this?

Oedipus

I thought I heard you say
that Laius was killed at a crossroads.   730

Jocasta

Yes, that was how the story went and still
that word goes round.

Oedipus

Where is this place, Jocasta,
where he was murdered?

Jocasta

Phocis is the country
and the road splits there, one of two roads from Delphi,
another comes from Daulia.

Oedipus

How long ago is this?   735

Jocasta

The news came to the city just before

you became king and all men's eyes looked to you.
What is it, Oedipus, that's in your mind?

Oedipus

What have you designed, O Zeus, to do with me?

Jocasta

What is the thought that troubles your heart?

Oedipus

Don't ask me yet—tell me of Laius—   740
How did he look? How old or young was he?

Jocasta

He was a tall man and his hair was grizzled
already—nearly white—and in his form
not unlike you.

Oedipus

            O God, I think I have
called curses on myself in ignorance.   745

Jocasta

What do you mean? I am terrified
when I look at you.

Oedipus

             I have a deadly fear
that the old seer had eyes. You'll show me more
if you can tell me one more thing.

Jocasta

            I will.
I'm frightened,—but if I can understand,
I'll tell you all you ask.

Oedipus

          How was his company?   750
Had he few with him when he went this journey,
or many servants, as would suit a prince?

Jocasta

In all there were but five, and among them
a herald; and one carriage for the king.

Oedipus

It's plain—its plain—who was it told you this?   755

Jocasta

The only servant that escaped safe home.

Oedipus

Is he at home now?

Jocasta

     No, when he came home again
and saw you king and Laius was dead,
he came to me and touched my hand and begged   760
that I should send him to the fields to be
my shepherd and so he might see the city
as far off as he might. So I
sent him away. He was an honest man,
as slaves go, and was worthy of far more
than what he asked of me.

Oedipus

O, how I wish that he could come back quickly!   765

Jocasta

He can. Why is your heart so set on this?

Oedipus

O dear Jocasta, I am full of fears
that I have spoken far too much; and therefore
I wish to see this shepherd.

Jocasta

     He will come;
but, Oedipus, I think I'm worthy too
to know what it is that disquiets you.   770

Oedipus

It shall not be kept from you, since my mind
has gone so far with its forebodings. Whom
should I confide in rather than you, who is there
of more importance to me who have passed
through such a fortune?

Polybus was my father, king of Corinth,
and Merope, the Dorian, my mother.   775
I was held greatest of the citizens
in Corinth till a curious chance befell me
as I shall tell you—curious, indeed,
but hardly worth the store I set upon it.
There was a dinner and at it a man,
a drunken man, accused me in his drink   780
of being bastard. I was furious
but held my temper under for that day.
Next day I went and taxed my parents with it;
they took the insult very ill from him,
the drunken fellow who had uttered it.
So I was comforted for their part, but   785
still this thing rankled always, for the story
crept about widely. And I went at last
to Pytho, though my parents did not know.
But Phoebus sent me home again unhonoured
in what I came to learn, but he foretold   790
other and desperate horrors to befall me,
that I was fated to lie with my mother,
and show to daylight an accursed breed
which men would not endure, and I was doomed
to be murderer of the father that begot me.
When I heard this I fled, and in the days
that followed I would measure from the stars   795
the whereabouts of Corinth—yes, I fled
to somewhere where I should not see fulfilled
the infamies told in that dreadful oracle.
And as I journeyed I came to the place
where, as you say, this king met with his death.
Jocasta, I will tell you the whole truth.   800
When I was near the branching of the crossroads,
going on foot, I was encountered by
a herald and a carriage with a man in it,
just as you tell me. He that led the way

and the old man himself wanted to thrust me   805
out of the road by force. I became angry
and struck the coachman who was pushing me.
When the old man saw this he watched his moment,
and as I passed he struck me from his carriage,
full on the head with his two pointed goad.
But he was paid in full and presently   810
my stick had struck him backwards from the car
and he rolled out of it. And then I killed them
all. If it happened there was any tie
of kinship twixt this man and Laius,
who is then now more miserable than I,   815
what man on earth so hated by the Gods,
since neither citizen nor foreigner
may welcome me at home or even greet me,
but drive me out of doors? And it is I,
I and no other have so cursed myself.   820
And I pollute the bed of him I killed
by the hands that killed him. Was I not born evil?
Am I not utterly unclean? I had to fly
and in my banishment not even see
my kindred nor set foot in my own country,
or otherwise my fate was to be yoked   825
in marriage with my mother and kill my father,
Polybus who begot me and had reared me.
Would not one rightly judge and say that on me
these things were sent by some malignant God?
O no, no, no—O holy majesty   830
of God on high, may I not see that day!
May I be gone out of men's sight before
I see the deadly taint of this disaster
come upon me.

Chorus

Sir, we too fear these things. But until you see this man face to
face and hear his story, hope.   835

Oedipus

Yes, I have just this much of hope—to wait until the herdsman comes.

Jocasta

And when he comes, what do you want with him?

Oedipus

I'll tell you; if I find that his story is the same as yours, I at least will be clear of this guilt.   840

Jocasta

Why what so particularly did you learn from my story?

Oedipus

You said that he spoke of highway *robbers* who killed Laius. Now if he uses the same number, it was not I who killed him. One man cannot be the same as many. But if he speaks of a man travelling   845 alone, then clearly the burden of the guilt inclines towards me.

Jocasta

Be sure, at least, that this was how he told the story. He cannot unsay it now, for every one in the city heard it—not I alone. But,   850 Oedipus, even if he diverges from what he said then, he shall never prove that the murder of Laius squares rightly with the prophecy—for Loxias declared that the king should be killed by his own son. And that poor creature did not kill him surely,—   855 for he died himself first. So as far as prophecy goes, henceforward I shall not look to the right hand or the left.

Oedipus

Right. But yet, send some one for the peasant to bring him here;   860 do not neglect it.

Jocasta

I will send quickly. Now let me go indoors. I will do nothing except what pleases you.

(*Exeunt.*)

Chorus

Strophe

May destiny ever find me

pious in word and deed   865
prescribed by the laws that live on high:
laws begotten in the clear air of heaven,
whose only father is Olympus;
no mortal nature brought them to birth,
no forgetfulness shall lull them to sleep;   870
for God is great in them and grows not old.

Antistrophe
Insolence breeds the tyrant, insolence
if it is glutted with a surfeit, unseasonable, unprofitable,   875
climbs to the roof-top and plunges
sheer down to the ruin that must be,
and there its feet are no service.
But I pray that the God may never   880
abolish the eager ambition that profits the state.
For I shall never cease to hold the God as our protector.

Strophe
If a man walks with haughtiness
of hand or word and gives no heed   885
to Justice and the shrines of Gods
despises—may an evil doom
smite him for his ill-starred pride of heart!—
if he reaps gains without justice
and will not hold from impiety   890
and his fingers itch for untouchable things.
When such things are done, what man shall contrive
to shield his soul from the shafts of the God?
When such deeds are held in honour,   895
why should I honour the Gods in the dance?

Antistrophe
No longer to the holy place,
to the navel of earth I'll go
to worship, nor to Abae
nor to Olympia,   900
unless the oracles are proved to fit,
for all men's hands to point at.

O Zeus, if you are rightly called
the sovereign lord, all-mastering,
let this not escape you nor your ever-living power! 905
The oracles concerning Laius
are old and dim and men regard them not.
Apollo is nowhere clear in honour; God's service perishes. 910

(*Enter Jocasta, carrying garlands.*)

Jocasta

Princes of the land, I have had the thought to go
to the Gods' temples, bringing in my hand
garlands and gifts of incense, as you see.
For Oedipus excites himself too much
at every sort of trouble, not conjecturing, 915
like a man of sense, what will be from what was,
but he is always at the speaker's mercy,
when he speaks terrors. I can do no good
by my advice, and so I came as suppliant
to you, Lycaean Apollo, who are nearest.
These are the symbols of my prayer and this 920
my prayer: grant us escape free of the curse.
Now when we look to him we are all afraid;
he's pilot of our ship and he is frightened.

(*Enter Messenger.*)

Messenger

Might I learn from you, sirs, where is the house of Oedipus? Or 925
best of all, if you know, where is the king himself?

Chorus

This is his house and he is within doors. This lady is his wife and
mother of his children.

Messenger

God bless you, lady, and God bless your household! God bless 930
Oedipus' noble wife!

Jocasta

God bless you, sir, for your kind greeting! What do you want
of us that you have come here? What have you to tell us?

Messenger

Good news, lady. Good for your house and for your husband.

Jocasta

What is your news? Who sent you to us?   935

Messenger

I come from Corinth and the news I bring will give you pleasure.
Perhaps a little pain too.

Jocasta

What is this news of double meaning?

Messenger

The people of the Isthmus will choose Oedipus to be their king.   940
That is the rumour there.

Jocasta

But isn't their king still old Polybus?

Messenger

No. He is in his grave. Death has got him.

Jocasta

Is that the truth? Is Oedipus' father dead?

Messenger

May I die myself if it be otherwise!

Jocasta (to a servant)

Be quick and run to the King with the news! O oracles of the   945
Gods, where are you now? It was from this man Oedipus fled, lest
he should be his murderer! And now he is dead, in the course of
nature, and not killed by Oedipus.

(Enter Oedipus.)

Oedipus

Dearest Jocasta, why have you sent for me?   950

Jocasta

Listen to this man and when you hear reflect what is the outcome
of the holy oracles of the Gods.

Oedipus

Who is he? What is his message for me?

Jocasta

He is from Corinth and he tells us that your father Polybus is   955
dead and gone.

Oedipus

What's this you say, sir? Tell me yourself.

Messenger

Since this is the first matter you want clearly told: Polybus has
gone down to death. You may be sure of it.

Oedipus

By treachery or sickness?   960

Messenger

A small thing will put old bodies asleep.

Oedipus

So he died of sickness, it seems,—poor old man!

Messenger

Yes, and of age—the long years he had measured.

Oedipus

Ha! Ha! O dear Jocasta, why should one
look to the Pythian hearth? Why should one look   965
to the birds screaming overhead? They prophesied
that I should kill my father! But he's dead,
and hidden deep in earth, and I stand here
who never laid a hand on spear against him,—
unless perhaps he died of longing for me,
and thus I am his murderer. But they,   970
the oracles, as they stand—he's taken them
away with him, they're dead as he himself is,
and worthless.

Jocasta

                    That I told you before now.

Oedipus

You did, but I was misled by my fear.

Jocasta

Then lay no more of them to heart, not one   975

Oedipus
>But surely I must fear my mother's bed?

Jocasta
>Why should man fear since chance is all in all
>for him, and he can clearly foreknow nothing?
>Best to live lightly, as one can, unthinkingly.
>As to your mother's marriage bed,—don't fear it.   980
>Before this, in dreams too, as well as oracles,
>many a man has lain with his own mother.
>But he to whom such things are nothing bears
>his life most easily.

Oedipus
>All that you say would be said perfectly
>if she were dead; but since she lives I must   985
>still fear, although you talk so well, Jocasta.

Jocasta
>Still in your father's death there's light of comfort?

Oedipus
>Great light of comfort; but I fear the living.

Messenger
>Who is the woman that makes you afraid?

Oedipus
>Merope, old man, Polybus' wife.   990

Messenger
>What about her frightens the queen and you?

Oedipus
>A terrible oracle, stranger, from the Gods.

Messenger
>Can it be told? Or does the sacred law
>forbid another to have knowledge of it?

Oedipus
>O no! Once on a time Loxias said
>that I should lie with my own mother and   995

take on my hands the blood of my own father.
And so for these long years I've lived away
from Corinth; it has been to my great happiness;
but yet it's sweet to see the face of parents.

Messenger
This was the fear which drove you out of Corinth?   1000

Oedipus
Old man, I did not wish to kill my father.

Messenger
Why should I not free you from this fear, sir,
since I have come to you in all goodwill?

Oedipus
You would not find me thankless if you did.

Messenger
Why, it was just for this I brought the news,—   1005
to earn your thanks when you had come safe home.

Oedipus
No, I will never come near my parents.

Messenger
                              Son,
it's very plain you don't know what you're doing.

Oedipus
What do you mean, old man? For God's sake, tell me.

Messenger
If your homecoming is checked by fears like these.   1010

Oedipus
Yes, I'm afraid that Phoebus may prove right.

Messenger
The murder and the incest?

Oedipus
                         Yes, old man;
that is my constant terror.

Messenger

Do you know
that all your fears are empty?

Oedipus

How is that,   1015
if they are father and mother and I their son?

Messenger

Because Polybus was no kin to you in blood.

Oedipus

What, was not Polybus my father?

Messenger

No more than I but just so much.

Oedipus

How can
my father be my father as much as one
that's nothing to me?

Messenger

Neither he nor I   1020
begat you.

Oedipus

Why then did he call me son?

Messenger

A gift he took you from these hands of mine.

Oedipus

Did he love so much what he took from another's hand?

Messenger

His childlessness before persuaded him.

Oedipus

Was I a child you bought or found when I   1025
was given to him?

Messenger

On Cithaeron's slopes
in the twisting thickets you were found.

Oedipus

And why
were you a traveller in those parts?

Messenger

I was
in charge of mountain flocks.

Oedipus

You were a shepherd?
A hireling vagrant?

Messenger

Yes, but at least at that time   1030
the man that saved your life, son.

Oedipus

What ailed me when you took me in your arms?

Messenger

In that your ankles should be witnesses.

Oedipus

Why do you speak of that old pain?

Messenger

I loosed you;
the tendons of your feet were pierced and fettered,—

Oedipus

My swaddling clothes brought me a rare disgrace.   1035

Messenger

So that from this you're called your present name.

Oedipus

Was this my father's doing or my mother's?
For God's sake, tell me.

Messenger

I don't know, but he
who gave you to me has more knowledge than I.

Oedipus

You yourself did not find me then? You took me
from someone else?

Messenger

Yes, from another shepherd.   1040

Oedipus

Who was he? Do you know him well enough
to tell?

Messenger

He was called Laius' man.

Oedipus

You mean the king who reigned here in the old days?

Messenger

Yes, he was that man's shepherd.

Oedipus

Is he alive   1045

still, so that I could see him?

Messenger

You who live here

would know that best.

Oedipus

Do any of you here

know of this shepherd whom he speaks about
in town or in the fields? Tell me. It's time   1050
that this was found out once for all.

Chorus

I think he is none other than the peasant
whom you have sought to see already; but
Jocasta here can tell us best of that.

Oedipus

Jocasta, do you know about this man
whom we have sent for? Is he the man he mentions?   1055

Jocasta

Why ask of whom he spoke? Don't give it heed;
nor try to keep in mind what has been said.
It will be wasted labour.

Oedipus

                With such clues
I could not fail to bring my birth to light.

Jocasta

  I beg you—do not hunt this out—I beg you,   1060
  if you have any care for your own life.
  What I am suffering is enough.

Oedipus

                Keep up
  your heart, Jocasta. Though I'm proved a slave,
  thrice slave, and though my mother is thrice slave,
  you'll not be shown to be of lowly lineage.

Jocasta

  O be persuaded by me, I entreat you;
  do not do this.

Oedipus

  I will not be persuaded to let be   1065
  the chance of finding out the whole thing clearly.

Jocasta

  It is because I wish you well that I
  give you this counsel—and it's the best counsel.

Oedipus

  Then the best counsel vexes me, and has
  for some while since.

Jocasta

             O Oedipus, God help you!
  God keep you from the knowledge of who you are!

Oedipus

  Here, some one, go and fetch the shepherd for me;
  and let her find her joy in her rich family!   1070

Jocasta

  O Oedipus, unhappy Oedipus!
  that is all I can call you, and the last thing
  that I shall ever call you.

                                 (*Exit.*)

Chorus

Why has the queen gone, Oedipus, in wild
grief rushing from us? I am afraid that trouble   1075
will break out of this silence.

Oedipus

Break out what will! I at least shall be
willing to see my ancestry, though humble.
Perhaps she is ashamed of my low birth,
for she has all a woman's high-flown pride.
But I account myself a child of Fortune,   1080
beneficent Fortune, and I shall not be
dishonoured. She's the mother from whom I spring;
the months, my brothers, marked me, now as small,
and now again as mighty. Such is my breeding,
and I shall never prove so false to it,   1085
as not to find the secret of my birth.

Chorus

  Strophe

If I am a prophet and wise of heart
you shall not fail, Cithaeron,   1090
by the limitless sky, you shall not!—
to know at tomorrow's full moon
that Oedipus honours you,
as native to him and mother and nurse at once;
and that you are honoured in dancing by us, as finding favour in
     sight of our king.
Apollo, to whom we cry, find these things pleasing!

  Antistrophe

Who was it bore you, child? One of   1098
the long-lived nymphs who lay with Pan—
the father who treads the hills?
Or was she a bride of Loxias, your mother? The grassy slopes
are all of them dear to him. Or perhaps Cyllene's king   1104
or the Bacchants' God that lives on the tops

of the hills received you a gift from some
one of the Helicon Nymphs, with whom he mostly plays?

(*Enter an old man, led by Oedipus' servants.*)

Oedipus

If some one like myself who never met him   1110
may make a guess,—I think this is the herdsman,
whom we were seeking. His old age is consonant
with the other. And besides, the men who bring him
I recognize as my own servants. You   1115
perhaps may better me in knowledge since
you've seen the man before.

Chorus
                        You can be sure
I recognize him. For if Laius
had ever an honest shepherd, this was he.

Oedipus

You, sir, from Corinth, I must ask you first,
is this the man you spoke of?   1120

Messenger
                        This is he
before your eyes.

Oedipus
                        Old man, look here at me
and tell me what I ask you. Were you ever
a servant of King Laius?

Herdsman
                        I was,—
no slave he bought but reared in his own house.

Oedipus

What did you do as work? How did you live?

Herdsman

Most of my life was spent among the flocks.   1125

Oedipus

In what part of the country did you live?

Herdsman

Cithaeron and the places near to it.

Oedipus

And somewhere there perhaps you knew this man?

Herdsman

What was his occupation? Who?

Oedipus

               This man here,   1130
have you had any dealings with him?

Herdsman

          No—
not such that I can quickly call to mind.

Messenger

That is no wonder, master. But I'll make him remember what he
does not know. For I know, that he well knows the country of
Cithaeron, how he with two flocks, I with one kept company for   1135
three years—each year half a year—from spring till autumn time
and then when winter came I drove my flocks to our fold home
again and he to Laius' steadings. Well—am I right or not in what   1140
I said we did?

Herdsman

You're right—although it's a long time ago.

Messenger

Do you remember giving me a child
to bring up as my foster child?

Herdsman

             What's this?
Why do you ask this question?

Messenger

            Look old man,   1145
here he is—here's the man who was that child!

Herdsman

Death take you! Won't you hold your tongue?

Oedipus
No, no,
do not find fault with him, old man. Your words
are more at fault than his.

Herdsman
O best of masters,
how do I give offense?

Oedipus
When you refuse   1150
to speak about the child of whom he asks you.

Herdsman
He speaks out of his ignorance, without meaning.

Oedipus
If you'll not talk to gratify me, you
will talk with pain to urge you.

Herdsman
O please, sir,
don't hurt an old man, sir.

Oedipus (*to the servants*)
Here, one of you,
twist his hands behind him.

Herdsman
Why, God help me, why?   1155
What do you want to know?

Oedipus
You gave a child
to him,—the child he asked you of?

Herdsman
I did.
I wish I'd died the day I did.

Oedipus
You will
unless you tell me truly.

Herdsman
                                And I'll die
far worse if I should tell you.

Oedipus
                                This fellow   1160
is bent on more delays, as it would seem.

Herdsman
O no, no! I have told you that I gave it.

Oedipus
Where did you get this child from? Was it your own or did you
get it from another?

Herdsman
                                Not
my own at all; I had it from some one.

Oedipus
One of these citizens? or from what house?

Herdsman
O master, please—I beg you, master, please   1165
don't ask me more.

Oedipus
                        You're a dead man if I
ask you again.

Herdsman
                        It was one of the children
of Laius.

Oedipus
                        A slave? Or born in wedlock?

Herdsman
O God, I am on the brink of frightful speech.

Oedipus
And I of frightful hearing. But I must hear.   1170

Herdsman
The child was called his child; but she within,
your wife would tell you best how all this was.

Oedipus
  She gave it to you?

Herdsman
                    Yes, she did, my lord.

Oedipus
  To do what with it?

Herdsman
                    Make away with it.

Oedipus
  She was so hard—its mother?   1175

Herdsman
                    Aye, through fear
  of evil oracles.

Oedipus
                    Which?

Herdsman
                    They said that he
  should kill his parents.

Oedipus
                    How was it that you
  gave it away to this old man?

Herdsman
                    O master,
  I pitied it, and thought that I could send it
  off to another country and this man
  was from another country. But he saved it   1180
  for the most terrible troubles. If you are
  the man he says you are, you're bred to misery.

Oedipus
  O, O, O, they will all come,
  all come out clearly! Light of the sun, let me
  look upon you no more after today!
  I who first saw the light bred of a match
  accursed, and accursed in my living
  with them I lived with, cursed in my killing.   1185

                    (*Exeunt all but the Chorus.*)

« 63 »

Chorus
>   *Strophe*
> O generations of men, how I
> count you as equal with those who live
> not at all!
> What man, what man on earth wins more   1190
> of happiness than a seeming
> and after that turning away?
> Oedipus, you are my pattern of this,
> Oedipus, you and your fate!
> Luckless Oedipus, whom of all men
> I envy not at all.   1196
>
>   *Antistrophe*
> In as much as he shot his bolt
> beyond the others and won the prize
> of happiness complete—
> O Zeus—and killed and reduced to nought
> the hooked taloned maid of the riddling speech,
> standing a tower against death for my land:
> hence he was called my king and hence
> was honoured the highest of all
> honours; and hence he ruled
> in the great city of Thebes.
>
>   *Strophe*
> But now whose tale is more miserable?   1204
> Who is there lives with a savager fate?
> Whose troubles so reverse his life as his?
>
> O Oedipus, the famous prince
> for whom a great haven
> the same both as father and son
> sufficed for generation,
> how, O how, have the furrows ploughed
> by your father endured to bear you, poor wretch,
> and hold their peace so long?

Antistrophe
Time who sees all has found you out   1213
against your will; judges your marriage accursed,
begetter and begot at one in it.

O child of Laius,
would I had never seen you.
I weep for you and cry
a dirge of lamentation.

To speak directly, I drew my breath
from you at the first and so now I lull   1222
my mouth to sleep with your name.

(Enter a second messenger.)

Second Messenger
O Princes always honoured by our country,
what deeds you'll hear of and what horrors see,
what grief you'll feel, if you as true born Thebans   1225
care for the house of Labdacus's sons.
Phasis nor Ister cannot purge this house,
I think, with all their streams, such things
it hides, such evils shortly will bring forth
into the light, whether they will or not;   1230
and troubles hurt the most
when they prove self-inflicted.

Chorus
What we had known before did not fall short
of bitter groaning's worth; what's more to tell?

Second Messenger
Shortest to hear and tell—our glorious queen   1235
Jocasta's dead.

Chorus
                            Unhappy woman! How?
Second Messenger
By her own hand. The worst of what was done
you cannot know. You did not see the sight.
Yet in so far as I remember it

you'll hear the end of our unlucky queen.   1240
When she came raging into the house she went
straight to her marriage bed, tearing her hair
with both her hands, and crying upon Laius   1245
long dead—Do you remember, Laius,
that night long past which bred a child for us
to send you to your death and leave
a mother making children with her son?
And then she groaned and cursed the bed in which
she brought forth husband by her husband, children   1250
by her own child, an infamous double bond.
How after that she died I do not know,—
for Oedipus distracted us from seeing.
He burst upon us shouting and we looked
to him as he paced frantically around,
begging us always: Give me a sword, I say,   1255
to find this wife no wife, this mother's womb,
this field of double sowing whence I sprang
and where I sowed my children! As he raved
some god showed him the way—none of us there.
Bellowing terribly and led by some   1260
invisible guide he rushed on the two doors,—
wrenching the hollow bolts out of their sockets,
he charged inside. There, there, we saw his wife
hanging, the twisted rope around her neck.
When he saw her, he cried out fearfully   1265
and cut the dangling noose. Then, as she lay,
poor woman, on the ground, what happened after,
was terrible to see. He tore the brooches—
the gold chased brooches fastening her robe—
away from her and lifting them up high
dashed them on his own eyeballs, shrieking out   1270
such things as: they will never see the crime
I have committed or had done upon me!
Dark eyes, now in the days to come look on
forbidden faces, do not recognize

those whom you long for—with such imprecations
he struck his eyes again and yet again   1275
with the brooches. And the bleeding eyeballs gushed
and stained his beard—no sluggish oozing drops
but a black rain and bloody hail poured down.

So it has broken—and not on one head   1280
but troubles mixed for husband and for wife.
The fortune of the days gone by was true
good fortune—but today groans and destruction
and death and shame—of all ills can be named   1285
not one is missing.

Chorus
  Is he now in any ease from pain?

Second Messenger
                    He shouts
for some one to unbar the doors and show him
to all the men of Thebes, his father's killer,
his mother's—no I cannot say the word,
it is unholy—for he'll cast himself,
out of the land, he says, and not remain   1290
to bring a curse upon his house, the curse
he called upon it in his proclamation. But
he wants for strength, aye, and some one to guide him;
his sickness is too great to bear. You, too,
will be shown that. The bolts are opening.   1295
Soon you will see a sight to waken pity
even in the horror of it.
                      (Enter the blinded Oedipus.)

Chorus
  This is a terrible sight for men to see!
  I never found a worse!
  Poor wretch, what madness came upon you!   1300
  What evil spirit leaped upon your life
  to your ill-luck—a leap beyond man's strength!
  Indeed I pity you, but I cannot

look at you, though there's much I want to ask
and much to learn and much to see. 1305
I shudder at the sight of you.

Oedipus
O, O,
where am I going? Where is my voice 1310
borne on the wind to and fro?
Spirit, how far have you sprung?

Chorus
To a terrible place whereof men's ears
may not hear, nor their eyes behold it.

Oedipus
Darkness!
Horror of darkness enfolding, resistless, unspeakable visitant sped
   by an ill wind in haste! 1315
madness and stabbing pain and memory
of evil deeds I have done!

Chorus
In such misfortunes it's no wonder
if double weighs the burden of your grief. 1320

Oedipus
My friend,
you are the only one steadfast, the only one that attends on me;
you still stay nursing the blind man.
Your care is not unnoticed. I can know 1325
your voice, although this darkness is my world.

Chorus
Doer of dreadful deeds, how did you dare
so far to do despite to your own eyes?
what spirit urged you to it?

Oedipus
It was Apollo, friends, Apollo,
that brought this bitter bitterness, my sorrows to completion. 1330
But the hand that struck me

was none but my own.
Why should I see
whose vision showed me nothing sweet to see?   1335

Chorus
These things are as you say.

Oedipus
What can I see to love?
What greeting can touch my ears with joy?
Take me away, and haste—to a place out of the way!   1340
Take me away, my friends, the greatly miserable,
the most accursed, whom God too hates   1345
above all men on earth!

Chorus
Unhappy in your mind and your misfortune,
would I had never known you!

Oedipus
Curse on the man who took
the cruel bonds from off my legs, as I lay in the field.   1350
He stole me from death and saved me,
no kindly service.
Had I died then
I would not be so burdensome to friends.   1355

Chorus
I, too, could have wished it had been so.

Oedipus
Then I would not have come
to kill my father and marry my mother infamously.
Now I am godless and child of impurity,   1360
begetter in the same seed that created my wretched self.
If there is any ill worse than ill,   1365
that is the lot of Oedipus.

Chorus
I cannot say your remedy was good;
you would be better dead than blind and living.

Oedipus

What I have done here was best done—don't tell me 1370
otherwise, do not give me further counsel.
I do not know with what eyes I could look
upon my father when I die and go
under the earth, nor yet my wretched mother—
those two to whom I have done things deserving
worse punishment than hanging. Would the sight 1375
of children, bred as mine are, gladden me?
No, not these eyes, never. And my city,
its towers and sacred places of the Gods,
of these I robbed my miserable self 1380
when I commanded all to drive *him* out,
the criminal since proved by God impure
and of the race of Laius.
To this guilt I bore witness against myself—
with what eyes shall I look upon my people? 1385
No. If there were a means to choke the fountain
of hearing I would not have stayed my hand
from locking up my miserable carcase,
seeing and hearing nothing; it is sweet 1390
to keep our thoughts out of the range of hurt.

Cithaeron, why did you receive me? why
having received me did you not kill me straight?
And so I had not shown to men my birth.

O Polybus and Corinth and the house,
the old house that I used to call my father's— 1395
what fairness you were nurse to, and what foulness
festered beneath! Now I am found to be
a sinner and a son of sinners. Crossroads,
and hidden glade, oak and the narrow way
at the crossroads, that drank my father's blood 1400
offered you by my hands, do you remember
still what I did as you looked on, and what
I did when I came here? O marriage, marriage!

you bred me and again when you had bred
bred children of your child and showed to men   1405
brides, wives and mothers and the foulest deeds
that can be in this world of ours.

Come—it's unfit to say what is unfit
to do.—I beg of you in God's name hide me   1410
somewhere outside your country, yes, or kill me,
or throw me into the sea, to be forever
out of your sight. Approach and deign to touch me
for all my wretchedness, and do not fear.
No man but I can bear my evil doom.   1415

Chorus

Here Creon comes in fit time to perform
or give advice in what you ask of us.
Creon is left sole ruler in your stead.

Oedipus

Creon! Creon! What shall I say to him?
How can I justly hope that he will trust me?   1420
In what is past I have been proved towards him
an utter liar.

                                            (*Enter Creon.*)

Creon

                        Oedipus, I've come
not so that I might laugh at you nor taunt you
with evil of the past. But if you still
are without shame before the face of men
reverence at least the flame that gives all life,   1425
our Lord the Sun, and do not show unveiled
to him pollution such that neither land
nor holy rain nor light of day can welcome.

                                            (*To a servant.*)

Be quick and take him in. It is most decent   1430
that only kin should see and hear the troubles
of kin.

Oedipus

           I beg you, since you've torn me from
my dreadful expectations and have come
in a most noble spirit to a man
that has used you vilely—do a thing for me.
I shall speak for your own good, not for my own.

Creon

  What do you need that you would ask of me?   1435

Oedipus

  Drive me from here with all the speed you can
to where I may not hear a human voice.

Creon

  Be sure, I would have done this had not I
wished first of all to learn from the God the course
of action I should follow.

Oedipus

              But his word   1440
has been quite clear to let the parricide,
the sinner, die.

Creon

              Yes, that indeed was said.
But in the present need we had best discover
what we should do.

Oedipus

            And will you ask about
a man so wretched?

Creon

           Now even you will trust   1445
the God.

Oedipus

         So. I command you—and will beseech you—
to her that lies inside that house give burial
as you would have it; she is yours and rightly
you will perform the rites for her. For me—

never let this my father's city have me   1450
living a dweller in it. Leave me live
in the mountains where Cithaeron is, that's called
my mountain, which my mother and my father
while they were living would have made my tomb.
So I may die by their decree who sought
indeed to kill me. Yet I know this much: 1455
no sickness and no other thing will kill me.
I would not have been saved from death if not
for some strange evil fate. Well, let my fate
go where it will.

                    Creon, you need not care   1460
about my sons; they're men and so wherever
they are, they will not lack a livelihood.
But my two girls—so sad and pitiful—
whose table never stood apart from mine,
and everything I touched they always shared—   1465
O Creon, have a thought for them! And most
I wish that you might suffer me to touch them
and sorrow with them.

        (Enter Antigone and Ismene, Oedipus' two daughters.)
O my lord! O true noble Creon! Can I   1470
really be touching them, as when I saw?
What shall I say?
Yes, I can hear them sobbing—my two darlings!
and Creon has had pity and has sent me
what I loved most?
Am I right?   1475

Creon

    You're right: it was I gave you this
    because I knew from old days how you loved them
    as I see now.

Oedipus

                God bless you for it, Creon,
    and may God guard you better on your road
    than he did me!

O children, 1480

where are you? Come here, come to my hands,
a brother's hands which turned your father's eyes,
those bright eyes you knew once, to what you see,
a father seeing nothing, knowing nothing,
begetting you from his own source of life. 1485
I weep for you—I cannot see your faces—
I weep when I think of the bitterness
there will be in your lives, how you must live
before the world. At what assemblages
of citizens will you make one? to what 1490
gay company will you go and not come home
in tears instead of sharing in the holiday?
And when you're ripe for marriage, who will he be,
the man who'll risk to take such infamy
as shall cling to my children, to bring hurt 1495
on them and those that marry with them? What
curse is not there? "Your father killed his father
and sowed the seed where he had sprung himself
and begot you out of the womb that held him."
These insults you will hear. Then who will marry you? 1500
No one, my children; clearly you are doomed
to waste away in barrenness unmarried.
Son of Menoeceus, since you are all the father
left these two girls, and we, their parents, both 1505
are dead to them—do not allow them wander
like beggars, poor and husbandless.
They are of your own blood.
And do not make them equal with myself
in wretchedness; for you can see them now
so young, so utterly alone, save for you only.
Touch my hand, noble Creon, and say yes. 1510
If you were older, children, and were wiser,
there's much advice I'd give you. But as it is,
let this be what you pray: give me a life

wherever there is opportunity
to live, and better life than was my father's.

Creon
  Your tears have had enough of scope; now go within the house.   1515

Oedipus
  I must obey, though bitter of heart.

Creon
  In season, all is good.

Oedipus
  Do you know on what conditions I obey?

Creon
                    You tell me them,
and I shall know them when I hear.

Oedipus
                    That you shall send me out
to live away from Thebes.

Creon
              That gift you must ask of the God.

Oedipus
  But I'm now hated by the Gods.

Creon
             So quickly you'll obtain your prayer.

Oedipus
  You consent then?   1520

Creon
            What I do not mean, I do not use to say.

Oedipus
  Now lead me away from here.

Creon
           Let go the children, then, and come.

Oedipus
  Do not take them from me.

Creon

        Do not seek to be master in everything,
for the things you mastered did not follow you throughout your
    life.

                  (As Creon and Oedipus go out.)

Chorus

You that live in my ancestral Thebes, behold this Oedipus,—
him who knew the famous riddles and was a man most masterful;   1525
not a citizen who did not look with envy on his lot—
see him now and see the breakers of misfortune swallow him!
Look upon that last day always. Count no mortal happy till
he has passed the final limit of his life secure from pain.   1530

OEDIPUS
AT
COLONUS

Translated by

ROBERT FITZGERALD

CHARACTERS

Oedipus

Antigone

A Stranger

Ismene

Theseus

Creon

Polyneices

A Messenger

Chorus

OEDIPUS AT COLONUS

Long after he had left Thebes, the blinded OEDIPUS *came with* ANTIGONE
to the Attic deme of COLONUS, *where the oracle of Apollo had prophesied
that he was to die.*

SCENE: *Like the theatre, is in the open air. In the background is the grove
of the Furies at Colonus in Attica, about a mile northwest of
Athens. A statue or stele of Colonus, a legendary horseman and
hero, can be seen stage left. Stage right, a flat rock jutting out
among the trees of the grove. Downstage, center, another ridge of
rock.*

TIME: *Early afternoon of a day about twenty years after the action of
King Oedipus.*

SCENE I

*(Oedipus, old, blind, bearded and ragged, but carrying
himself well, enters stage right, led by Antigone.)*

Oedipus
  My daughter—daughter of the blind old man—
  Where, I wonder, have we come to now?
  What place is this, Antigone? What people?
  Who will be kind to Oedipus this evening
  And give the wanderer charity?

  Though he ask little and receive still less,   5
  It is sufficient:
                    Suffering and time,
  Vast time, have been instructors in contentment,
  Which kingliness teaches too.
                    But now, child,
  If you can see a place where we might rest,
  Some public place or consecrated park,   10
  Let me stop and sit down there.
  And then let us inquire where we may be.

As foreigners and strangers we must learn
From the local people, and do as they direct.

Antigone

Father, poor tired Oedipus, the towers
That crown the city still seem far away;   15
As for this place, it is clearly a holy one,
Shady with vines and olive trees and laurel;
Snug in their wings within, the nightingales
Make a sweet music.
                        Rest on this rough stone.
It was a long road for an old man to travel.   20

Oedipus

Help me sit down; take care of the blind man.

Antigone

After so long, you need not tell me, father.

Oedipus

And now have you any idea where we are?

Antigone

This place I do not know; the city is Athens.

Oedipus

Yes, everyone we met has told us that.   25

Antigone

Then shall I go and ask?

Oedipus

Do, child, if there is any life near-by.

Antigone

Oh, but indeed there is; I need not leave you;
I see a man, now, not far away from us.

Oedipus

Is he coming this way? Has he started towards us?   30

                        (*The Stranger enters, left.*)

Antigone

Here he is now.

                        Say what seems best to you,
    Father; the man is here.

Oedipus
    Friend, my daughter's eyes serve for my own.
    She tells me we are fortunate enough to meet you,
    And no doubt you will inform us—   35

Stranger
                        Do not go on;
    First move from where you sit; the place is holy;
    It is forbidden to walk upon that ground.

Oedipus
    What ground is this? What god is honored here?

Stranger
    It is not to be touched, no one may live upon it;
    Most dreadful are its divinities, most feared,
    Daughters of darkness and mysterious earth.   40

Oedipus
    Under what solemn name shall I invoke them?

Stranger
    The people here prefer to address them as Gentle
    All-seeing Ones; elsewhere there are other names.

Oedipus
    Then may they be gentle to the suppliant.
    For I shall never leave this resting place.   45

Stranger
    What is the meaning of this?

Oedipus
                        It was ordained;
    I recognize it now.

Stranger
                        Without authority
    From the city government I dare not move you;
    First I must show them what it is you are doing.

Oedipus

    Friend, in the name of God, bear with me now!
    I turn to you for light; answer the wanderer.   50

Stranger

    Speak. You will not find me discourteous.

Oedipus

    What is this region into which I've come?

Stranger

    Whatever I can tell you, I will tell.
    This country, all of it, is blessed ground;
    The god of the sea loves it; in it the firecarrier   55
    Prometheus has his influence; in particular
    That spot you rest on has been called this earth's
    Doorsill of Brass, and buttress of great Athens.
    All men of this land claim descent from him
    Whose statue stands near-by: Colonus the horseman,
    And bear his name in common with their own.   60
    That is this country, stranger: honored less
    In histories than in the hearts of the people.

Oedipus

    Then people live in the land?

Stranger

                      Yes, certainly,
    The clan of those descended from that hero.   65

Oedipus

    Ruled by a king? Or do the people rule?

Stranger

    The land is governed from Athens, by Athens' king.

Oedipus

    And who is he whose word has power here?

Stranger

    Theseus, son of Aegeus, the king before him.

Oedipus

    Ah. Would someone then go to this king for me?   70

Stranger
  To tell him what? Perhaps to urge his coming?

Oedipus
  To tell him a small favor will gain him much.

Stranger
  What service can a blind man render him?

Oedipus
  All I shall say will be clear-sighted indeed.

Stranger
  Listen, stranger: I wish you no injury;   75
  You seem well-born, though obviously unlucky;
  Stay where you are, exactly where I found you,
  And I'll inform the people of what you say—
  Not in the town, but here—it rests with them
  To decide if you should stay or must move on.   80

                             (*Exit Stranger, left.*)

Oedipus
  Child, has he gone?

Antigone
  Yes, father. Now you may speak tranquilly,
  For only I am with you.

Oedipus (*praying*)
                     Ladies whose eyes
  Are terrible: Spirits: upon your sacred ground
  I have first bent my knees in this new land;   85
  Therefore be mindful of me and of Apollo,
  For when he gave me oracles of evil,
  He also spoke of this:
                   A resting place,
  After long years, in the last country, where
  I should find home among the sacred Furies: 90
  That there I might round out my bitter life,
  Conferring benefit on those who received me,
  A curse on those who have driven me away.

Portents, he said, would make me sure of this:
Earthquake, thunder, or God's smiling lightning;   95
But I am sure of it now, sure that you guided me
With feathery influence upon this road,
And led me here into your hallowed wood.

How otherwise could I, in my wandering,
Have sat down first with you in all this land,   100
I who drink not, with you who love not wine?

How otherwise had I found this chair of stone?
Grant me then, goddesses, passage from life at last,
And consummation, as the unearthly voice foretold;
Unless indeed I seem not worth your grace:
Slave as I am to such unending pain   105
As no man had before.
                            O hear my prayer,
Sweet children of original Darkness! Hear me,
Athens, city named for great Athena,
Honored above all cities in the world!
Pity a man's poor carcase and his ghost,
For Oedipus is not the strength he was.   110

Antigone

Be still. Some elderly men are coming this way,
Looking for the place where you are seated.

Oedipus

I shall be still. You get me clear of the path,
And hide me in the wood, so I may hear
What they are saying. If we know their temper   115
We shall be better able to act with prudence.
                    (*Oedipus and Antigone withdraw into the grove.*)

CHORAL DIALOGUE
(*The Chorus enters from the left. Here, and throughout the
play, its lines may be taken by various members as
seems suitable.*)

Chorus

  Look for him. Who could he be? Where
  Is he? Where is the stranger
  Impious, blasphemous, shameless!   120
  Use your eyes, search him out!
  Cover the ground and uncover him!
          Vagabond!
  The old man must be a vagabond,
  Not of our land, for he'd never   125
  Otherwise dare to go in there,
  In the inviolate thicket
  Of those whom it's futile to fight,
  Those whom we tremble to name.
  When we pass we avert our eyes—
          Close our eyes!—   130
  In silence, without conversation,
  Shaping our prayers with our lips.
  But now, if the story is credible,
  Some alien fool has profaned it;
  Yet I have looked over all the grove and   135
          Still cannot see him;
  Cannot say where he has hidden.

          (*Oedipus comes forward from the wood.*)

Oedipus

  That stranger is I. As they say of the blind,
  Sounds are the things I see.

Chorus

          Ah!   140
  His face is dreadful! His voice is dreadful!

Oedipus

  Do not regard me, please, as a law-breaker.

Chorus

  Zeus defend us, who is this old man?

Oedipus

  One whose fate is not quite to be envied,

O my masters, and men of this land;   145
That must be evident: why, otherwise,
   Should I need this girl
To lead me, her frailty to put my weight on?

Chorus

Ah! His eyes are blind!   150
And were you brought into the world so?
Unhappy life—and so long!
Well, not if I can help it,
Will you have this curse besides.—
   Stranger! you   155
Trespass there! But beyond there,
In the glade where the grass is still,
Where the honeyed libations drip
In the rill from the brimming spring,
You must not step! O stranger,   160
It is well to be careful about it!
   Most careful!
Stand aside and come down then!
There is too much space between us!
Say, wanderer, can you hear?   165
If you have a mind to tell us
Your business, or wish to converse with our council,
   Come down from that place!
Only speak where it's proper to do so!

Oedipus

Now, daughter, what is the way of wisdom?   170

Antigone

We must do just as they do here, father;
We should give in now, and listen to them.

Oedipus

Stretch out your hand to me.

Antigone

   There, I am near you.

Oedipus
  Sirs, let there be no injustice done me,
  Once I have trusted you, and left my refuge.   175

                    (*Led by Antigone, he starts downstage.*)

Chorus
  Never, never, will anyone drive you away
  From rest in this land, old man!

Oedipus
  Shall I come further?

Chorus
                    Yes, further.

Oedipus
  And now?

Chorus
                    You must guide him, girl;   180
  You can see how much further to come.

Antigone
  Come with your blind step, father;
  This way; come where I lead you.

Chorus
  Though the land is strange, newcomer,
  You've weathered much; take heart;   185
  What the state has long held hateful,
  Hate, and respect what it loves.

Oedipus
  Lead me on, then, child,
  To where we may speak or listen respectfully;   190
  Let us not fight necessity.

Chorus
  Now! Go no further than that platform there,
  Formed of the natural rock.

Oedipus
  This?

Chorus
> Far enough; you can hear us.

Oedipus
  Shall I sit down?

Chorus
> Yes, sit there   195
  To the left on the ridge of the rock.

Antigone
  Father, this is where I can help you;
  You must keep step with me; gently now.

Oedipus
  Ah, me!

Antigone
  Lean your old body on my arm;   200
  It is I who love you; let yourself down.

Oedipus
  How bitter blindness is!

> *(He is seated on the rock downstage, center.)*

Chorus
  Now that you are at rest, poor man,
  Tell us, what is your name?
  Who are you, wanderer?   205
  What is the land of your ancestors?

Oedipus
  I am an exile, friends; but do not ask me . . .

Chorus
  What is it you fear to say, old man?

Oedipus
  No, no, no! Do not go on   210
  Questioning me! Do not ask my name!

Chorus
  Why not?

Oedipus
>My star was unspeakable.

Chorus
>>>>Speak!

Oedipus
>My child, what can I say to them?

Chorus
>Answer us, stranger; what is your race,
>Who was your father?   215

Oedipus
>God help me, what will become of me, child?

Antigone
>Tell them; there is no other way.

Oedipus
>Well, then, I will; I cannot hide it.

Chorus
>Between you, you greatly delay. Speak up!

Oedipus
>Have you heard of Laius' family?

Chorus
>>>Ah!   220

Oedipus
>Of the race of Labdacidae?

Chorus
>>>Ah, Zeus!

Oedipus
>And ruined Oedipus?

Chorus
>>>You are he!

Oedipus
>Do not take fright from what I say—

Chorus
>Oh, dreadful!

Oedipus
> I am accursed.

Chorus
> > Oh, fearful!

Oedipus
> Antigone, what will happen now?   225

Chorus
> Away with you! Out with you! Leave our country!

Oedipus
> And what of the promises you made me?

Chorus
> God will not punish the man
> Who makes return for an injury:
> Deceivers may be deceived: 230
> They play a game that ends
> In grief, and not in pleasure.
> Leave this grove at once!
> Our country is not for you!
> Wind no further   235
> Your clinging evil upon us!

Antigone
> O men of reverent mind!
> Since you will not suffer my father,
> Old man though he is,
> And though you know his story—
> He never knew what he did—   240
> Take pity still on my unhappiness,
> And let me intercede with you for him.
> Not with lost eyes, but looking in your eyes
> As if I were a child of yours, I beg   245
> Mercy for him, the beaten man! O hear me!
> We are thrown upon your mercy as on God's;
> > Be kinder than you seem!
> By all you have and own that is dear to you:
> Children, wives, possessions, gods, I pray you!   250

For you will never see in all the world
    A man whom God has led
    Escape his destiny!

SCENE 2

Chorus

Child of Oedipus, indeed we pity you,
Just as we pity him for his misfortune;   255
But we tremble to think of what the gods may do;
We could not dare to speak more generously!

Oedipus

What use is reputation then? What good
Comes of a noble name? A noble fiction!
For Athens, so they say, excels in piety;   260
Has power to save the wretched of other lands;
Can give them refuge; is unique in this.
Yet, when it comes to me, where is her refuge?
You pluck me from these rocks and cast me out,
All for fear of a name!
                 Or do you dread   265
My strength? my actions? I think not, for I
Suffered those deeds more than I acted them,
As I might show if it were fitting here
To tell my father's and my mother's story . . .
For which you fear me, as I know too well.

And yet, how was I evil in myself?   270
I had been wronged, I retaliated; even had I
Known what I was doing, was that evil?
Then, knowing nothing, I went on. Went on.
But those who wronged me knew, and ruined me.

Therefore I beg of you before the gods,   275
For the same cause that made you move me—
In reverence of your gods—give me this shelter,
And thus accord those powers what is theirs.
Think: their eyes are fixed upon the just,

Fixed on the unjust, too; no impious man 280
Can twist away from them forever.
Now, in their presence, do not blot your city's
Luster by bending to unholy action;
As you would receive an honest petitioner,
Give me, too, sanctuary; though my face 285
Be dreadful in its look, yet honor me!

For I come here as one endowed with grace
By those who are over Nature; and I bring
Advantage to this race, as you may learn
More fully when some lord of yours is here. 290
Meanwhile be careful to be just.

Chorus

              Old man,
This argument of yours compels our wonder.
It was not feebly worded. I am content
That higher authorities should judge this matter. 295

Oedipus

And where is he who rules the land, strangers?

Chorus

In his father's city; but the messenger
Who sent us here has gone to fetch him also.

Oedipus

Do you think a blind man will so interest him
As to bring him such a distance? 300

Chorus

I do, indeed, when he has heard your name.

Oedipus

But who will tell him that?

Chorus

It is a long road, and the rumors of travellers
Have a way of wandering. He will have word of them;
Take heart—he will be here. Old man, your name 305

Has gone over all the earth; though he may be
At rest when the news comes, he will come quickly.

Oedipus

Then may he come with luck for his own city,
As well as for me. . . . The good befriend themselves.

Antigone

O Zeus! What shall I say? How interpret this?   310

Oedipus

Antigone, my dear child, what is it?

Antigone

A woman
Riding a Sicilian pony and coming towards us;
She is wearing the wide Thessalian sun-hat;
I don't know!   315
Is it or isn't it? Or am I dreaming?
I think so; yes!—No. I can't be sure. . . .

Ah, poor child,
It is no one else but she! And she is smiling   320
Now as she comes! It is my dear Ismene!

Oedipus

What did you say, child?

(Ismene enters, with one Attendant.)

Antigone

That I see your daughter!
My sister! Now you can tell her by her voice.

Ismene

O father and sister together! Dearest voices!
Now I have found you—how, I scarcely know—   325
I don't know how I shall see you through my tears!

Oedipus

Child, you have come?

Ismene

Father, how old you seem!

Oedipus
  Child, are you here?

Ismene
                    And such a time I had!

Oedipus
  Touch me, little one.

Ismene
                    I shall hold you both!

Oedipus
  My children . . . and sisters.

Ismene
                    Oh, unhappy people!   330

Oedipus
  She and I?

Ismene
                    And I with you, unhappy.

Oedipus
  But, child, why have you come?

Ismene
                    For your sake, father.

Oedipus
  You missed me?

Ismene
                    Yes; and I have news for you.
  I came with the one person I could trust.

Oedipus
  Why, where are your brothers? Could they not do it?   335

Ismene
  They are—where they are. It is a hard time for them.

Oedipus
  Ah! They behave as if they were Egyptians,
  Bred the Egyptian way! Down there, the men
  Sit indoors all day long, weaving;
  The women go out and attend to business.   340
  Just so your brothers, who should have done this work

Sit by the fire like home-loving girls,
And you two, in their place, must bear my hardships.

One, since her childhood ended and her body
Gained its power, has wandered ever with me,   345
An old man's governess; often in the wild
Forest going without shoes, and hungry,
Beaten by many rains, tired by the sun;   350
Yet she rejected the sweet life of home
So that her father should have sustenance.

And you, my daughter, once before came out,
Unknown to Thebes, bringing me news of all
The oracle had said concerning me;   355
And you remained my faithful outpost there,
When I was driven from that land.
                                    But now,
What news, Ismene, do you bring your father?
Why have you left your house to make this journey?
You came for no light reason, I know that;
It must be something serious for me.   360

Ismene

I will pass over the troubles I have had
Searching for your whereabouts, father.
They were hard enough to bear; and I will not
Go through it all again in telling of them.
In any case, it is your sons' troubles   365
That I have come to tell you.
First it was their desire, as it was Creon's,
That the throne should pass to him; that thus the city
Should be defiled no longer: such was their reasoning
When they considered our people's ancient curse
And how it enthralled your pitiful family.   370
But then some fury put it in their hearts—
O pitiful again!—to itch for power:
For seizure of prerogative and throne;
And it was the younger and the less mature

Who stripped his elder brother, Polyneices,   375
Of place and kingship, and then banished him.

But now the people hear he has gone to Argos,
Into the valley land, has joined that nation,
And is enlisting friends among its warriors,
Telling them Argos shall honorably win   380
Thebes and her plain, or else eternal glory.
This is not a mere recital, father;
But terrible truth!
                      How long will it be, I wonder,
Before the gods take pity on your distress?

Oedipus
You have some hope then that they are concerned   385
With my deliverance?

Ismene
                      I have, father.
The latest sentences of the oracle . . .

Oedipus
How are they worded? What do they prophesy?

Ismene
That you shall be much solicited by our people
Before your death—and after—for their welfare.   390

Oedipus
And what could anyone hope from such as I?

Ismene
The oracles declare their strength's in you—

Oedipus
When I am finished, I suppose I am strong!

Ismene
For the gods who threw you down sustain you now.

Oedipus
Slight favor, now I am old! My doom was early.   395

Ismene

    The proof of it is that Creon is coming to you
    For that same reason, and soon: not by and by.

Oedipus

    To do what, daughter? Tell me about this.

Ismene

    To settle you near the land of Thebes, and so
    Have you at hand; but you may not cross the border.   400

Oedipus

    What good am I to them outside the country?

Ismene

    It is merely that if your burial were unlucky,
    That would be perilous for them.

Oedipus

                Ah, then!
    No god's assistance is needed in comprehending.

Ismene

    Therefore they want to keep you somewhere near,
    Just at the border, where you'll not be free.   405

Oedipus

    And will they compose my shade with Theban dust?

Ismene

    Ah, father! No. Your father's blood forbids it.

Oedipus

    Then they shall never hold me in their power!

Ismene

    If so, some day it will be bitter for them.

Oedipus

    How will that be, my child?

Ismene

             When they shall stand   410
    Where you are buried, and feel your anger there.

Oedipus

What you have said—from whom did you hear it, child?

Ismene

The envoys told me when they returned from Delphi.

Oedipus

Then all this about me was spoken there?

Ismene

According to those men, just come to Thebes.   415

Oedipus

Has either of my sons had word of this?

Ismene

They both have, and they understand it well.

Oedipus

The scoundrels! So they knew all this, and yet
Would not give up the throne to have me back?

Ismene

It hurts me to hear it, but I can't deny it.   420

Oedipus

Gods!
Put not their fires of ambition out!
Let the last word be mine upon this battle
They are about to join, with the spears lifting!
I'd see that the one who holds the sceptre now   425
Would not have power long, nor would the other,
The banished one, return!
                              These were the two
Who saw me in disgrace and banishment
And never lifted a hand for me. They heard me
Howled from the country, heard the thing proclaimed!   430

And will they say I wanted exile then,
An appropriate clemency, granted by the state?
That is all false! The truth is that at first

My mind was a boiling caldron; nothing so sweet
As death, death by stoning, could have been given me;　　435
Yet no one there would grant me that desire.
It was only later, when my madness cooled,
And I had begun to think my rage excessive,
My punishment too great for what I had done;
Then it was that the city—in its good time!—　　440
Decided to be harsh, and drove me out.
They could have helped me then; they could have
Helped him who begot them! Would they do it?
For lack of a little word from that fine pair
Out I went, like a beggar, to wander forever!　　445
Only by grace of these two girls, unaided,
Have I got food or shelter or devotion;
The others held their father of less worth
Than sitting on a throne and being king.

Well, they shall never win me in their fight!　　450
Nor will they profit from the rule of Thebes.
I am sure of that; I have heard the prophecies
Brought by this girl; I think they fit those others
Spoken so long ago, and now fulfilled.
So let Creon be sent to find me: Creon,　　455
Or any other of influence in the state.
If you men here consent—as do those powers
Holy and awful, the spirits of this place—
To give me refuge, then shall this city have
A great savior; and woe to my enemies!　　460

Chorus

Oedipus: you are surely worth our pity:
You, and your children, too. And since you claim
Also to be a savior of our land,
I'd like to give you counsel for good luck.

Oedipus

Dear friend! I'll do whatever you advise.　　465

Chorus

Make expiation to these divinities
Whose ground you violated when you came.

Oedipus

In what way shall I do so? Tell me, friends.

Chorus

First you must bring libations from the spring
That runs forever; and bring them with clean hands. 470

Oedipus

And when I have that holy water, then?

Chorus

There are some bowls there, by a skillful potter;
Put chaplets round the brims, over the handles.

Oedipus

Of myrtle springs, or woolen stuff, or what?

Chorus

Take the fleeces cropped from a young lamb. 475

Oedipus

Just so; then how must I perform the rite?

Chorus

Facing the quarter of the morning light,
Pour your libations out.

Oedipus

Am I to pour them from the bowls you speak of?

Chorus

In three streams, yes; the last one, empty it.

Oedipus

With what should it be filled? Tell me this, too. 480

Chorus

With water and honey; but with no wine added.

Oedipus
  And when the leaf-dark earth receives it?

Chorus
  Lay three times nine young shoots of olive on it
  With both your hands; meanwhile repeat this prayer:

Oedipus
  This I am eager to hear: it has great power.   485

Chorus
  That as we call them Eumenides,
  Which means the gentle of heart,
  May they accept with gentleness
  The suppliant and his wish.

  So you, or he who prays for you, address them;

  But do not speak aloud or raise a cry;
  Then come away, and do not turn again.   490
  If you will do all this, I shall take heart
  And stand up for you; otherwise, O stranger,
  I should be seriously afraid for you.

Oedipus
  Children, you hear the words of these good people?

Antigone
  Yes; now tell us what we ought to do.

Oedipus
  It need not be performed by me; I'm far   495
  From having the strength or sight for it—I have neither.
  Let one of you go and carry out the ritual.
  One soul, I think, often can make atonement
  For many others, if it be sincere.
  Now do it quickly.—Yet do not leave me alone!   500
  I could not move without the help of someone.

Ismene
  I'll go and do it. But where am I to go?
  Where shall I find the holy place, I wonder?

Chorus

On the other side of the wood, girl. If you need it, 505
You may get help from the attendant there.

Ismene

I am going now. Antigone, you'll stay
And care for father. Even if it were hard,
I should not think it so, since it is for him.

(Ismene goes out, right. The chorus draws nearer to Oedipus.)

CHORAL DIALOGUE

Chorus

What evil things have slept since long ago 510
 It is not sweet to awaken;
 And yet I long to be told—

Oedipus
      What?

Chorus

Of that heartbreak for which there was no help,
 The pain you have had to suffer.

Oedipus

 For kindness' sake, do not open 515
 My old wound, and my shame.

Chorus

It is told everywhere, and never dies;
 I only want to hear it truly told.

Oedipus

 Ah! Ah!

Chorus

     Consent I beg you;
Give me my wish, and I shall give you yours. 520

Oedipus

I had to face a thing most terrible,
 Not willed by me, I swear;
 I would have abhorred it all.

Chorus
                    So?

Oedipus
   Though I did not know, Thebes married me to evil;   525
   Fate and I were joined there.

Chorus
   Then it was indeed your mother
   With whom the thing was done?

Oedipus
   Ah! It is worse than death to have to hear it!
   Strangers! Yes: and these two girls of mine . . .   530

Chorus
   Go on—

Oedipus
                    These luckless two
   Were given birth by her who gave birth to me.

Chorus
   These then are daughters; they are also—

Oedipus
   Sisters: yes, their father's sisters . . .   535

Chorus
   Ah, pity!

Oedipus
                    Pity, indeed. What throngs
   Of pities come into my mind!

Chorus
   You suffered—

Oedipus
                    Yes, unspeakably.

Chorus
   You sinned—

Oedipus
                No, I did not sin!

Chorus

How not?

Oedipus

I thought
Of her as my reward. Ah, would I had never won it!   540
Would I had never served the State that day!

Chorus

Unhappy man—and you also killed—

Oedipus

What is it now? What are you after?

Chorus

Killed your father!

Oedipus

God in heaven!
You strike again where I am hurt.

Chorus

You killed him.

Oedipus

Killed him. Yet, there is—   545

Chorus

What more?

Oedipus

A just extenuation.
This:
I did not know him; and he wished to murder me.
Before the law—before God—I am innocent!

(*The Chorus turns at the approach of Theseus.*)

SCENE 3

Chorus

The king is coming! Aegeus' eldest son,
Theseus: news of you has brought him here.   550

(*Theseus enters with soldiers, left.*)

Theseus

    In the old time I often heard men tell
    Of the bloody extinction of your eyes.
    Even if on my way I were not informed,
    I'd recognize you, son of Laius.
    The garments and the tortured face   555
    Make plain your identity. I am sorry for you.
    And I should like to know what favor here
    You hope for from the city and from me:
    Both you and your unfortunate companion.
    Tell me. It would be something dire indeed   560
    To make me leave you comfortless; for I
    Too was an exile. I grew up abroad,
    And in strange lands I fought as few men have
    With danger and with death.
    Therefore no wanderer shall come, as you do,   565
    And be denied my audience or aid.
    I know I am only a man; I have no more
    To hope for in the end than you have.

Oedipus

    Theseus, in those few words your nobility
    Is plain to me. I need not speak at length;   570
    You have named me and my father accurately,
    Spoken with knowledge of my land and exile.
    There is, then, nothing left for me to tell
    But my desire; and then the tale is ended.

Theseus

    Tell me your wish, then; let me hear it now.   575

Oedipus

    I come to give you something, and the gift
    Is my own beaten self: no feast for the eyes;
    Yet in me is a more lasting grace than beauty.

Theseus

    What grace is this you say you bring to us?

Oedipus

In time you'll learn, but not immediately.　　　　　　580

Theseus

How long, then, must we wait to be enlightened?

Oedipus

Until I am dead, and you have buried me.

Theseus

Your wish is burial? What of your life meanwhile?
Have you forgotten that?—or do you care?

Oedipus

It is all implicated in my burial.　　　　　　585

Theseus

But this is a brief favor you ask of me.

Oedipus

See to it, nevertheless! It is not simple.

Theseus

You mean I shall have trouble with your sons?

Oedipus

Those people want to take me back there now.

Theseus

Will you not go? Is exile admirable?　　　　　　590

Oedipus

No. When I would have returned, they would not have it.

Theseus

What childishness! You are surely in no position—

Oedipus

When you know me, rebuke me; not till then!

Theseus

Well, tell me more. I must not speak in ignorance.

Oedipus

Theseus, I have been wounded more than once.　　　　　　595

Theseus

    Is it your family's curse that you refer to?

Oedipus

    Not merely that; for all Greece buzzes with it.

Theseus

    Then what is the wound that is so pitiless?

Oedipus

    Think how it is with me. I was expelled

    From my own land by my own sons; and now,   600

    As a parricide, my return is not allowed.

Theseus

    How can they summon you, if this is so?

Oedipus

    The sacred oracle compels them to.

Theseus

    They fear some punishment from his forebodings?

Oedipus

    They fear they will be struck down in this land!   605

Theseus

    And how could war arise between these nations?

Oedipus

    Most gentle son of Aegeus! The immortal

    Gods alone have neither age nor death!

    All other things almighty Time disquiets.

    Earth wastes away; the body wastes away;   610

    Faith dies; distrust is born.

    And imperceptibly the spirit changes

    Between a man and his friend, or between two cities.

    For some men soon, for others in later time,

    Their pleasure sickens; or love comes again.   615

    And so with you and Thebes: the sweet season

    Holds between you now; but time goes on,

    Unmeasured Time, fathering numberless

Nights, unnumbered days: and on one day
They'll break apart with spears this harmony—   620
All for a trivial word.
And then my sleeping and long-hidden corpse,
Cold in the earth, will drink hot blood of theirs,
If Zeus endures; if his son's word is true . . .

However: there's no felicity in speaking
Of hidden things. Let me come back to this: 625
Be careful that you keep your word to me;
For if you do you'll never say of Oedipus
That he was given refuge uselessly—
Or if you say it, then the gods have lied.

Chorus

My lord: before you came this man gave promise
Of having power to make his words come true.   630

Theseus

Who would reject his friendship? Is he not
One who would have, in any case, an ally's
Right to our hospitality?
Moreover he has asked grace of our deities,
And offers no small favor in return.   635
As I value that favor, I shall not refuse
This man's desire; I declare him a citizen.

And if it should please our friend to remain here,
I direct you to take care of him;
Or else he may come with me.
                          Whatever you choose,
Oedipus, we shall be happy to accord.   640
You know your own needs best; I accede to them.

Oedipus

May God bless men like these!

Theseus

What do you say then? Shall it be my house?

Oedipus
If it were right for me. But the place is here . . .

Theseus
And what will you do here?—Not that I oppose you.   645

Oedipus
Here I shall prevail over those who banished me.

Theseus
Your presence, as you say, is a great blessing.

Oedipus
If you are firm in doing what you promise.

Theseus
You can be sure of me; I'll not betray you.

Oedipus
I'll not ask pledges, as I would of scoundrels.   650

Theseus
You'd get no more assurance than by my word.

Oedipus
I wonder how you will behave?

Theseus
                              You fear?
Oedipus
That men will come—

Theseus
                              These men will attend to them.

Oedipus
Look: when you leave me—

Theseus
                              I know what to do!

Oedipus
I am oppressed by fear!

Theseus
                              I feel no fear.   655

Oedipus

    You do not know the menace!

Theseus

                     I do know

    No man is going to take you against my will.

    Angry men are liberal with threats

    And bluster generally. When the mind

    Is master of itself, threats are no matter.   660

    These people may have dared to talk quite fiercely

    Of taking you; perhaps, as I rather think,

    They'll find a sea of troubles in the way.

    Therefore I should advise you to take heart.

    Even aside from me and my intentions,

    Did not Apollo send and guide you here?   665

    However it may be, I can assure you,

    While I'm away, my name will be your shield.

        (Exit Theseus and soldiers. The Chorus turns to the audience.)

CHORAL POEM

Chorus

    The land beloved of horsemen, fair

    Colonus takes a guest;

    He shall not seek another home,   670

    For this, in all the earth and air,

    Is most secure and loveliest.

    In the god's untrodden vale

    Where leaves and berries throng,

    And wine-dark ivy climbs the bough,

    The sweet, sojourning nightingale

    Murmurs all day long.   675

    No sun nor wind may enter there

    Nor the winter's rain;

    But ever through the shadow goes

    Dionysus reveler,

    Immortal maenads in his train.   680

Here with drops of heaven's dews
At daybreak all the year,
The clusters of narcissus bloom,
Time-hallowed garlands for the brows
Of those great ladies whom we fear.   685

The crocus like a little sun
Blooms with its yellow ray;
The river's fountains are awake,
And his nomadic streams that run
Unthinned forever, and never stay;   690

But like perpetual lovers move
On the maternal land.
And here the choiring Muses come,
And the divinity of love
With the gold reins in her hand.

> (*The Chorus may now shift its grouping or otherwise
> indicate a change of theme.*)

Chorus

And our land has a thing unknown
On Asia's sounding coast   695
Or in the sea-surrounded west
Where Agamemnon's race has sway:
The olive, fertile and self-sown,
The terror of our enemies
That no hand tames nor tears away—
The blessed tree that never dies!—
But it will mock the swordsman in his rage.

Ah, how it flourishes in every field,
Most beautifully here!   700
The gray-leafed tree, the children's nourisher!
No young man nor one partnered by his age
Knows how to root it out nor make
Barren its yield;
For Zeus the Father smiles on it with sage

Eyes that forever are awake, 705
And Pallas watches with her sea-pale eyes.

Last and grandest praise I sing
To Athens, nurse of men,
For her great pride and for the splendor
Destiny has conferred on her. 710
Land from which fine horses spring!
Land where foals are beautiful!
Land of the sea and the sea-farer!
Upon whose lovely littoral
The god of the sea moves, the son of Time.

That lover of our land I praise again,
Who found our horsemen fit
For first bestowal of the curb and bit, 715
To discipline the stallion in his prime;
And strokes to which our oarsmen sing,
Well-fitted, oak and men,
Whose long sea-oars in wondrous rhyme
Flash from the salt foam, following
The hundred-footed sea-wind and the gull.

> *(At the conclusion of this, Antigone is standing stage*
> *right, looking off-stage attentively.)*

Scene 4

Antigone

Land so well spoken of and praised so much! 720
Now is the time to show those words are true.

Oedipus

What now, my child?

Antigone (returning to him)

A man is coming towards us,
And it is Creon—not unaccompanied, father.

Oedipus

Most kindly friends! I hope you may give proof,
And soon, of your ability to protect me! 725

Chorus

    Don't be afraid: you'll see. I may be old,
    But the nation's strength has not grown old.

                          (Enter Creon, right, with guards.)

Creon

    Gentlemen, and citizens of this land:
    I can see from your eyes that my arrival
    Has been a cause of sudden fear to you;   730
    Do not be fearful. And say nothing hostile!
    I have not come for any hostile action,
    For I am old, and know this city has
    Power, if any city in Hellas has.

    But for this man here: I, despite my age,   735
    Am sent to bring him to the land of Thebes.
    This is not one man's mission, but was ordered
    By the whole Theban people. I am their emissary
    Because it fell to me as a relative
    To mourn his troubles more than anyone.

    So, now, poor Oedipus, come home.   740
    You have heard my message. The people of the city
    Are right in summoning you—I most of all,
    For most of all, unless I am worst of men,
    I grieve for your unhappiness, old man.
    I see you ravaged as you are, a stranger   745
    Everywhere, never at rest,
    With only a girl to serve you in your need.—
    I never thought she'd fall to such indignity,
    Poor child! And yet she has;   750
    Forever tending you, leading a beggar's
    Life with you; a grown-up girl who knows
    Nothing of marriage; whoever comes can take her. . . .

    Is not this a disgrace? I weep to see it!
    Disgrace for you, for me, for all our people!
    We cannot hide what is so palpable,   755
    But you, if you will listen to me, Oedipus—

And in the name of your father's gods, listen!—
Bury the whole thing now; agree with me
To go back to your city and your home!

Take friendly leave of Athens, for she deserves it;
But you should have more reverence for Thebes,
Since long ago she was your kindly nurse.   760

Oedipus

You brazen rascal! Playing your rascal's tricks
In righteous speeches, as you always would!
Why do you try it? How can you think to take me
Into that snare I should so hate if taken?

That time when I was sick with my private   765
Agony: when I would lightly have left the earth—
You had no mind to give me what I wanted!
But when at long last I had had my fill
Of rage and grief, and in my quiet house
Began to find some comfort: that was the time
You chose to rout me out.   770
How precious was this kinship to you then?
It is the same thing now: you see this city
And all its people being kind to me,
So you attempt to coax me away from them!
A cruel thing, for all your soothing words.

What pleasure is there in being amiable   775
To those who do not want your amiability?

Suppose that when you wanted something terribly
A man should neither grant it you nor give
Sympathy even; but later when you were glutted
With all your heart's desire, should give it then,
When charity was no charity at all?
Would you not think the kindness somewhat hollow?   780
That is the sort of kindness you offer me:
Generous in words, but in reality evil.

Now I will tell these men, and prove you evil.
You come to take me, but not to take me home;
Rather to settle me outside the city
So that the city may escape my curse,   785
Escape from punishment by Athens.
                         Yes;
But you'll not have it. What you'll have is this:
My vengeance active in that land forever;
And what my sons will have of my old kingdom
Is just so much room as they need to die in!   790

Now who knows better the destiny of Thebes?
I do, for I have had the best informants:
Apollo, and Zeus himself who is his father.
And yet you come here with your fraudulent speech
All whetted up! The more you talk, the more   795
Harm, not good, you'll get by it!—
However, I know you'll never believe that.—

Only leave us! Let us live here in peace!
Is it a bad life, if it gives us pleasure?

Creon

Which of us do you consider is more injured   800
By talk like this? You hurt only yourself.

Oedipus

I am perfectly content, so long as you
Can neither wheedle me nor fool these others.

Creon

Unhappy man! Shall it be plain that time
Brings you no wisdom? that you shame your age?   805

Oedipus

What repartee! I know no honest man
Able to speak so well under all conditions!

Creon

To speak much is one thing; to speak to the point's another!

Oedipus
As if you spoke so little but so fittingly!

Creon
No, not fittingly for a mind like yours!   810

Oedipus
Go away! I speak for these men also!
Stop busybodying here where I must live!

Creon
I call on these—not you!—as witnesses
Of what rejoinder you have made to friends.—
If I ever take you—

Oedipus
      With these men fighting for me,
Who is going to take me by violence?   815

Creon
You'll have pain enough without that, I promise you!

Oedipus
What are you up to? What is behind that brag?

Creon
Your two daughters: one of them I have just now
Had seized and carried off, and I'll take this one!

Oedipus
Ah!

Creon
   You'll soon have better reason to groan about it!   820

Oedipus
You have my child?

Creon
      And this one in a moment!

Oedipus
Ah, friends! What will you do? Will you betray me?
Are you not going to drive this thief away?

Chorus
  Go, stranger! Off with you! You have no right
  To do what you are doing, or what you have done!   825

Creon (to Guards)
  You there: it would be well to take her now,
  Whether she wants to go with you or not.

                (Two Guards approach Antigone.)

Antigone
  Oh, God, where shall I run? What help is there
  From gods or men?

Chorus
             What are you doing, stranger?

Creon
  I will not touch this man; only her who is mine.   830

Oedipus
  O masters of this land!

Chorus
            This is unjust!

Creon
  No, just!

Chorus
     Why so?

Creon
        I take what belongs to me!

Oedipus
  O Athens!
             (The Guards pinion Antigone's arms.)

Chorus
  What are you doing, stranger? Will you
  Let her go? Must we have a test of strength?   835

Creon
  Hold off!

Chorus
             Not while you persist in doing this!

Creon
Your city will have war if you hurt me!

Oedipus
Did I not proclaim this?

Chorus (*to Guards*)
      Take your hands
Off the child at once!

Creon
      What you cannot enforce,
Do not command!

Chorus
I tell you, let go!

Creon
      And I tell you—on your way!   840

(The Guards pull Antigone toward the right.)

Chorus
Help! Here, men of Colonus! Help! Help!
The city, my city, is pillaged!
Hurry! Help, ho!

Antigone
They drag me away. How wretched! O friends, friends!

Oedipus (*groping*)
Where are you, child?

Antigone
      They have overpowered me!   845

Oedipus
Give me your hands, little one!

Antigone
      I cannot do it!

Creon (*to Guards*)
Will you get on with her?

        (They go out, right.)

Oedipus
      God help me now!

Creon

    With these two sticks at any rate you'll never
    Guide yourself again! But since you wish
    To conquer your own people—by whose command,   850
    Though I am royal, I have performed this act—
    Go on and conquer! Later, I think, you'll learn
    That now as before you have done yourself no good
    By gratifying your temper against your friends!
    Anger has always been your greatest sin!   855

Chorus (approaching Creon)

    Control yourself, stranger!

Creon

    Don't touch me, I say!

Chorus

    I'll not release you! Those two girls were stolen!

Creon

    By God, I'll have more booty in a moment
    To bring my city! I'll not stop with them!

Chorus

    Now what are you about?

Creon

                    I'll take him, too!   860

Chorus

    A terrible thing to say!

Creon

                    It will be done!

Chorus

    Not if the ruler of our land can help it!

Oedipus

    Voice of shamelessness! Will you touch me?

Creon

    Silence, I say!

Oedipus

No! May the powers here
Not make me silent until I say this curse: 865
You scoundrel, who have cruelly taken her
Who served my naked eyepits as their eyes!
On you and yours forever may the sun god,
Watcher of all the world, confer such days
As I have had, and such an age as mine!   870

Creon

Do you see this, citizens of this country?

Oedipus

They see both me and you; and they see also
That when I am hurt I have only words to avenge it!

Creon

I'll not stand for it longer! Alone as I am,
And slow with age, I'll try my strength to take him!   875

(*Creon goes slowly toward Oedipus.*)

Oedipus

Ah!

Chorus

You are a bold man, friend,
If you think you can do this!

Creon

I do think so!

Chorus

If you could do it, our city would be finished!

Creon

In a just cause the weak will beat the strong!   880

Oedipus

You hear his talk?

Chorus

By Zeus, he shall not do it!

Creon

Zeus may determine that, but you will not.

Chorus
>Is this not criminal!

Creon (laying hold of Oedipus)
>If so, you'll bear it!

Chorus
>Ho, everyone! Captains, ho!
>Hurry up! Come on the run!   885
>They are well on their way by now!

>>>>>(*Theseus enters, left, with armed men.*)
Theseus
>Why do you shout? What is the matter here?
>Of what are you afraid?
>You have interrupted me as I was sacrificing
>To the great god of the sea, Colonus's patron.
>Tell me everything, so I may know;
>I do not care to make such haste for nothing.   890

Oedipus
>O dearest friend—I recognize your voice—
>A despicable thing has just been done to me!

Theseus
>What is it? Who is the man who did it? Tell me.

Oedipus
>This Creon has had my daughters bound and stolen.   895

Theseus
>What's that you say?

Oedipus
>>>>>Yes; now you know my loss.
Theseus (to his men)
>One of you go on the double
>To the altar place and rouse the people there;
>Make them leave the sacrifice at once
>And run full speed, both foot and cavalry
>As hard as they can gallop, for the place   900
>Where the two highways come together.

The girls must not be permitted to pass there,
Or I will be a laughing-stock to this fellow,
As if I were a man to be handled roughly!
Go on, do as I tell you! Quick!

(Exit Soldier, left.)

This fellow—
If I should act in anger, as he deserves,   905
I wouldn't let him go without chastisement;
But he shall be subject to the sort of laws
He has himself imported here.—

(To Creon)

You: you shall never leave this land of Attica
Until you produce those girls here in my presence;   910
For your behavior is an affront to me,
A shame to your own people and your nation.

You come to a city-state that practices justice,
A state that rules by law, and by law only;
And yet you cast aside her authority,   915
Take what you please, and worse, by violence,
As if you thought there were no men among us,
Or only slaves; and as if I were nobody.

I doubt that Thebes is responsible for you:
She has no propensity for breeding rascals.   920
And Thebes would not applaud you if she knew
You tried to trick me and to rob the gods
By dragging helpless people from their sanctuary!

Were I a visitor in your country—
No matter how immaculate my claims—   925
Without consent from him who ruled the land,
Whoever he might be, I'd take nothing.
I think I have some notion of the conduct
Proper to one who visits a friendly city.
You bring disgrace upon an honorable
Land—your own land, too; a long life   930
Seems to have left you witless as you are old.

I said it once and say it now again:
Someone had better bring those girls here quickly,
Unless you wish to prolong your stay with us
Under close guard, and not much liking it.   935
This is not just a speech; I mean it, friend.

Chorus

Now do you see where you stand? Thebes is just,
But you are adjudged to have acted wickedly.

Creon

It was not that I thought this state unmanly,
Son of Aegeus; nor ill-governed, either;   940
Rather I did this thing in the opinion
That no one here would love my citizens
So tenderly as to keep them against my will . . .
And surely, I thought, no one would give welcome
To an unholy man, a parricide,   945
A man with whom his mother had been found!
Such at least was my estimate of the wisdom
Native to the Areopagus; I thought
Athens was not a home for such exiles.
In that belief I considered him my prize.   950
Even so, I'd not have touched him had he not
Called down curses on my race and me;
That was an injury that deserved reprisal.
There is no old age for a man's anger,
Only death; the dead cannot be hurt.   955

You'll do whatever you wish in this affair,
For even though my case is right and just,
I am weak, without support. Nevertheless,
Old as I am, I'll try to hold you answerable.

Oedipus

O arrogance unashamed! Whose age do you   960
Think you are insulting, mine or yours?
The bloody deaths, the incest, the calamities
You speak so glibly of: I suffered them,

By fate, against my will! It was God's pleasure,
And perhaps our race had angered him long ago.   965
In me myself you could not find such evil
As would have made me sin against my own.
And tell me this: if there were prophecies
Repeated by the oracles of the gods,
That father's death should come through his own son,   970
How could you justly blame it upon me?
On me, who was yet unborn, yet unconceived,
Not yet existent for my father and mother?
If then I came into the world—as I did come—
In wretchedness, and met my father in fight,   975
And knocked him down, not knowing that I killed him
Nor whom I killed—again, how could you find
Guilt in that unmeditated act?
As for my mother—damn you, you have no shame,
Though you are her own brother, in forcing me   980
To speak of that unspeakable marriage;
But I shall speak, I'll not be silent now
After you've let your foul talk go so far!
Yes, she gave me birth—incredible fate!—
But neither of us knew the truth; and she
Bore my children also—and then her shame.
But one thing I do know: you are content   985
To slander her as well as me for that;
While I would not have married her willingly
Nor willingly would I ever speak of it.

No: I shall not be judged an evil man,
Neither in that marriage nor in that death
Which you forever charge me with so bitterly.—   990
Just answer me one thing:
If someone tried to kill you here and now,
You righteous gentleman, what would you do,
Inquire first if the stranger was your father?
Or would you not first try to defend yourself?

I think that since you like to be alive 995
You'd treat him as the threat required; not
Look around for assurance that you were right.
Well, that was the sort of danger I was in,
Forced into it by the gods. My father's soul,
Were it on earth, I know would bear me out.

You, however, being a knave—and since you 1000
Think it fair to say anything you choose,
And speak of what should not be spoken of—
Accuse me of all this before these people.
You also think it clever to flatter Theseus,
And Athens—her exemplary government;
But in your flattery you have forgotten this: 1005
If any country comprehends the honors
Due to the gods, this country knows them best;
Yet you would steal me from Athens in my age
And in my time of prayer; indeed, you seized me,
And you have taken and carried off my daughters.

Now for that profanation I make my prayer, 1010
Calling on the divinities of the grove
That they shall give me aid and fight for me;
So you may know what men defend this town.

Chorus
My lord, our friend is worthy; he has had
Disastrous fortune; yet he deserves our comfort. 1015

Theseus
Enough of speeches. While the perpetrators
Flee, we who were injured loiter here.

Creon
What will you have me do?—since I am worthless.

Theseus
You lead us on the way. You can be my escort.
If you are holding the children in this neighborhood 1020
You yourself will uncover them to me.

If your retainers have taken them in flight,
The chase is not ours; others are after them.
And they will never have cause to thank their gods
For getting free out of this country.
All right. Move on. And remember that the captor 1025
Is now the captive; the hunter is in the snare.
What was won by stealth will not be kept.

In this you'll not have others to assist you;
And I know well you had them, for you'd never
Dare to go so far in your insolence 1030
Were you without sufficient accomplices.
You must have had a reason for your confidence,
And I must reckon with it. The whole city
Must not seem overpowered by one man.
Do you understand at all? Or do you think
That what I say is still without importance? 1035

Creon
To what you say I make no objection here.
At home we, too, shall determine what to do.

Theseus
If you must threaten, do so on the way.
Oedipus, you stay here, and rest assured
That unless I perish first I'll not draw breath 1040
Until I put your children in your hands.

Oedipus
Bless you for your noble heart, Theseus!
And good luck to you in what you do for us!

(Two Soldiers take Creon by the arms and march him out,
right, followed by Theseus and the rest of his men.
The Chorus follows a short way and stands
gazing after them.)

CHORAL POEM
Chorus
Ah, God, to be where the pillagers make stand!
To hear the shout and brazen sound of war! 1045

Or maybe on Apollo's sacred strand,
Or by that torchlit Eleusinian shore

Where pilgrims come, whose lips the golden key   1050
Of sweet-voiced ministers has rendered still,
To cherish there with grave Persephone
Consummate rest from death and mortal ill;

For even to those shades the warrior king   1055
Will press the fighting on—until he take
The virgin sisters from the foemen's ring,
Within his country, for his country's sake!

It may be they will get beyond the plain
And reach the snowy mountain's western side,   1060
If their light chariots have the racing rein,
If they have ponies, and if they can ride;

Yet they'll be taken: for the god they fear
Fights for our land, and Theseus sends forth   1065
His breakneck cavalry with all its gear
Flashing like mountain lightning to the north.

These are the riders of Athens, conquered never;
They honor her whose glory all men know,
And honor the god of the sea, who loves forever   1070
The feminine earth that bore him long ago.

*(A shift of grouping, and the four following stanzas
taken each by a separate voice.)*

Chorus

Has the fight begun? May it begin!
The presentiment enchants my mind   1075
That they shall soon give in!
And free the daughters of the blind
From hurt by their own kind!

*For God will see some noble thing
Before this day is over.*

Forevisioning the fight, and proud,   1080
Would I could be a soaring dove

And circle the tail cloud;
So might I gaze down from above
On the mêlée I love.

For God will see some noble thing
Before this day is over.

All highest of immortals! Hail,   1085
Great Zeus who see all things below!
Let not our troopers fail;
But give them luck to snare and throw
And bring the quarry low!

And you shall see some noble thing
Before this day is over.

Stern Pallas, hear us! Apollo, hear!   1090
Hunter and sister who give chase
To the swift and dappled deer:
Be our protectors! Lend your grace
To our land and our race!

And you shall see some noble thing
Before this day is over.

> (*There is a long pause, and then the Chorus turns*
> *to Oedipus in joy.*)

SCENE 5

Chorus

O wanderer! You will not say I lied;
I who kept lookout for you!
I see them now—the two girls—here they come
With our armed men around them!

Oedipus

Ah, where? Do you really mean it?

> (*Theseus comes in leading by the hand Antigone and*
> *Ismene, followed by Soldiers.*)

Antigone
                        Father, father!
I wish some god would give you eyes to see   1100
The noble prince who brings us back to you!

Oedipus
Ah, child! You are really here?

Antigone
                        Yes, for the strength
Of Theseus and his kind followers saved us.

Oedipus
Come to your father, child, and let me touch you
Whom I had thought never to touch again!   1105

Antigone
It shall be as you ask; I wish it as much as you.

Oedipus
Where are you?

Antigone
                        We are coming to you together.
Oedipus
My sweet children!

Antigone
                        To our father, sweet indeed.
Oedipus
My staff and my support!

Antigone
                        And partners in sorrow.
Oedipus
I have what is dearest to me in the world.   1110
To die, now, would not be so terrible,
Since you are near me.
                        Press close to me, child,
Be rooted in your father's arms; rest now
From the cruel separation, the going and coming;
And tell me the story as briefly as you can: 1115
A little talk is enough for girls so tired.

Antigone

    Theseus saved us: he is the one to tell you;
    Neither you nor I had much to do with it!

Oedipus

    Dear friend: don't be offended if I continue
    To talk to these two children overlong;   1120
    I had scarce thought they would be seen again!
    Be sure I understand that you alone
    Made this joy possible for me.
    You are the one that saved them, no one else.
    And may the gods give you such destiny
    As I desire for you: and for your country.   1125
    For I have found you truly reverent,
    Decent, and straight in speech: you only
    Of all mankind.
    I know it, and I thank you with these words.
    All that I have I owe to your courtesy;—
    Now give me your right hand, my lord,   1130
    And if it be permitted, let me kiss you. . . .

    What am I saying? How can a wretch like me
    Desire to touch a man who has no stain
    Of evil in him? No, no; I will not do it;
    And neither shall you touch me. The only ones   1135
    Fit to be fellow suffers of mine
    Are those with such experience as I have.
    Receive my salutation where you are.
    And for the rest, be kindly to me still
    As you have been up to now.

Theseus

    That you should talk a long time to your children
    In joy at seeing them—why, that's no wonder!   1140
    Or that you should address them before me—
    There's no offense in that. It is not in words
    That I should wish my life to be distinguished,
    But rather in things done.

Have I not shown that? I was not a liar   1145
In what I swore I'd do for you, old man.
I am here; and I have brought them back
Alive and safe, for all they were threatened with.
As to how I found them, how I took them, why
Brag of it? You will surely learn from them.

However, there is a matter that just now   1150
Came to my attention on my way here—
A trivial thing to speak of, and yet puzzling;
I want your opinion on it.
It is best for a man not to neglect such things.

Oedipus
 What is it, son of Aegeus? Tell me,
 So I may know on what you desire counsel.   1155

Theseus
 They say some man is here who claims to be
 A relative of yours, though not of Thebes;
 For some reason he has thrown himself in prayer
 Before Poseidon's altar, where I was making
 Sacrifice before I came.

Oedipus
 What is his country? What is he praying for?   1160

Theseus
 All I know is this: he asks, they tell me,
 A brief interview with you, and nothing more.

Oedipus
 What about, I wonder?
 It can't be a slight matter, if he is praying.

Theseus
 They say he only asks to speak to you
 And then to depart safely by the same road.   1165

Oedipus
 Who could it be who would come here to pray?

Theseus
 Think: have you any relative in Argos
 Who might desire this favor of you?

Oedipus
                    Dear friend!
 Say no more!

Theseus
                    What is the matter with you?

Oedipus
 No more!

Theseus
                    But: what is the matter? Tell me.   1170

Oedipus
 When I heard "Argos" I knew the petitioner.

Theseus
 And who is he whom I must prepare to dislike?

Oedipus
 A son of mine, my lord, and a hated one.
 Nothing could be more painful than to listen to him.

Theseus
 But why? Is it not possible to listen   1175
 Without doing anything you need not do?
 Why should it annoy you so to hear him?

Oedipus
 My lord, even his voice is hateful to me.
 Don't beat me down; don't make me yield in this!

Theseus
 But now consider if you are not obliged
 To do so by his supplication here:
 Perhaps you have a duty to the god.   1180

Antigone
 Father: listen to me, even if I am young.
 Allow this man to satisfy his conscience
 And give the gods whatever he thinks their due.
 And let our brother come here, for my sake.

Don't be afraid: he will not throw you off   1185
In your resolve, nor speak offensively.
What is the harm in hearing what he says?
If he has ill intentions, he'll betray them.
You sired him; even had he wronged you, father,
And wronged you impiously, still you could not   1190
Rightfully wrong him in return!
Do let him come!
                   Other men have bad sons,
And other men are swift to anger; yet
They will accept advice, they will be swayed
By their friends' pleading, even against their nature.
Reflect, not on the present, but on the past;   1195
Think of your mother's and your father's fate
And what you suffered through them! If you do,
I think you'll see how terrible an end
Terrible wrath may have.
You have, I think, a permanent reminder
In your lost, irrecoverable eyes. . . .   1200
Ah, yield to us! If our request is just,
We need not, surely, be importunate;
And you, to whom I have not yet been hard,
Should not be obdurate with me!

Oedipus
    Child, your talk wins you a pleasure
    That will be pain for me. If you have set   1205
    Your heart on it, so be it.

    Only, Theseus: if he is to come here,
    Let no one have power over my life!

Theseus
    That is the sort of thing I need hear only
    Once, not twice, old man. I do not boast,
    But you should know your life is safe while mine is.   1210

*(Theseus goes out, left, with his Soldiers, leaving two on
guard. The Chorus turns to address the audience.)*

« 133 »

Choral Poem

Chorus

Though he has watched a decent age pass by,
A man will sometimes still desire the world.
I swear I see no wisdom in that man.
The endless hours pile up a drift of pain
More unrelieved each day; and as for pleasure,   1215
When he is sunken in excessive age,
You will not see his pleasure anywhere.
The last attendant is the same for all,
Old men and young alike, as in its season   1220
Man's heritage of underworld appears:
There being then no epithalamion,
No music and no dance. Death is the finish.

Not to be born surpasses thought and speech.
The second best is to have seen the light   1225
And then to go back quickly whence we came.
The feathery follies of his youth once over,   1230
What trouble is beyond the range of man?
What heavy burden will he not endure?
Jealousy, faction, quarreling, and battle—
The bloodiness of war, the grief of war.
And in the end he comes to strengthless age,   1235
Abhorred by all men, without company,
Unfriended in that uttermost twilight
Where he must live with every bitter thing.

This is the truth, not for me only,
But for this blind and ruined man.
Think of some shore in the north the   1240
Concussive waves make stream
This way and that in the gales of winter:
It is like that with him:
The wild wrack breaking over him
From head to foot, and coming on forever;
Now from the plunging down of the sun,   1245

Now from the sunrise quarter,
Now from where the noonday gleams,
Now from the night and the north.

> (*Antigone and Ismene have been looking off-stage, left.*
> *Antigone turns.*)

SCENE 6

Antigone

I think I see the stranger near us now,
And no men with him, father; but his eyes   1250
Swollen with weeping as he comes.

> (*Polyneices enters, left.*)

Oedipus
                    Who comes?

Antigone

The one whom we have had so long in mind;
It is he who stands here; it is Polyneices.

Polyneices

Ah, now what shall I do? Sisters, shall I
Weep for my misfortunes or for those   1255
I see in the old man, my father,
Whom I have found here in an alien land,
With you two girls, an outcast for so long,
And with such garments! The abominable
Filth grown old with him, rotting his sides!
And on his sightless face the ragged hair   1260
Streams in the wind. There's the same quality
In the food he carries for his thin old belly.
All this I learn too late.
And I swear now that I have been villainous   1265
In not supporting you! You need not wait
To hear it said by others!
                    Only, think:
Compassion limits even the power of God;
So may there be a limit for you, father!

For all that has gone wrong may still be healed,
And surely the worst is over!   1270

Why are you silent?
Speak to me, father! Don't turn away from me!
Will you not answer me at all? Will you
Send me away without a word?
                          Not even
Tell me why you are enraged against me?

Daughters of Oedipus, my own sisters,   1275
Try to move your so implacable father;
Do not let him reject me in such contempt!
Make him reply!
                          I am here on pilgrimage. . . .

Antigone

Poor brother: you yourself must tell him why.   1280
As men speak on they may sometimes give pleasure,
Sometimes annoy, or sometimes touch the heart;
And so somehow provide the mute with voices.

Polyneices

I will speak out then; your advice is fair.
First, however, I must claim the help   1285
Of that same god, Poseidon, from whose altars
The governor of this land has lifted me
And sent me here, giving me leave to speak
And to await response, and a safe passage.
These are the favors I desire from you,
Stranger, and from my sisters and my father.   1290

And now, father, I will tell you why I came.
I am a fugitive, driven from my country,
Because I thought fit, as the eldest born,
To take my seat upon your sovereign throne.
For that, Eteocles, the younger of us,   1295
Banished me—but not by a decision
In argument or ability or arms;
Merely because he won the city over.

Of this I believe the Furies that pursue you
Were indeed the cause: and so I hear   1300
From clairvoyants whom I afterwards consulted. . . .

Then, when I went into the Dorian land,
I took Adrastus as my father-in-law,
And bound to me by oath whatever men
Were known as leaders or as fighters there;
My purpose being to form an expedition
Of seven troops of spearmen against Thebes.—   1305
With which enlistment may I die for justice
Or else expel the men who exiled me!

So it is. Then why should I come here now?
Father, my prayers must be made to you!
Mine and those of all who fight with me!   1310
Their seven columns under seven captains
Even now complete the encirclement of Thebes:
Men like Amphiareus, the hard spear thrower,
Expert in spears and in the ways of eagles;
Second is Tydeus, the Aetolian,   1315
Son of Oeneus; third is Eteoclus,
Born in Argos; fourth is Hippomedon
(His father, Talaus, sent him); Capaneus,
The fifth, has sworn he'll raze the town of Thebes
With fire-brands; and sixth is Parthenopaeus,   1320
An Arcadian who roused himself to war—
Son of that virgin famous in the old time
Who long years afterward conceived and bore him—
Parthenopaeus, Atalanta's son.
And it is I, your son—or if I am not
Truly your son, since evil fathered me,
At least I am called your son—it is I who lead
The fearless troops of Argos against Thebes.   1325

Now in the name of these two children, father,
And for your own soul's sake, we all implore
And beg you to give up your heavy wrath

Against me! I go forth to punish him,
The brother who robbed me of my fatherland!   1330
If we can put any trust in oracles,
They say that those you bless shall come to power.

Now by the gods and fountains of our people,
I pray you, listen and comply! Are we not beggars
Both of us, and exiles, you and I?   1335
We live by paying court to other men;
The same fate follows us.
But as for him—how insupportable!—
He lords it in our house, luxuriates there,
Laughs at us both!

If you will stand by me in my resolve,
I'll waste no time or trouble whipping him;   1340
And then I'll re-establish you at home,
And settle there myself, and throw him out.
If your will is the same as mine, it's possible
To promise this. If not, I can't be saved.   1345

Chorus

For the sake of the one who sent him, Oedipus,
Speak to this man before you send him back.

Oedipus

Yes, gentlemen: but were it not Theseus,
The sovereign of your land, who sent him here,   1350
Thinking it right that he should have an answer,
You never would have heard a sound from me.

Well: he has asked, and he shall hear from me
A kind of answer that will not overjoy him.
You scoundrel!
               When it was you who held
Throne and authority—as your brother now   1355
Holds them in Thebes—you drove me into exile:
Me, your own father: made me a homeless man,
Insuring me these rags you blubber over

When you behold them now—now that you, too,
Have fallen on evil days and are in exile.

Weeping is no good now. However long   1360
My life may last, I have to see it through;
But I regard you as a murderer!
For you reduced me to this misery,
You made me an alien. Because of you
I have begged my daily bread from other men.
If I had not these children to sustain me,   1365
I might have lived or died for all your interest.
But they have saved me, they are my support,
And are not girls, but men, in faithfulness.
As for you two, you are no sons of mine!

And so it is that there are eyes that watch you   1370
Even now; though not as they shall watch
If those troops are in fact marching on Thebes.
You cannot take that city. You'll go down
All bloody, and your brother, too.
                            For I
Have placed that curse upon you before this,   1375
And now I invoke that curse to fight for me,
That you may see a reason to respect
Your parents, though your birth was as it was;
And though I am blind, not to dishonor me.
These girls did not.

And so your supplication and your throne   1380
Are overmastered surely,—if accepted
Justice still has place in the laws of God.
Now go! For I abominate and disown you!
You utter scoundrel! Go with the malediction
I here pronounce for you: that you shall never   1385
Master your native land by force of arms,
Nor ever see your home again in Argos,
The land below the hills; but you shall die
By your own brother's hand, and you shall kill

The brother who banished you. For this I pray.
And I cry out to the hated underworld   1390
That it may take you home; cry out to those
Powers indwelling here; and to that Power
Of furious War that filled your hearts with hate!

Now you have heard me. Go: tell it to Thebes,
Tell all the Thebans; tell your faithful fighting
Friends what sort of honors   1395
Oedipus has divided among his sons!

Chorus

Polyneices, your coming here has given me
No joy at all. Now go away at once.

Polyneices

Ah, what a journey! What a failure!
My poor companions! See the finish now   1400
Of all we marched from Argos for! See me . . .
For I can neither speak of this to anyone
Among my friends, nor lead them back again;
I must go silently to meet this doom.

O sisters—daughters of his, sisters of mine!   1405
You heard the hard curse of our father:
For God's sweet sake, if father's curse comes true,
And if you find some way to return home,
Do not, at least, dishonor me in death!
But give me a grave and what will quiet me.   1410
Then you shall have, besides the praise he now
Gives you for serving him, an equal praise
For offices you shall have paid my ghost.

Antigone

Polyneices, I beseech you, listen to me!

Polyneices

Dearest—what is it? Tell me, Antigone.   1415

Antigone
>Withdraw your troops to Argos as soon as you can.
>Do not go to your own death and your city's!

Polyneices
>But that is impossible. How could I command
>That army, even backward, once I faltered?

Antigone
>Now why, boy, must your anger rise again?   1420
>What is the good of laying waste your homeland?

Polyneices
>It is shameful to run; and it is also shameful
>To be a laughing-stock to a younger brother.

Antigone
>But see how you fulfill his prophecies!
>Did he not cry that you should kill each other?   1425

Polyneices
>He wishes that. But I cannot give way.

Antigone
>Ah, I am desolate! But who will dare
>Go with you, after hearing the prophecies?

Polyneices
>I'll not report this trifle. A good commander
>Tells what is encouraging, not what is not.   1430

Antigone
>Then you have made up your mind to this, my brother?

Polyneices
>Yes. And do not try to hold me back.
>The dark road is before me; I must take it,
>Doomed by my father and his avenging Furies.
>God bless you if you do what I have asked: 1435
>It is only in death that you can help me now.
>Now let me go. Good-bye! You will not ever
>Look in my eyes again.

Antigone

You break my heart!

Polyneices

Do not grieve for me.

Antigone

Who would not grieve for you,
Sweet brother! You go with open eyes to death!   1440

Polyneices

Death, if that must be.

Antigone

No! Do as I ask!

Polyneices

You ask the impossible.

Antigone

Then I am lost,
If I must be deprived of you!

Polyneices

All that
Rests with the powers that are over us,—
Whether it must be so or otherwise.
You two—I pray no evil comes to you,   1445
For all men know you merit no more pain.

> (*Polyneices goes out, left. There is a dead silence;*
> *then the Chorus meditates.*)

CHORAL POEM AND DIALOGUE

Chorus

So in this new event we see
New forms of terror working through the blind,
Or else inscrutable destiny.   1450
I am not one to say "This is in vain"
Of anything allotted to mankind.
Though some must fall, or fall to rise again,
Time watches all things steadily—   1455

> (*A terrific peal of thunder.*)

Ah, Zeus! Heaven's height has cracked!

(*Thunder and lightning.*)

Oedipus

O my child, my child! Could someone here—
Could someone bring the hero, Theseus?

Antigone

Father, what is your reason for calling him?

Oedipus

God's beating thunder, any moment now,   1460
Will clap me underground: send for him quickly!

(*Thunder and lightning.*)

Chorus

Hear it cascading down the air!
The god-thrown, the gigantic, holy sound!
Terror crawls to the tips of my hair!   1465
My heart shakes!
             There the lightning flames again!
What heavenly marvel is it bringing 'round?
I fear it, for it never comes in vain,
But for man's luck or his despair. . . .   1470

(*Another terrific peal.*)

Ah, Zeus! Majestic heaven!

Oedipus

My children, the appointed end has come;
I can no longer turn away from it.

Antigone

How do you know? What is the sign that tells you?

Oedipus

I know it clearly now. Let someone quickly   1475
Send for the king and bring him here to me!

(*Thunder and lightning.*)

Chorus

Hear the wild thunder fall!
Towering Nature is transfixed!

Be merciful, great spirit, if you run 1480
This sword of darkness through our mother land;
Come not for our confusion,
And deal no blows to me,
Though your tireless Furies stand
By him whom I have looked upon.
Great Zeus, I make my prayer to thee! 1485

Oedipus

Is the king near by? Will he come in time
To find me still alive, my mind still clear?

Antigone

Tell me what it is you have in mind!

Oedipus

To give him now, in return for his great kindness,
The blessing that I promised I would give. 1490
                                    (*Thunder.*)

Chorus

O noble son, return!
No matter if you still descend
In the deep fastness of the sea god's grove,
To make pure offering at his altar fire:
Come back quickly, for God's love! 1495
Receive from this strange man
Whatever may be his heart's desire
That you and I and Athens are worthy of.
My lord, come quickly as you can!

(*The thunder continues, until it stops abruptly with
the entrance of Theseus, left.*)

SCENE 7

Theseus

Now why do you all together 1500
Set up this shout once more?
I see it comes from you, as from our friend.
Is it a lightning bolt from God? a squall

Of rattling hail? Those are familiar things
When such a tempest rages over heaven.

Oedipus

My lord, I longed for you to come! This is   1505
God's work, your lucky coming.

Theseus

                              Now, what new
Circumstance has arisen, son of Laius?

Oedipus

My life sinks in the scale: I would not die
Without fulfilling what I promised Athens.

Theseus

What proof have you that your hour has come?   1510

Oedipus

The great, incessant thunder and continuous
Flashes of lightning from the hand of God.   1515

Theseus

I believe you. I have seen you prophesy
Many things, none falsely. What must be done?

Oedipus

I shall disclose to you, O son of Aegeus,
What is appointed for you and for your city:
A thing that age will never wear away.
Presently now, without a soul to guide me,   1520
I'll lead you to the place where I must die;
But you must never tell it to any man,
Not even the neighborhood in which it lies.
If you obey, this will count more for you
Than many shields and many neighbors' spears.   1525
These things are mysteries, not to be explained;
But you will understand when you come there
Alone. Alone, because I cannot disclose it
To any of your men or to my children,
Much as I love and cherish them. But you

Keep it secret always, and when you come   1530
To the end of life, then you must hand it on
To your most cherished son, and he in turn
Must teach it to his heir, and so forever.
That way you shall forever hold this city
Safe from the men of Thebes, the dragon's sons.

For every nation that lives peaceably,
There will be many others to grow hard
And push their arrogance to extremes: the gods   1535
Attend to these things slowly. But they attend
To those who put off God and turn to madness!
You have no mind for that, child of Aegeus;
Indeed, you know already all that I teach.

Let us proceed then to that place   1540
And hesitate no longer; I am driven
By an insistent voice that comes from God.
Children, follow me this way: see, now,
I have become your guide, as you were mine!
Come: do not touch me: let me alone discover
The holy and funereal ground where I   1545
Must take this fated earth to be my shroud.

This way, O come! The angel of the dead,
Hermes, and veiled Persephone lead me on!

            (*He leads them, firmly and slowly, to the left.*)
O sunlight of no light! Once you were mine!
This is the last my flesh will feel of you;   1550
For now I go to shade my ending day
In the dark underworld. Most cherished friend!
I pray that you and this your land and all
Your people may be blessed: remember me,
Be mindful of my death, and be
Fortunate in all the time to come!   1555

        (*Oedipus goes out, followed by his children and by Theseus
            with his Soldiers. The Chorus lifts its arms to pray.*)

CHORAL POEM

Chorus

If I may dare to adore that Lady
The living never see,
And pray to the master of spirits plunged in night,
Who of vast Hell has sovereignty;
Let not our friend go down in grief and weariness   1560
To that all-shrouding cold,
The dead men's plain, the house that has no light.
Because his sufferings were great, unmerited and untold,   1565
Let some just god relieve him from distress!

O powers under the earth, and tameless
Beast in the passage way,   1570
Rumbler prone at the gate of the strange hosts,
Their guard forever, the legends say:
I pray you, even Death, offspring of Earth and Hell,
To let the descent be clear   1575
As Oedipus goes down among the ghosts
On those dim fields of underground that all men living fear.
Eternal sleep, let Oedipus sleep well!

(A long pause. A Messenger comes in, left.)

SCENE 8

Messenger

Citizens, the briefest way to tell you
Would be to say that Oedipus is no more;   1580
But what has happened cannot be told so simply—
It was no simple thing.

Chorus

                    He is gone, poor man?

Messenger

You may be sure that he has left this world.

Chorus

By God's mercy, was his death a painless one?   1585

Messenger

That is the thing that seems so marvelous.

You know, for you were witnesses, how he
Left this place with no friend leading him,
Acting, himself, as guide for all of us.
Well, when he came to the steep place in the road,   1590
The embankment there, secured with steps of brass,
He stopped in one of the many branching paths.

This was not far from the stone bowl that marks
Theseus' and Pirithous' covenant.

Half-way between that place of stone
With its hollow pear tree, and the marble tomb,   1595
He sat down and undid his filthy garments;
Then he called his daughters and commanded
That they should bring him water from a fountain
For bathing and libation to the dead.
From there they could see the hill of Demeter,   1600
Freshener of all things: so they ascended it
And soon came back with water for their father;
Then helped him properly to bathe and dress.

When everything was finished to his pleasure,
And no command of his remained undone,   1605
Then the earth groaned with thunder from the god below;
And as they heard the sound, the girls shuddered,
And dropped to their father's knees, and began wailing,
Beating their breasts and weeping as if heartbroken.
And hearing them cry out so bitterly,   1610
He put his arms around them, and said to them:

"Children, this day your father is gone from you.
All that was mine is gone. You shall no longer
Bear the burden of taking care of me—
I know it was hard, my children.—And yet one word   1615
Makes all those difficulties disappear:
That word is love. You never shall have more

From any man than you have had from me.
And now you must spend the rest of life without me."

That was the way of it. They clung together   1620
And wept, all three. But when they finally stopped,
And no more sobs were heard, then there was
Silence, and in the silence suddenly
A voice cried out to him—of such a kind
It made our hair stand up in panic fear: 1625
Again and again the call came from the god:
"Oedipus! Oedipus! Why are we waiting?
You delay too long; you delay too long to go!"

Then, knowing himself summoned by the spirit,
He asked that the lord Theseus come to him;   1630
And when he had come, said: "O beloved one,
Give your right hand now as a binding pledge
To my two daughters; children, give him your hands.
Promise that you will never willingly
Betray them, but will carry out in kindness
Whatever is best for them in the days to come."   1635

And Theseus swore to do it for his friend,
With such restraint as fits a noble king.
And when he had done so, Oedipus at once
Laid his blind hands upon his daughters, saying:
"Children, you must show your nobility,   1640
And have the courage now to leave this spot.
You must not wish to see what is forbidden,
Or hear what may not afterward be told.
But go—go quickly. Only the lord Theseus
May stay to see the thing that now begins."

This much every one of us heard him say,   1645
And then we came away with the sobbing girls.
But after a little while as we withdrew
We turned around—and nowhere saw that man,
But only the king, his hands before his face,   1650

Shading his eyes as if from something awful,
Fearful and unendurable to see.
Then very quickly we saw him do reverence
To Earth and to the powers of the air,
With one address to both.

But in what manner   1655
Oedipus perished, no one of mortal men
Could tell but Theseus. It was not lightning,
Bearing its fire from God, that took him off;
No hurricane was blowing.   1660
But some attendant from the train of Heaven
Came for him; or else the underworld
Opened in love the unlit door of earth.
For he was taken without lamentation,
Illness or suffering; indeed his end
Was wonderful if mortal's ever was.   1665

Should someone think I speak intemperately,
I make no apology to him who thinks so.

Chorus
But where are his children and the others with them?

Messenger
They are not far away; the sound of weeping
Should tell you now that they are coming here.

(*Antigone and Ismene enter together.*)

CHORAL DIALOGUE

Antigone
Now we may weep, indeed.   1670
Now, if ever, we may cry
In bitter grief against our fate,
Our heritage still unappeased.
In other days we stood up under it,
Endured it for his sake,
The unrelenting horror. Now the finish   1675
Comes, and we know only

In all that we have seen and done
Bewildering mystery.

Chorus
　What happened?

Antigone
　　　　　　We can only guess, my friends.

Chorus
　He has gone?

Antigone
　　　　　　He has; as one could wish him to.
　Why not? It was not war
　Nor the deep sea that overtook him,　　　　　　　　　　　1680
　But something invisible and strange
　Caught him up—or down—
　Into a space unseen.
　But we are lost. A deathly
　Night is ahead of us.
　For how, in some far country wandering,　　　　　　　　　1685
　Or on the lifting seas,
　Shall we eke out our lives?

Ismene
　I cannot guess. But as for me
　I wish that charnel Hell would take me　　　　　　　　　　1690
　In one death with our father.
　This is such desolation
　I cannot go on living.

Chorus
　Most admirable sisters:
　Whatever God has brought about
　Is to be borne with courage.
　You must not feed the flames of grief.　　　　　　　　　　1695
　No blame can come to you.

Antigone
　One may long for the past
　Though at the time indeed it seemed

Nothing but wretchedness and evil.
Life was not sweet, yet I found it so
When I could put my arms around my father.
O father! O my dear!   1700
Now you are shrouded in eternal darkness,
Even in that absence
You shall not lack our love,
Mine and my sister's love.

Chorus

He lived his life.

Antigone

He did as he had wished!

Chorus

What do you mean?

Antigone

In this land among strangers   1705
He died where he chose to die.
He has his eternal bed well shaded,
And in his death is not unmourned.
My eyes are blind with tears
From crying for you, father.   1710
The terror and the loss
Cannot be quieted.
I know you wished to die in a strange country,
Yet your death was so lonely!
Why could I not be with you?

Ismene

O pity! What is left for me?   1715
What destiny awaits us both
Now we have lost our father?

Chorus

Dear children, remember   1720
That his last hour was free and blessed.
So make an end of grieving!

Is anyone in all the world
Safe from unhappiness?

Antigone
Let us run back there!

Ismene
Why, what shall we do?

Antigone
I am carried away with longing—

Ismene
For what,—tell me!   1725

Antigone
To see the resting place in the earth—

Ismene
Of whom?

Antigone
Oh, father's! O dear God, I am so unhappy!

Ismene
But that is not permitted. Do you not see?

Antigone
Do not rebuke me!

Ismene
—And remember, too—   1730

Antigone
Oh, what?

Ismene
He had no tomb, there was no one near!

Antigone
Take me there and you can kill me, too!

Ismene
Ah! I am truly lost!
Helpless and so forsaken!   1735
Where shall I go and how shall I live?

Chorus
Don't be afraid, now.

Antigone
                        Yes, but where is a refuge?

Chorus
    A refuge has been found—

Antigone
                                Where do you mean?

Chorus
    A place where you will be unharmed!

Antigone
                                No . . .   1740

Chorus
    What are you thinking?

Antigone
                                I think there is no way
    For me to get home again.

Chorus
                        Do not go home!

Antigone
    My home is in trouble.

Chorus
                        So it has been before.

Antigone
    There was no help for it then: but now it is worse.   1745

Chorus
    A wide and desolate world it is for you.

Antigone
    Great God! What way is there?
    Do the powers that rule our lives
    Still press me on to hope at all?   1750
                        (*Theseus comes in, with attendants.*)

Theseus
    Mourn no more, children. Those to whom
    The night of earth gives benediction
    Should not be mourned. Retribution comes.

Antigone
    Theseus: we fall on our knees to you!

Theseus
What is it that you desire, children?   1755

Antigone
We wish to see the place ourselves
In which our father rests.

Theseus
                              No, no.
It is not permissible to go there.

Antigone
My lord and ruler of Athens, why?

Theseus
Because your father told me, children,   1760
That no one should go near the spot,
No mortal man should tell of it,
Since it is holy, and is his.
And if I kept this pledge, he said,
I should preserve my land from its enemies.   1765
I swore I would, and the god heard me:
The oathkeeper who keeps track of all.

Antigone
If this was our father's cherished wish,
We must be satisfied.
Send us back, then, to ancient Thebes,   1770
And we may stop the bloody war
From coming between our brothers!

Theseus
I will do that, and whatever else
I am able to do for your happiness,
For his sake who has gone just now   1775
Beneath the earth. I must not fail.

Chorus
Now let the weeping cease;
Let no one mourn again.
These things are in the hands of God.

ANTIGONE

Translated by

ELIZABETH WYCKOFF

CHARACTERS

Antigone

Ismene

Chorus of Theban Elders

Creon

A Guard

Haemon

Teiresias

A Messenger

Eurydice

ANTIGONE

Scene: *Thebes, before the royal palace. Antigone and Ismene emerge from its great central door.*

Antigone

My sister, my Ismene, do you know
of any suffering from our father sprung
that Zeus does not achieve for us survivors?
There's nothing grievous, nothing free from doom,
not shameful, not dishonored, I've not seen.
Your sufferings and mine.
And now, what of this edict which they say
the commander has proclaimed to the whole people?
Have you heard anything? Or don't you know
that the foes' trouble comes upon our friends?   10

Ismene

I've heard no word, Antigone, of our friends.
Not sweet nor bitter, since that single moment
when we two lost two brothers
who died on one day by a double blow.
And since the Argive army went away
this very night, I have no further news
of fortune or disaster for myself.

Antigone

I knew it well, and brought you from the house
for just this reason, that you alone may hear.

Ismene

What is it? Clearly some news has clouded you.   20

Antigone

It has indeed. Creon will give the one
of our two brothers honor in the tomb;
the other none.

Eteocles, with just entreatment treated,
as law provides he has hidden under earth
to have full honor with the dead below.
But Polyneices' corpse who died in pain,
they say he has proclaimed to the whole town
that none may bury him and none bewail,
but leave him unwept, untombed, a rich sweet sight
for the hungry birds' beholding.   30
Such orders they say the worthy Creon gives
to you and me—yes, yes, I say to *me*—
and that he's coming to proclaim it clear
to those who know it not.
Further: he has the matter so at heart
that anyone who dares attempt the act
will die by public stoning in the town.
So there you have it and you soon will show
if you are noble, or fallen from your descent.

Ismene
If things have reached this stage, what can I do,
poor sister, that will help to make or mend?   40

Antigone
Think will you share my labor and my act.

Ismene
What will you risk? And where is your intent?

Antigone
Will you take up that corpse along with me?

Ismene
To bury him you mean, when it's forbidden?

Antigone
My brother, and yours, though you may wish he were not.
I never shall be found to be his traitor.

Ismene
O hard of mind! When Creon spoke against it!

Antigone

    It's not for him to keep me from my own.

Ismene

    Alas. Remember, sister, how our father
    perished abhorred, ill-famed.   50
    Himself with his own hand, through his own curse
    destroyed both eyes.
    Remember next his mother and his wife
    finishing life in the shame of the twisted strings.
    And third two brothers on a single day,
    poor creatures, murdering, a common doom
    each with his arm accomplished on the other.
    And now look at the two of us alone.
    We'll perish terribly if we force law
    and try to cross the royal vote and power.   60
    We must remember that we two are women
    so not to fight with men.
    And that since we are subject to strong power
    we must hear these orders, or any that may be worse.
    So I shall ask of them beneath the earth
    forgiveness, for in these things I am forced,
    and shall obey the men in power. I know
    that wild and futile action makes no sense.

Antigone

    I wouldn't urge it. And if now you wished
    to act, you wouldn't please me as a partner.   70
    Be what you want to; but that man shall I
    bury. For me, the doer, death is best.
    Friend shall I lie with him, yes friend with friend,
    when I have dared the crime of piety.
    Longer the time in which to please the dead
    than that for those up here.
    There shall I lie forever. You may see fit
    to keep from honor what the gods have honored.

Ismene

    I shall do no dishonor. But to act
    against the citizens. I cannot.

Antigone

    That's your protection. Now I go, to pile   80
    the burial-mound for him, my dearest brother.

Ismene

    Oh my poor sister. How I fear for you!

Antigone

    For me, don't borrow trouble. Clear your fate.

Ismene

    At least give no one warning of this act;
    you keep it hidden, and I'll do the same.

Antigone

    Dear God! Denounce me. I shall hate you more
    if silent, not proclaiming this to all.

Ismene

    You have a hot mind over chilly things.

Antigone

    I know I please those whom I most should please.

Ismene

    If but you can. You crave what can't be done.   90

Antigone

    And so, when strength runs out, I shall give over.

Ismene

    Wrong from the start, to chase what cannot be.

Antigone

    If that's your saying, I shall hate you first,
    and next the dead will hate you in all justice.
    But let me and my own ill-counselling
    suffer this terror. I shall suffer nothing
    as great as dying with a lack of grace.

Ismene

Go, since you want to. But know this: you go
senseless indeed, but loved by those who love you.

> (*Ismene returns to the palace; Antigone leaves by one of the side
> entrances. The Chorus now enters from the other side.*)

Chorus

Sun's own radiance, fairest light ever shone on the gates of
   Thebes,   100
then did you shine, O golden day's
eye, coming over Dirce's stream,
on the Man who had come from Argos with all his armor
running now in headlong fear as you shook his bridle free.

He was stirred by the dubious quarrel of Polyneices.   110
So, screaming shrill,
like an eagle over the land he flew,
covered with white-snow wing,
with many weapons,
with horse-hair crested helms.

He who had stood above our halls, gaping about our seven gates,
with that circle of thirsting spears.
Gone, without our blood in his jaws,   120
before the torch took hold on our tower-crown.
Rattle of war at his back; hard the fight for the dragon's foe.

The boasts of a proud tongue are for Zeus to hate.
So seeing them streaming on
in insolent clangor of gold,   130
he struck with hurling fire him who rushed
for the high wall's top,
to cry conquest abroad.

Swinging, striking the earth he fell
fire in hand, who in mad attack,
had raged against us with blasts of hate.
He failed. He failed of his aim.

For the rest great Ares dealt his blows about,
first in the war-team.   140

The captains stationed at seven gates
fought with seven and left behind
their brazen arms as an offering
to Zeus who is turner of battle.
All but those wretches, sons of one man,
one mother's sons, who sent their spears
each against each and found the share
of a common death together.

Great-named Victory comes to us
answering Thebe's warrior-joy.
Let us forget the wars just done   150
and visit the shrines of the gods.
All, with night-long dance which Bacchus will lead,
who shakes Thebe's acres.

                              (*Creon enters from the palace.*)

Now here he comes, the king of the land,
Creon, Menoeceus' son,
newly named by the gods' new fate.
What plan that beats about his mind
has made him call this council-session,   160
sending his summons to all?

Creon
My friends, the very gods who shook the state
with mighty surge have set it straight again.
So now I sent for you, chosen from all,
first that I knew you constant in respect
to Laius' royal power; and again
when Oedipus had set the state to rights,
and when he perished, you were faithful still
in mind to the descendants of the dead.
When they two perished by a double fate,   170
on one day struck and striking and defiled
each by his own hand, now it comes that I

hold all the power and the royal throne
through close connection with the perished men.
You cannot learn of any man the soul,
the mind, and the intent until he shows
his practise of the government and law.
For I believe that who controls the state
and does not hold to the best plans of all,
but locks his tongue up through some kind of fear,   180
that he is worst of all who are or were.
And he who counts another greater friend
than his own fatherland, I put him nowhere.
So I—may Zeus all-seeing always know it—
could not keep silent as disaster crept
upon the town, destroying hope of safety.
Nor could I count the enemy of the land
friend to myself, not I who know so well
that she it is who saves us, sailing straight,
and only so can we have friends at all.   190
With such good rules shall I enlarge our state.
And now I have proclaimed their brother-edict.
In the matter of the sons of Oedipus,
citizens, know: Eteocles who died,
defending this our town with champion spear,
is to be covered in the grave and granted
all holy rites we give the noble dead.
But his brother Polyneices whom I name
the exile who came back and sought to burn   200
his fatherland, the gods who were his kin,
who tried to gorge on blood he shared, and lead
the rest of us as slaves—
it is announced that no one in this town
may give him burial or mourn for him.
Leave him unburied, leave his corpse disgraced,
a dinner for the birds and for the dogs.
Such is my mind. Never shall I, myself,
honor the wicked and reject the just.

The man who is well-minded to the state
from me in death and life shall have his honor. 210

Chorus

This resolution, Creon, is your own,
in the matter of the traitor and the true.
For you can make such rulings as you will
about the living and about the dead.

Creon

Now you be sentinels of the decree.

Chorus

Order some younger man to take this on.

Creon

Already there are watchers of the corpse.

Chorus

What other order would you give us, then?

Creon

Not to take sides with any who disobey.

Chorus

No fool is fool as far as loving death. 220

Creon

Death is the price. But often we have known
men to be ruined by the hope of profit.

(*Enter, from the side, a guard.*)

Guard

Lord, I can't claim that I am out of breath
from rushing here with light and hasty step,
for I had many haltings in my thought
making me double back upon my road.
My mind kept saying many things to me:
"Why go where you will surely pay the price?"
"Fool, are you halting? And if Creon learns
from someone else, how shall you not be hurt?" 230
Turning this over, on I dilly-dallied.

And so a short trip turns itself to long.
Finally, though, my coming here won out.
If what I say is nothing, still I'll say it.
For I come clutching to one single hope
that I can't suffer what is not my fate.

Creon

What is it that brings on this gloom of yours?

Guard

I want to tell you first about myself.
I didn't do it, didn't see who did it.
It isn't right for me to get in trouble.   240

Creon

Your aim is good. You fence the fact around.
It's clear you have some shocking news to tell.

Guard

Terrible tidings make for long delays.

Creon

Speak out the story, and then get away.

Guard

I'll tell you. Someone left the corpse just now,
burial all accomplished, thirsty dust
strewn on the flesh, the ritual complete.

Creon

What are you saying? What man has dared to do it?

Guard

I wouldn't know. There were no marks of picks,
no grubbed-out earth. The ground was dry and hard,   250
no trace of wheels. The doer left no sign.
When the first fellow on the day-shift showed us,
we all were sick with wonder.
For he was hidden, not inside a tomb,
light dust upon him, enough to turn the curse,
no wild beast's track, nor track of any hound

having been near, nor was the body torn.
We roared bad words about, guard against guard, 260
and came to blows. No one was there to stop us.
Each man had done it, nobody had done it
so as to prove it on him—we couldn't tell.
We were prepared to hold to red-hot iron,
to walk through fire, to swear before the gods
we hadn't done it, hadn't shared the plan,
when it was plotted or when it was done.
And last, when all our sleuthing came out nowhere,
one fellow spoke, who made our heads to droop
low toward the ground. We couldn't disagree. 270
We couldn't see a chance of getting off.
He said we had to tell you all about it.
We couldn't hide the fact.
So he won out. The lot chose poor old me
to win the prize. So here I am unwilling,
quite sure you people hardly want to see me.
Nobody likes the bringer of bad news.

Chorus

Lord, while he spoke, my mind kept on debating.
Isn't this action possibly a god's?

Creon

Stop now, before you fill me up with rage, 280
or you'll prove yourself insane as well as old.
Unbearable, your saying that the gods
take any kindly forethought for this corpse.
Would it be they had hidden him away,
honoring his good service, his who came
to burn their pillared temples and their wealth,
even their land, and break apart their laws?
Or have you seen them honor wicked men?
It isn't so.
No, from the first there were some men in town 290
who took the edict hard, and growled against me,

who hid the fact that they were rearing back,
not rightly in the yoke, no way my friends.
These are the people—oh it's clear to me—
who have bribed these men and brought about the deed.
No current custom among men as bad
as silver currency. This destroys the state;
this drives men from their homes; this wicked teacher
drives solid citizens to acts of shame.
It shows men how to practise infamy   300
and know the deeds of all unholiness.
Every least hireling who helped in this
brought about then the sentence he shall have.
But further, as I still revere great Zeus,
understand this, I tell you under oath,
if you don't find the very man whose hands
buried the corpse, bring him for me to see,
not death alone shall be enough for you
till living, hanging, you make clear the crime.
For any future grabbings you'll have learned   310
where to get pay, and that it doesn't pay
to squeeze a profit out of every source.
For you'll have felt that more men come to doom
through dirty profits than are kept by them.

Guard
  May I say something? Or just turn and go?

Creon
  Aren't you aware your speech is most unwelcome?

Guard
  Does it annoy your hearing or your mind?

Creon
  Why are you out to allocate my pain?

Guard
  The doer hurts your mind. I hurt your ears.

Creon

You are a quibbling rascal through and through.   320

Guard

But anyhow I never did the deed.

Creon

And you the man who sold your mind for money!

Guard

Oh!
How terrible to guess, and guess at lies!

Creon

Go pretty up your guesswork. If you don't
show me the doers you will have to say
that wicked payments work their own revenge.

Guard

Indeed, I pray he's found, but yes or no,
taken or not as luck may settle it,
you won't see me returning to this place.
Saved when I neither hoped nor thought to be,   330
I owe the gods a mighty debt of thanks.

(Creon enters the palace. The Guard leaves by the way he came.)

Chorus

Many the wonders but nothing walks stranger than man.
This thing crosses the sea in the winter's storm,
making his path through the roaring waves.
And she, the greatest of gods, the earth—
ageless she is, and unwearied—he wears her away
as the ploughs go up and down from year to year   340
and his mules turn up the soil.

Gay nations of birds he snares and leads,
wild beast tribes and the salty brood of the sea,
with the twisted mesh of his nets, this clever man.
He controls with craft the beasts of the open air,
walkers on hills. The horse with his shaggy mane   350

he holds and harnesses, yoked about the neck,
and the strong bull of the mountain.

Language, and thought like the wind
and the feelings that make the town,
he has taught himself, and shelter against the cold,
refuge from rain. He can always help himself.
He faces no future helpless. There's only death
that he cannot find an escape from. He has contrived   360
refuge from illnesses once beyond all cure.

Clever beyond all dreams
the inventive craft that he has
which may drive him one time or another to well or ill.
When he honors the laws of the land and the gods' sworn right
high indeed is his city; but stateless the man   370
who dares to dwell with dishonor. Not by my fire,
never to share my thoughts, who does these things.

(The Guard enters with Antigone.)

My mind is split at this awful sight.
I know her. I cannot deny
Antigone is here.
Alas, the unhappy girl,
her unhappy father's child.   380
Oh what is the meaning of this?
It cannot be you that they bring
for breaking the royal law,
caught in open shame.

Guard

This is the woman who has done the deed.
We caught her at the burying. Where's the king?

(Creon enters.)

Chorus

Back from the house again just when he's needed.

Creon

What must I measure up to? What has happened?

Guard

 Lord, one should never swear off anything.
 Afterthought makes the first resolve a liar.
 I could have vowed I wouldn't come back here   390
 after your threats, after the storm I faced.
 But joy that comes beyond the wildest hope
 is bigger than all other pleasure known.
 I'm here, though I swore not to be, and bring
 this girl. We caught her burying the dead.
 This time we didn't need to shake the lots;
 mine was the luck, all mine.
 So now, lord, take her, you, and question her
 and prove her as you will. But I am free.
 And I deserve full clearance on this charge.   400

Creon

 Explain the circumstance of the arrest.

Guard

 She was burying the man. You have it all.

Creon

 Is this the truth? And do you grasp its meaning?

Guard

 I saw her burying the very corpse
 you had forbidden. Is this adequate?

Creon

 How was she caught and taken in the act?

Guard

 It was like this: when we got back again
 struck with those dreadful threatenings of yours,
 we swept away the dust that hid the corpse.   410
 We stripped it back to slimy nakedness.
 And then we sat to windward on the hill
 so as to dodge the smell.
 We poked each other up with growling threats
 if anyone was careless of his work.

For some time this went on, till it was noon.
The sun was high and hot. Then from the earth
up rose a dusty whirlwind to the sky,
filling the plain, smearing the forest-leaves,
clogging the upper air. We shut our eyes,   420
sat and endured the plague the gods had sent.
So the storm left us after a long time.
We saw the girl. She cried the sharp and shrill
cry of a bitter bird which sees the nest
bare where the young birds lay.
So this same girl, seeing the body stripped,
cried with great groanings, cried a dreadful curse
upon the people who had done the deed.
Soon in her hands she brought the thirsty dust,
and holding high a pitcher of wrought bronze   430
she poured the three libations for the dead.
We saw this and surged down. We trapped her fast;
and she was calm. We taxed her with the deeds
both past and present. Nothing was denied.
And I was glad, and yet I took it hard.
One's own escape from trouble makes one glad;
but bringing friends to trouble is hard grief.
Still, I care less for all these second thoughts
than for the fact that I myself am safe.   440

Creon
  You there, whose head is drooping to the ground,
  do you admit this, or deny you did it?

Antigone
  I say I did it and I don't deny it.

Creon (to the guard)
  Take yourself off wherever you wish to go
  free of a heavy charge.

Creon (to Antigone)
  You—tell me not at length but in a word.
  You knew the order not to do this thing?

Antigone

  I knew, of course I knew. The word was plain.

Creon

  And still you dared to overstep these laws?

Antigone

  For me it was not Zeus who made that order.   450
  Nor did that Justice who lives with the gods below
  mark out such laws to hold among mankind.
  Nor did I think your orders were so strong
  that you, a mortal man, could over-run
  the gods' unwritten and unfailing laws.
  Not now, nor yesterday's, they always live,
  and no one knows their origin in time.
  So not through fear of any man's proud spirit
  would I be likely to neglect these laws,
  draw on myself the gods' sure punishment.
  I knew that I must die; how could I not?   460
  even without your warning. If I die
  before my time, I say it is a gain.
  Who lives in sorrows many as are mine
  how shall he not be glad to gain his death?
  And so, for me to meet this fate, no grief.
  But if I left that corpse, my mother's son,
  dead and unburied I'd have cause to grieve
  as now I grieve not.
  And if you think my acts are foolishness
  the foolishness may be in a fool's eye.   470

Chorus

  The girl is bitter. She's her father's child.
  She cannot yield to trouble; nor could he.

Creon

  These rigid spirits are the first to fall.
  The strongest iron, hardened in the fire,
  most often ends in scraps and shatterings.

Small curbs bring raging horses back to terms.
Slave to his neighbor, who can think of pride?
This girl was expert in her insolence   480
when she broke bounds beyond established law.
Once she had done it, insolence the second,
to boast her doing, and to laugh in it.
I am no man and she the man instead
if she can have this conquest without pain.
She is my sister's child, but were she child
of closer kin than any at my hearth,
she and her sister should not so escape
their death and doom. I charge Ismene too.
She shared the planning of this burial.   490
Call her outside. I saw her in the house,
maddened, no longer mistress of herself.
The sly intent betrays itself sometimes
before the secret plotters work their wrong.
I hate it too when someone caught in crime
then wants to make it seem a lovely thing.

Antigone

Do you want more than my arrest and death?

Creon

No more than that. For that is all I need.

Antigone

Why are you waiting? Nothing that you say
fits with my thought. I pray it never will.   500
Nor will you ever like to hear my words.
And yet what greater glory could I find
than giving my own brother funeral?
All these would say that they approved my act
did fear not mute them.
(A king is fortunate in many ways,
and most, that he can act and speak at will.)

Creon

None of these others see the case this way.

Antigone
They see, and do not say. You have them cowed.

Creon
And you are not ashamed to think alone?   510

Antigone
No, I am not ashamed. When was it shame
to serve the children of my mother's womb?

Creon
It was not your brother who died against him, then?

Antigone
Full brother, on both sides, my parents' child.

Creon
Your act of grace, in his regard, is crime.

Antigone
The corpse below would never say it was.

Creon
When you honor him and the criminal just alike?

Antigone
It was a brother, not a slave, who died.

Creon
Died to destroy this land the other guarded.

Antigone
Death yearns for equal law for all the dead.

Creon
Not that the good and bad draw equal shares.   520

Antigone
Who knows that this is holiness below?

Creon
Never the enemy, even in death, a friend.

Antigone
I cannot share in hatred, but in love.

Creon

    Then go down there, if you must love, and love
    the dead. No woman rules me while I live.

                      (Ismene is brought from the palace under guard.)

Chorus

    Look there! Ismene is coming out.
    She loves her sister and mourns,
    with clouded brow and bloodied cheeks,
    tears on her lovely face.   530

Creon

    You, lurking like a viper in the house,
    who sucked me dry. I looked the other way
    while twin destruction planned against the throne.
    Now tell me, do you say you shared this deed?
    Or will you swear you didn't even know?

Ismene

    I did the deed, if she agrees I did.
    I am accessory and share the blame.

Antigone

    Justice will not allow this. You did not
    wish for a part, nor did I give you one.

Ismene

    You are in trouble, and I'm not ashamed   540
    to sail beside you into suffering.

Antigone

    Death and the dead, they know whose act it was.
    I cannot love a friend whose love is words.

Ismene

    Sister, I pray, don't fence me out from honor,
    from death with you, and honor done the dead.

Antigone

    Don't die along with me, nor make your own
    that which you did not do. My death's enough.

Ismene

When you are gone what life can be my friend?

Antigone

Love Creon. He's your kinsman and your care.

Ismene

Why hurt me, when it does yourself no good?   550

Antigone

I also suffer, when I laugh at you.

Ismene

What further service can I do you now?

Antigone

To save yourself. I shall not envy you.

Ismene

Alas for me. Am I outside your fate?

Antigone

Yes. For you chose to live when I chose death.

Ismene

At least I was not silent. You were warned.

Antigone

Some will have thought you wiser. Some will not.

Ismene

And yet the blame is equal for us both.

Antigone

Take heart. You live. My life died long ago.
And that has made me fit to help the dead.   560

Creon

One of these girls has shown her lack of sense
just now. The other had it from her birth.

Ismene

Yes, lord. When people fall in deep distress
their native sense departs, and will not stay.

Creon

You chose your mind's distraction when you chose
to work out wickedness with this wicked girl.

Ismene

What life is there for me to live without her?

Creon

Don't speak of her. For she is here no more.

Ismene

But will you kill your own son's promised bride?

Creon

Oh, there are other furrows for his plough.

Ismene

But where the closeness that has bound these two?   570

Creon

Not for my sons will I choose wicked wives.

Ismene

Dear Haemon, your father robs you of your rights.

Creon

You and your marriage trouble me too much.

Ismene

You will take away his bride from your own son?

Creon

Yes. Death will help me break this marriage off.

Chorus

It seems determined that the girl must die.

Creon

You helped determine it. Now, no delay!
Slaves, take them in. They must be women now.
No more free running.
Even the bold will fly when they see Death   580
drawing in close enough to end their life.

(Antigone and Ismene are taken inside.)

Chorus

Fortunate they whose lives have no taste of pain.
For those whose house is shaken by the gods
escape no kind of doom. It extends to all the kin
like the wave that comes when the winds of Thrace
run over the dark of the sea.
The black sand of the bottom is brought from the depth;   590
the beaten capes sound back with a hollow cry.

Ancient the sorrow of Labdacus' house, I know.
Dead men's grief comes back, and falls on grief.
No generation can free the next.
One of the gods will strike. There is no escape.
So now the light goes out
for the house of Oedipus, while the bloody knife   600
cuts the remaining root. Folly and Fury have done this.

What madness of man, O Zeus, can bind your power?
Not sleep can destroy it who ages all,
nor the weariless months the gods have set. Unaged in time
monarch you rule of Olympus' gleaming light.   610
Near time, far future, and the past,
one law controls them all:
any greatness in human life brings doom.

Wandering hope brings help to many men.
But others she tricks from their giddy loves,
and her quarry knows nothing until he has walked into flame.
Word of wisdom it was when someone said,   620
"The bad becomes the good
to him a god would doom."
Only briefly is that one from under doom.

(Haemon enters from the side.)

Here is your one surviving son.
Does he come in grief at the fate of his bride,
in pain that he's tricked of his wedding?   630

Creon

    Soon we shall know more than a seer could tell us.
    Son, have you heard the vote condemned your bride?
    And are you here, maddened against your father,
    or are we friends, whatever I may do?

Haemon

    My father, I am yours. You keep me straight
    with your good judgment, which I shall ever follow.
    Nor shall a marriage count for more with me
    than your kind leading.

Creon

    There's my good boy. So should you hold at heart
    and stand behind your father all the way.   640
    It is for this men pray they may beget
    households of dutiful obedient sons,
    who share alike in punishing enemies,
    and give due honor to their father's friends.
    Whoever breeds a child that will not help
    what has he sown but trouble for himself,
    and for his enemies laughter full and free?
    Son, do not let your lust mislead your mind,
    all for a woman's sake, for well you know
    how cold the thing he takes into his arms   650
    who has a wicked woman for his wife.
    What deeper wounding than a friend no friend?
    Oh spit her forth forever, as your foe.
    Let the girl marry somebody in Hades.
    Since I have caught her in the open act,
    the only one in town who disobeyed,
    I shall not now proclaim myself a liar,
    but kill her. Let her sing her song of Zeus
    who guards the kindred.
    If I allow disorder in my house
    I'd surely have to licence it abroad.   660
    A man who deals in fairness with his own,

he can make manifest justice in the state.
But he who crosses law, or forces it,
or hopes to bring the rulers under him,
shall never have a word of praise from me.
The man the state has put in place must have
obedient hearing to his least command
when it is right, and even when it's not.
He who accepts this teaching I can trust,
ruler, or ruled, to function in his place,
to stand his ground even in the storm of spears,   670
a mate to trust in battle at one's side.
There is no greater wrong than disobedience.
This ruins cities, this tears down our homes,
this breaks the battle-front in panic-rout.
If men live decently it is because
discipline saves their very lives for them.
So I must guard the men who yield to order,
not let myself be beaten by a woman.
Better, if it must happen, that a man
should overset me.
I won't be called weaker than womankind.   680

Chorus
    We think—unless our age is cheating us—
    that what you say is sensible and right.

Haemon
    Father, the gods have given men good sense,
    the only sure possession that we have.
    I couldn't find the words in which to claim
    that there was error in your late remarks.
    Yet someone else might bring some further light.
    Because I am your son I must keep watch
    on all men's doing where it touches you,
    their speech, and most of all, their discontents.
    Your presence frightens any common man   690
    from saying things you would not care to hear.

But in dark corners I have heard them say
how the whole town is grieving for this girl,
unjustly doomed, if ever woman was,
to die in shame for glorious action done.
She would not leave her fallen, slaughtered brother
there, as he lay, unburied, for the birds
and hungry dogs to make an end of him.
Isn't her real desert a golden prize?
This is the undercover speech in town.   700
Father, your welfare is my greatest good.
What loveliness in life for any child
outweighs a father's fortune and good fame?
And so a father feels his children's faring.
Then, do not have one mind, and one alone
that only your opinion can be right.
Whoever thinks that he alone is wise,
his eloquence, his mind, above the rest,
come the unfolding, shows his emptiness.
A man, though wise, should never be ashamed   710
of learning more, and must unbend his mind.
Have you not seen the trees beside the torrent,
the ones that bend them saving every leaf,
while the resistant perish root and branch?
And so the ship that will not slacken sail,
the sheet drawn tight, unyielding, overturns.
She ends the voyage with her keel on top.
No, yield your wrath, allow a change of stand.
Young as I am, if I may give advice,
I'd say it would be best if men were born   720
perfect in wisdom, but that failing this
(which often fails) it can be no dishonor
to learn from others when they speak good sense.

Chorus
    Lord, if your son has spoken to the point
    you should take his lesson. He should do the same.
    Both sides have spoken well.

Creon

  At my age I'm to school my mind by his?
  This boy instructor is my master, then?

Haemon

  I urge no wrong. I'm young, but you should watch
  my actions, not my years, to judge of me.

Creon

  A loyal action, to respect disorder?   730

Haemon

  I wouldn't urge respect for wickedness.

Creon

  You don't think she is sick with that disease?

Haemon

  Your fellow-citizens maintain she's not.

Creon

  Is the town to tell me how I ought to rule?

Haemon

  Now there you speak just like a boy yourself.

Creon

  Am I to rule by other mind than mine?

Haemon

  No city is property of a single man.

Creon

  But custom gives possession to the ruler.

Haemon

  You'd rule a desert beautifully alone.

Creon (to the Chorus)

  It seems he's firmly on the woman's side.   740

Haemon

  If you're a woman. It is you I care for.

Creon

  Wicked, to try conclusions with your father.

Haemon

When you conclude unjustly, so I must.

Creon

Am I unjust, when I respect my office?

Haemon

You tread down the gods' due. Respect is gone.

Creon

Your mind is poisoned. Weaker than a woman!

Haemon

At least you'll never see me yield to shame.

Creon

Your whole long argument is but for her.

Haemon

And you, and me, and for the gods below.

Creon

You shall not marry her while she's alive. 750

Haemon

Then she shall die. Her death will bring another.

Creon

Your boldness has made progress. Threats, indeed!

Haemon

No threat, to speak against your empty plan.

Creon

Past due, sharp lessons for your empty brain.

Haemon

If you weren't father, I should call you mad.

Creon

Don't flatter me with "father," you woman's slave.

Haemon

You wish to speak but never wish to hear.

Creon

You think so? By Olympus, you shall not
revile me with these tauntings and go free.

Bring out the hateful creature; she shall die
full in his sight, close at her bridegroom's side.   760

Haemon

Not at my side her death, and you will not
ever lay eyes upon my face again.
Find other friends to rave with after this.

(*Haemon leaves, by one of the side entrances.*)

Chorus

Lord, he has gone with all the speed of rage.
When such a man is grieved his mind is hard.

Creon

Oh, let him go, plan superhuman action.
In any case the girls shall not escape.

Chorus

You plan for both the punishment of death?   770

Creon

Not her who did not do it. You are right.

Chorus

And what death have you chosen for the other?

Creon

To take her where the foot of man comes not.
There shall I hide her in a hollowed cave
living, and leave her just so much to eat
as clears the city from the guilt of death.
There, if she prays to Death, the only god
of her respect, she may manage not to die.
Or she may learn at last and even then
how much too much her labor for the dead.   780

(*Creon returns to the palace.*)

Chorus

Love unconquered in fight, love who falls on our havings.
You rest in the bloom of a girl's unwithered face.
You cross the sea, you are known in the wildest lairs.

Not the immortal gods can fly,
nor men of a day. Who has you within him is mad. 790

You twist the minds of the just. Wrong they pursue and are
ruined.
You made this quarrel of kindred before us now.
Desire looks clear from the eyes of a lovely bride:
power as strong as the founded world.
For there is the goddess at play with whom no man can fight. 800

(*Antigone is brought from the palace under guard.*)

Now I am carried beyond all bounds.
My tears will not be checked.
I see Antigone depart
to the chamber where all men sleep.

Antigone

Men of my fathers' land, you see me go
my last journey. My last sight of the sun,
then never again. Death who brings all to sleep 810
takes me alive to the shore
of the river underground.
Not for me was the marriage-hymn, nor will anyone start the
song
at a wedding of mine. Acheron is my mate.

Chorus

With praise as your portion you go
in fame to the vault of the dead.
Untouched by wasting disease,
not paying the price of the sword, 820
of your own motion you go.
Alone among mortals will you descend
in life to the house of Death.

Antigone

Pitiful was the death that stranger died,
our queen once, Tantalus' daughter. The rock
it covered her over, like stubborn ivy it grew.

Still, as she wastes, the rain
and snow companion her.
Pouring down from her mourning eyes comes the water that
   soaks the stone.   830
My own putting to sleep a god has planned like hers.

Chorus

   God's child and god she was.
   We are born to death.
   Yet even in death you will have your fame,
   to have gone like a god to your fate,
   in living and dying alike.

Antigone

   Laughter against me now. In the name of our fathers' gods,
   could you not wait till I went? Must affront be thrown in my
      face?   840
   O city of wealthy men.
   I call upon Dirce's spring,
   I call upon Thebe's grove in the armored plain,
   to be my witnesses, how with no friend's mourning,
   by what decree I go to the fresh-made prison-tomb.
   Alive to the place of corpses, an alien still,   850
   never at home with the living nor with the dead.

Chorus

   You went to the furthest verge
   of daring, but there you found
   the high foundation of justice, and fell.
   Perhaps you are paying your father's pain.

Antigone

   You speak of my darkest thought, my pitiful father's fame,
   spread through all the world, and the doom that haunts our
      house,   860
   the royal house of Thebes.
   My mother's marriage-bed.
   Destruction where she lay with her husband-son,
   my father. These are my parents and I their child.

I go to stay with them. My curse is to die unwed.
My brother, you found your fate when you found your bride,   870
found it for me as well. Dead, you destroy my life.

Chorus

You showed respect for the dead.
So we for you: but power
is not to be thwarted so.
Your self-sufficiency has brought you down.

Antigone

Unwept, no wedding-song, unfriended, now I go
the road laid down for me.
No longer shall I see this holy light of the sun.   880
No friend to bewail my fate.

(Creon enters from the palace.)

Creon

When people sing the dirge for their own deaths
ahead of time, nothing will break them off
if they can hope that this will buy delay.
Take her away at once, and open up
the tomb I spoke of. Leave her there alone.
There let her choose: death, or a buried life.
No stain of guilt upon us in this case,
but she is exiled from our life on earth.   890

Antigone

O tomb, O marriage-chamber, hollowed out
house that will watch forever, where I go.
To my own people, who are mostly there;
Persephone has taken them to her.
Last of them all, ill-fated past the rest,
shall I descend, before my course is run.
Still when I get there I may hope to find
I come as a dear friend to my dear father,
to you, my mother, and my brother too.
All three of you have known my hand in death.   900
I washed your bodies, dressed them for the grave,

poured out the last libation at the tomb.
Last, Polyneices knows the price I pay
for doing final service to his corpse.
And yet the wise will know my choice was right.
Had I had children or their father dead,
I'd let them moulder. I should not have chosen
in such a case to cross the state's decree.
What is the law that lies behind these words?
One husband gone, I might have found another,
or a child from a new man in first child's place,   910
but with my parents hid away in death,
no brother, ever, could spring up for me.
Such was the law by which I honored you.
But Creon thought the doing was a crime,
a dreadful daring, brother of my heart.
So now he takes and leads me out by force.
No marriage-bed, no marriage-song for me,
and since no wedding, so no child to rear.
I go, without a friend, struck down by fate,
live to the hollow chambers of the dead.   920
What divine justice have I disobeyed?
Why, in my misery, look to the gods for help?
Can I call any of them my ally?
I stand convicted of impiety,
the evidence my pious duty done.
Should the gods think that this is righteousness,
in suffering I'll see my error clear.
But if it is the others who are wrong
I wish them no greater punishment than mine.

Chorus
    The same tempest of mind
    as ever, controls the girl.   930

Creon
    Therefore her guards shall regret
    the slowness with which they move.

Antigone

That word comes close to death.

Creon

You are perfectly right in that.

Antigone

O town of my fathers in Thebe's land,
O gods of our house.
I am led away at last.
Look, leaders of Thebes,   940
I am last of your royal line.
Look what I suffer, at whose command,
because I respected the right.

> (*Antigone is led away. The slow procession should begin during
> the preceding passage.*)

Chorus

Danaë suffered too.
She went from the light to the brass-built room,
chamber and tomb together. Like you, poor child,
she was of great descent, and more, she held and kept
the seed of the golden rain which was Zeus.   950
Fate has terrible power.
You cannot escape it by wealth or war.
No fort will keep it out, no ships outrun it.

Remember the angry king,
son of Dryas, who raged at the god and paid,
pent in a rock-walled prison. His bursting wrath
slowly went down. As the terror of madness went,
he learned of his frenzied attack on the god.   960
Fool, he had tried to stop
the dancing women possessed of god,
the fire of Dionysus, the songs and flutes.

Where the dark rocks divide
sea from sea in Thrace
is Salmydessus whose savage god   970

beheld the terrible blinding wounds
dealt to Phineus' sons by their father's wife.
Dark the eyes that looked to avenge their mother.
Sharp with her shuttle she struck, and blooded her hands.

Wasting they wept their fate,
settled when they were born   980
to Cleopatra, unhappy queen.
She was a princess too, of an ancient house,
reared in the cave of the wild north wind, her father.
Half a goddess but, child, she suffered like you.

> (*Enter, from the side Teiresias, the blind prophet,*
> *led by a boy attendant.*)

Teiresias
  Elders of Thebes, we two have come one road,
  two of us looking through one pair of eyes.
  This is the way of walking for the blind.   990

Creon
  Teiresias, what news has brought you here?

Teiresias
  I'll tell you. You in turn must trust the prophet.

Creon
  I've always been attentive to your counsel.

Teiresias
  And therefore you have steered this city straight.

Creon
  So I can say how helpful you have been.

Teiresias
  But now you are balanced on a razor's edge.

Creon
  What is it? How I shudder at your words!

Teiresias
  You'll know, when you hear the signs that I have marked
  I sat where every bird of heaven comes   1000

in my old place of augury, and heard
bird-cries I'd never known. They screeched about
goaded by madness, inarticulate.
I marked that they were tearing one another
with claws of murder. I could hear the wing-beats.
I was afraid, so straight away I tried
burnt sacrifice upon the flaming altar.
No fire caught my offerings. Slimy ooze
dripped on the ashes, smoked and sputtered there.
Gall burst its bladder, vanished into vapor;   1010
the fat dripped from the bones and would not burn.
These are the omens of the rites that failed,
as my boy here has told me. He's my guide
as I am guide to others.
Why has this sickness struck against the state?
Through your decision.
All of the altars of the town are choked
with leavings of the dogs and birds; their feast
was on that fated, fallen Polyneices.
So the gods will have no offering from us,
not prayer, nor flame of sacrifice. The birds   1020
will not cry out a sound I can distinguish,
gorged with the greasy blood of that dead man.
Think of these things, my son. All men may err
but error once committed, he's no fool
nor yet unfortunate, who gives up his stiffness
and cures the trouble he has fallen in.
Stubbornness and stupidity are twins.
Yield to the dead. Why goad him where he lies?
What use to kill the dead a second time?   1030
I speak for your own good. And I am right.
Learning from a wise counsellor is not pain
if what he speaks are profitable words.

Creon
Old man, you all, like bowmen at a mark,
have bent your bows at me. I've had my share

of seers. I've been an item in your accounts.
Make profit, trade in Lydian silver-gold,
pure gold of India; that's your chief desire.
But you will never cover up that corpse.
Not if the very eagles tear their food   1040
from him, and leave it at the throne of Zeus.
I wouldn't give him up for burial
in fear of that pollution. For I know
no mortal being can pollute the gods.
O old Teiresias, human beings fall;
the clever ones the furthest, when they plead
a shameful case so well in hope of profit.

Teiresias
  Alas!
  What man can tell me, has he thought at all . . .

Creon
  What hackneyed saw is coming from your lips?

Teiresias
  How better than all wealth is sound good counsel.   1050

Creon
  And so is folly worse than anything.

Teiresias
  And you're infected with that same disease.

Creon
  I'm reluctant to be uncivil to a seer . . .

Teiresias
  You're that already. You have said I lie.

Creon
  Well, the whole crew of seers are money-mad.

Teiresias
  And the whole tribe of tyrants grab at gain.

Creon
  Do you realize you are talking to a king?

Teiresias

I know. Who helped you save this town you hold?

Creon

You're a wise seer, but you love wickedness.

Teiresias

You'll bring me to speak the unspeakable, very soon.   1060

Creon

Well, speak it out. But do not speak for profit.

Teiresias

No, there's no profit in my words for you.

Creon

You'd better realise that you can't deliver
my mind, if you should sell it, to the buyer.

Teiresias

Know well, the sun will not have rolled its course
many more days, before you come to give
corpse for these corpses, child of your own loins.
For you've confused the upper and lower worlds.
You sent a life to settle in a tomb;
you keep up here that which belongs below   1070
the corpse unburied, robbed of its release.
Not you, nor any god that rules on high
can claim him now.
You rob the nether gods of what is theirs.
So the pursuing horrors lie in wait
to track you down. The Furies sent by Hades
and by all gods will even you with your victims.
Now say that I am bribed! At no far time
shall men and women wail within your house.
And all the cities that you fought in war   1080
whose sons had burial from wild beasts, or dogs,
or birds that brought the stench of your great wrong
back to each hearth, they move against you now.
A bowman, as you said, I send my shafts,

now you have moved me, straight. You'll feel the wound.
Boy, take me home now. Let him spend his rage
on younger men, and learn to calm his tongue,
and keep a better mind than now he does.   1090

(*Exit.*)

Chorus

Lord, he has gone. Terrible prophecies!
And since the time when I first grew grey hair
his sayings to the city have been true.

Creon

I also know this. And my mind is torn.
To yield is dreadful. But to stand against him.
Dreadful to strike my spirit to destruction.

Chorus

Now you must come to counsel, and take advice.

Creon

What must I do? Speak, and I shall obey.

Chorus

Go free the maiden from that rocky house.   1100
Bury the dead who lies in readiness.

Creon

This is your counsel? You would have me yield?

Chorus

Quick as you can. The gods move very fast
when they bring ruin on misguided men.

Creon

How hard, abandonment of my desire.
But I can fight necessity no more.

Chorus

Do it yourself. Leave it to no one else.

Creon

I'll go at once. Come, followers, to your work.
You that are here round up the other fellows.

Take axes with you, hurry to that place
that overlooks us.   1110
Now my decision has been overturned
shall I, who bound her, set her free myself.
I've come to fear it's best to hold the laws
of old tradition to the end of life.

                                                          (*Exit.*)

Chorus

God of the many names, Semele's golden child,
child of Olympian thunder, Italy's lord.
Lord of Eleusis, where all men come   1120
to mother Demeter's plain.
Bacchus, who dwell in Thebes,
by Ismenus' running water,
where wild Bacchic women are at home,
on the soil of the dragon seed.

Seen in the glaring flame, high on the double mount,
with the nymphs of Parnassus at play on the hill,
seen by Kastalia's flowing stream.   1130
You come from the ivied heights,
from green Euboea's shore.
In immortal words we cry
your name, lord, who watch the ways,
the many ways of Thebes.

This is your city, honored beyond the rest,
the town of your mother's miracle-death.
Now, as we wrestle our grim disease,   1140
come with healing step from Parnassus' slope
or over the moaning sea.

Leader in dance of the fire-pulsing stars,
overseer of the voices of night,
child of Zeus, be manifest,
with due companionship of Maenad maids   1150
whose cry is but your name.

          (*Enter one of those who left with Creon, as messenger.*)

Messenger

Neighbors of Cadmus, and Amphion's house,
there is no kind of state in human life
which I now dare to envy or to blame.
Luck sets it straight, and luck she overturns
the happy or unhappy day by day.
No prophecy can deal with .nen's affairs.　　　　　　1160
Creon was envied once, as I believe,
for having saved this city from its foes
and having got full power in this land.
He steered it well. And he had noble sons.
Now everything is gone.
Yes, when a man has lost all happiness,
he's not alive. Call him a breathing corpse.
Be very rich at home. Live as a king.
But once your joy has gone, though these are left
they are smoke's shadow to lost happiness.　　　　　　1170

Chorus

What is the grief of princes that you bring?

Messenger

They're dead. The living are responsible.

Chorus

Who died? Who did the murder? Tell us now.

Messenger

Haemon is gone. One of his kin drew blood.

Chorus

But whose arm struck? His father's or his own?

Messenger

He killed himself. His blood is on his father.

Chorus

Seer, all too true the prophecy you told!

Messenger

This is the state of things. Now make your plans.

(*Enter, from the palace, Eurydice.*)

Chorus

Eurydice is with us now, I see.　　　　　　　　　1180
Creon's poor wife. She may have come by chance.
She may have heard something about her son.

Eurydice

I heard your talk as I was coming out
to greet the goddess Pallas with my prayer.
And as I moved the bolts that held the door
I heard of my own sorrow.
I fell back fainting in my women's arms.
But say again just what the news you bring.　　　　1190
I, whom you speak to, have known grief before.

Messenger

Dear lady, I was there, and I shall tell,
leaving out nothing of the true account.
Why should I make it soft for you with tales
to prove myself a liar? Truth is right.
I followed your husband to the plain's far edge,
where Polyneices' corpse was lying still
unpitied. The dogs had torn him all apart.　　　　1200
We prayed the goddess of all journeyings,
and Pluto, that they turn their wrath to kindness,
we gave the final purifying bath,
then burned the poor remains on new-cut boughs,
and heaped a high mound of his native earth.
Then turned we to the maiden's rocky bed,
death's hollow marriage-chamber.
But, still far off, one of us heard a voice
in keen lament by that unblest abode.
He ran and told the master. As Creon came
he heard confusion crying. He groaned and spoke:　1210
"Am I a prophet now, and do I tread
the saddest of all roads I ever trod?
My son's voice crying! Servants, run up close,

stand by the tomb and look, push through the crevice
where we built the pile of rock, right to the entry.
Find out if that is Haemon's voice I hear
or if the gods are tricking me indeed."
We obeyed the order of our mournful master.
In the far corner of the tomb we saw   1220
her, hanging by the neck, caught in a noose
of her own linen veiling.
Haemon embraced her as she hung, and mourned
his bride's destruction, dead and gone below,
his father's actions, the unfated marriage.
When Creon saw him, he groaned terribly,
and went toward him, and called him with lament:
"What have you done, what plan have you caught up,
what sort of suffering is killing you?
Come out, my child, I do beseech you, come!"   1230
The boy looked at him with his angry eyes,
spat in his face and spoke no further word.
He drew his sword, but as his father ran,
he missed his aim. Then the unhappy boy,
in anger at himself, leant on the blade.
It entered, half its length, into his side.
While he was conscious he embraced the maiden,
holding her gently. Last, he gasped out blood,
red blood on her white cheek.
Corpse on a corpse he lies. He found his marriage.   1240
Its celebration in the halls of Hades.
So he has made it very clear to men
that to reject good counsel is a crime.

(Eurydice returns to the house.)

Chorus

What do you make of this? The queen has gone
in silence. We know nothing of her mind.

Messenger

I wonder at her, too. But we can hope
that she has gone to mourn her son within

with her own women, not before the town.
She knows discretion. She will do no wrong.   1250

Chorus

I am not sure. This muteness may portend
as great disaster as a loud lament.

Messenger

I will go in and see if some deep plan
hides in her heart's wild pain. You may be right.
There can be heavy danger in mute grief.

> (*The messenger goes into the house. Creon enters with his
> followers. They are carrying Haemon's body on a bier.*)

Chorus

But look, the king draws near.
His own hand brings
the witness of his crime,
the doom he brought on himself.   1260

Creon

O crimes of my wicked heart,
harshness bringing death.
You see the killer, you see the kin he killed.
My planning was all unblest.
Son, you have died too soon.
Oh, you have gone away
through my fault, not your own.

Chorus

You have learned justice, though it comes too late.   1270

Creon

Yes, I have learned in sorrow. It was a god who struck,
who has weighted my head with disaster; he drove me to wild
    strange ways,
his heavy heel on my joy.
Oh sorrows, sorrows of men.

> (*Re-enter the messenger, from a side door of the palace.*)

Messenger

Master, you hold one sorrow in your hands
but you have more, stored up inside the house. 1280

Creon

What further suffering can come on me?

Messenger

Your wife has died. The dead man's mother in deed,
poor soul, her wounds are fresh.

Creon

Hades, harbor of all,
you have destroyed me now.
Terrible news to hear, horror the tale you tell. 1290
I was dead, and you kill me again.
Boy, did I hear you right?
Did you say the queen was dead,
slaughter on slaughter heaped?

      (*The central doors of the palace begin to open.*)

Chorus

Now you can see. Concealment is all over.

    (*The doors are open, and the corpse of Eurydice is revealed.*)

Creon

My second sorrow is here. Surely no fate remains
which can strike me again. Just now, I held my son in my arms.
And now I see her dead.
Woe for the mother and son. 1300

Messenger

There, by the altar, dying on the sword,
her eyes fell shut. She wept her older son
who died before, and this one. Last of all
she cursed you as the killer of her children.

Creon

I am mad with fear. Will no one strike
and kill me with cutting sword?
Sorrowful, soaked in sorrow to the bone! 1310

Messenger

    Yes, for she held you guilty in the death
    of him before you, and the elder dead.

Creon

    How did she die?

Messenger

                Struck home at her own heart
    when she had heard of Haemon's suffering.

Creon

    This is my guilt, all mine. I killed you, I say it clear.
    Servants, take me away, out of the sight of men.   1320
    I who am nothing more than nothing now.

Chorus

    Your plan is good—if any good is left.
    Best to cut short our sorrow.

Creon

    Let me go, let me go. May death come quick,
    bringing my final day.   1330
    O let me never see tomorrow's dawn.

Chorus

    That is the future's. We must look to now.
    What will be is in other hands than ours.

Creon

    All my desire was in that prayer of mine.

Chorus

    Pray not again. No mortal can escape
    the doom prepared for him.

Creon

    Take me away at once, the frantic man who killed   1340
    my son, against my meaning. I cannot rest.
    My life is warped past cure. My fate has struck me down.

                  (Creon and his attendants enter the house.)

Chorus

Our happiness depends
on wisdom all the way.
The gods must have their due.
Great words by men of pride   1350
bring greater blows upon them.
So wisdom comes to the old.

A NOTE ON THE TEXT

THE foregoing is a translation of the text of Jebb's third edition (Cambridge, 1900). In the dialogue, I have tried to bring into English almost all that I thought I saw in the Greek, even though this was to run the risk of a clumsy literalism. In the choruses, I have taken more freedom.

The following are the places where my rendering is of another text than Jebb's.

486 ὁμαιμονεστέρας A, other MSS, and the scholiast in L. ὁμαιμονεστέρα L, as corrected from -αις, Jebb.

The extravagance of imagining the impossible possibility of closer blood kin than a sister seems to me in character for Creon at this point. (For a similar use of language, cf. Aeschylus *Septem* 197.)

519 τούτους MSS and Jebb. ἴσους is recorded by L's scholiast and read by Pearson. Line 520 seems even more pointed if Creon is picking up Antigone's own term to throw at her.

572. This line is Ismene's in all the manuscripts. The only traditional evidence for giving it to Antigone is that the Aldine edition (1502) and Turnebus (1553) gave it to her. These editors may have had manuscript evidence lost to us. But they may also, like most modern editors, including Jebb, have been exercising their own sense of fitness. It is touching to have an Antigone stung from her silence to defend her lover. Further, if the line is not hers, we are faced with an Antigone who never mentions him; and much has been built on this.

The best argument for giving her the line is Creon's reply to it (573). If Ismene has 572 "your marriage" must mean "the marriage you talk of," or words to that effect. This is possible, but the phrase would certainly come out more naturally to Antigone.

Confusions of speakers in stichomythia are many, and I see no possibility of certainty here. It is our misfortune that the line in question is an important one. I have stayed with the manuscripts, which seems to me all one can do.

574. This is Ismene's line in all MSS. Boeckh, followed by Jebb, gave it to the chorus. I have followed my own precedent in 572, and stayed with the MSS. The question might come, as Jebb argues, more reasonably from the chorus than from Ismene, who has had her answer already. But she is not too logical to ask the same appalling question twice.

600 κόνις MSS, Jebb. κοπίς Reiske and others, Jebb in earlier editions, Pearson. See Jebb's note and appendix. He was of two minds here. My own final feeling is that for dust to be doing the reaping is too much, even for a tragic chorus.

609 παντογήρως L, the MSS generally, L's scholiast. παντ᾽ἀγρεύων, Jebb. This image was too strained for Jebb (and many others), as the dust in 600 was for me. De gustibus. . . .

904–20. Jebb (following and followed by many) brackets these lines, which are in all the MSS, and were known to Aristotle as Antigone's. I think he is wrong, but he should not be pilloried as a prudish Victorian for this. The positions of his note and appendix are well taken and held. Some sensible contemporaries (e.g., Fitts and Fitzgerald) are with him still. For those, like myself, who are sure the lines are Antigone's, there is drama in her abandoning her moralities and clinging to her irrational profundity of feeling for her lost and irreplaceable brother, devising legalistic arguments for her intellectual justification. Jebb finds the syntax of 909–12 strained past all bearing, but I believe Antigone's obscurity here a touch of realism parallel to the confused and contradictory negatives of her opening lines, which Jebb allows her.

AJAX

Translated and with an Introduction by

JOHN MOORE

INTRODUCTION TO *AJAX*

THE *Ajax* is probably the earliest of the seven plays by Sophocles which are preserved. The *Antigone* is generally thought to have been produced in 442 or 441 B.C., and the *Ajax* appears to belong to the same period of Sophocles' work. In dramatic technique these plays have not the suppleness of the *Oedipus*, but they are in no sense to be regarded as immature works. At the time he produced the *Antigone*, Sophocles was already fifty-five years old and had been producing tragedies in the Theatre of Dionysus for a quarter of a century. The *Ajax*, too, is the work not of a novice but of a seasoned dramatist. It is a play of very remarkable beauties and likewise of some perplexities.

The subject which Sophocles has chosen is the shame and death of Ajax, which follow on his defeat in the contest for Achilles' armor, and the growth, in and after this shame and death and triumphing over them, of a revealed sense of his heroic virtue and magnanimity. It will be seen that this subject is a single subject: the death of Ajax, taken quite simply in itself, completes nothing; the play's action is complete only when the spectator is brought to an altered estimate of the meaning of Ajax' career and destiny.

Throughout the drama, Ajax remains the central issue and our principal concern. Sophocles' judgment of him is not simple: he sees that Ajax and the Ajax-world of value and aspiration have their limitations in point of sympathy and insight; and the sense of these limitations is in part conveyed to us by means of the figure of Odysseus. Yet to imagine, as some writers have done, that the structure of the play is a polarity, so to speak, between Ajax and Odysseus is surely a distortion. The major dramatic subject, the weight and heft of it, is Ajax. The greatness of his demand upon life is the thing that we must, above all, be made to feel; and Sophocles places this theme before us by the full dramatization he gives of Ajax' suffering and resolution, of the dismay and pathetic dependence of those around him, and of their desolation when his protection is removed.

Sophocles' version of the myth is not original with him; he chose it from among the epic treatments which were already familiar. It is interesting, though, that he chose the version of the story which is most discreditable to Ajax. Pindar, writing a generation before Sophocles, follows a different version in which there is no hint of any attempt by Ajax to murder the Greek chieftains, no lunacy, and no assault upon the livestock. Ajax is simply filled with chagrin because of his disappointment and falls upon his sword. This version suited Pindar's artistic purpose very well: it provided him with a single arresting picture of outraged merit which could serve for a telling allusion and no more. For a dramatist, though, there were richer possibilities in the ghastlier version of the story which emphasized Ajax' criminality and disgrace. In choosing this version Sophocles incurred one serious embarrassment: his hero has *ex hypothesi* been guilty of a foul and treacherous attempt to assassinate the men who have wronged him, and in the prosecution of his plan he has come to grief in a most unseemly way. Sophocles surmounts the difficulty with his usual dexterity. He contrives in the main to make us lose sight of Ajax' criminality, while making of his ignominy a capital dramatic resource. The disclosure of Ajax in his tent, fouled by the animals he has insanely tormented and killed, is more than a powerful *coup de théâtre;* it is a fearful and summary image of total degradation not merely of heroic, but of all human, value. The process by which this image is transformed and Ajax' disaster irradiated by his recovery of heroic strength and human relatedness is the true action of the play.

This process is already well begun by the end of the long scene in which Ajax is disclosed among the slaughtered animals. The scene ends harshly, and, indeed, it is marked throughout by a certain acerbity. Nevertheless, out of his chagrin and misery Ajax is able to reaffirm some part of his former image of himself: rather than endure disgrace, he is resolved to die. There is a moment of tenderness for Eurysaces, none at all for Tecmessa; and even the address to Eurysaces, one feels, is an uncompromising assertion of the quality of Ajax more than a response to the child.

In the next scene he appears an altered man. Not wholly so: his purpose is unchanged. But he discovers in himself, rather to his surprise, a softening of his former harshness. He is touched now by the plight of his wife and child; they must be deceived, so that he may have an opportunity of doing in peace what he has to do; but he deceives them tenderly, expressing his true intentions, but in ambiguous words which they are bound to misunderstand. Thus the speech is a farewell to them, while at the same time it expresses a new attitude in him. His suicide is not to be a frantic gesture of despair: it will be performed composedly, on the seashore, and, when the act is done, he, or something of him, will be saved (*sesômenon*). The softening of temper which this scene registers is therefore a necessary step in the development of the drama; and the splendid lines in which Ajax compares the softening of his own severity to the yielding of the great stern things in Nature before their gentler opposites have a deep psychological appropriateness.

The scenes which now follow are an impressive example of Sophocles' skill in dramatic organization. As Ajax leaves, sword in hand, bent as we know upon suicide, the Chorus break into an ecstatic song of joy, for they have been deceived by Ajax' words no less than Tecmessa and Eurysaces. At once the messenger arrives with news of the alarming prognostications of Calchas: if Ajax has left his tent, there is no hope for him. Joy and relief are now replaced by terror; Tecmessa understands that she has been deceived; and she and the Chorus in great agitation leave the scene, in haste to forestall Ajax' death.

But Ajax appears, calmly making his preparations (we understand that the scene has changed, as it does sometimes, though rarely, in Greek tragedy—we are now in the place Ajax has chosen by the shore). His death speech is long, eloquent, and handsome. He prays for a quiet death and for his body to be discovered first by Teucer; he calls the Sun-God to carry the news to his home, and the Erinyes to pursue his enemies; and, lastly, he makes his farewell to the world above and his addresses to the world below. Athena is not present by even a mention to disturb the harmonious order of the scene. True, he does not forgive his enemies: to forgive your enemies when you are dying and they surviving is an impulse which lies outside the ethical universe of Sophocles, unless there is a hint of it, and that doubtful, in *Antigone*.

Upon this splendid and now silent solitude Tecmessa and the Chorus urgently break in: the search, the discovery, the broken-hearted cries of grief come rapidly, one upon the other. Those whom Ajax has left are now helpless. They are threatened in every conceivable way; they cannot vindicate Ajax or protect themselves. Only for us Tecmessa's beautiful words (which this translator is helpless to render) may express a portion of the response that seems to be appropriate. Evidently the drama cannot end here; and if Sophocles has not found an entirely happy solution to the problem of how to conclude it, that is not because no conclusion was necessary. Beyond question, we attend to the long wrangle between Teucer and the Atridae with a sense of diminished tragic feeling, not, however, for the reason that the question of Ajax' burial cannot concern us but because the mode selected or enforced upon Sophocles here, that of the set debate, entails a disastrous lowering of tone. The right argument for burial is Odysseus' argument, not Teucer's; and in the *Antigone* the heroine makes no corresponding defense of Polynices.

The *Ajax* has, then, its imperfections and defects. The role of Athena is perplexing, not to say fiendish. Sophocles ignores with perhaps somewhat too ready a skill our repugnance at Ajax' conduct. The wrangle at the end seems unduly prolonged and at times undignified. But all this counts for little in comparison with the admirable and central virtue of the *Ajax*, its sustained and noble affirmation of the heroic in human life, as expressed in Ajax himself, and its rendering in Tecmessa of the beauty of entire devotion.

In making this translation I have followed the text of Sir Richard Jebb.

CHARACTERS

Athena

Odysseus

Ajax

Chorus of Salaminian Sailors

Tecmessa

Messenger

Teucer

Menelaus

Agamemnon

AJAX

SCENE: *Before the "tent" of Ajax, a fairly considerable structure covered with canvas and equipped with a large principal door and a second door on the flank, which gives access to a lower lateral extension of the structure. As the play opens, the goddess Athena is revealed on a high platform which may be conveniently placed over the lateral extension of the tent. Odysseus enters and moves eagerly across the stage as though tracing footprints.*

Athena

    Odysseus, I have always seen and marked you
    Stalking to pounce upon your enemies;
    And now by the tent of Ajax, where he keeps
    Last place upon the shore, I find you busy
    Tracing and scanning these fresh tracks of his,
    New-printed on the sand, to guess if he's inside.
    You've coursed him like a keen Laconian hound.
    In fact, he has just come in. His head is moist with sweat,
    His murderous hands are moistened too. . . . But now   10
    You need not go on peering in—no, tell me,
    What is the reason for your eager search?
    For I have knowledge and can set you right.

Odysseus

    Voice of Athena, dearest utterance
    Of all the gods' to me—I cannot see you,
    And yet how clearly I can catch your words,
    That speak as from a trumpet's throat of bronze!
    You guess my purpose; I have been circling
    Steadily on the trail of a man I hate,
    Shield-bearing Ajax.   20
    He has done a thing—sometime last night it was—
    An act of staggering horror . . . aimed at us,

If it all can be believed; nothing about it
Is surely known—we are floundering in conjecture,
And I have volunteered to search it out.
This much is sure: we found not long ago
Our flocks and herds of captured beasts all ruined
And struck with havoc by some butchering hand.
Their guards were slaughtered with them. Everyone
Puts the blame of it on Ajax. One man saw him
Alone, bounding over the plain and carrying   30
A sword still wet with blood—this man informed me
And set me on the track. I leapt to the scent
At once; and partly I can trace it still,
Though partly, too, I'm baffled. How can these prints be his?
You come just as I need you. Now and always,
As heretofore, your hand shall be my guide.

Athena
I know, Odysseus;
Some time ago I felt your need and came
On the path to guard and help you in your chase.

Odysseus
Tell me, dear mistress: am I working to some purpose?

Athena
Yes, this is the man that did the things you speak of.

Odysseus
What motive, though, prompted that senseless hand?   40

Athena
He was aggrieved, because of Achilles' armor.

Odysseus
But why this wild assault upon the flocks?

Athena
Ah, he thought it was your murder that fouled his hands.

Odysseus
It was a stroke, then, aimed at the whole Greek army?

Athena

    A successful one, if I had not been watchful.

Odysseus

    What desperate daring nerved him to the thing?

Athena

    In the night he was moving upon you, stealthily and alone.

Odysseus

    Did he come close? Was he reaching near his goal?

Athena

    To the very doors of the two supreme commanders.

Odysseus

    And how did he check that hand that yearned for murder? 50

Athena

    I checked him; I threw before his eyes
    Obsessive notions, thoughts of insane joy,
    To fall on the mingled droves of captured livestock,
    The undistributed loot which the herdsmen had in charge.
    He hit them,
    Hewed out a weltering shambles of horned beasts,
    Cleaving them down in a circle all around him.
    Sometimes he thought he held the sons of Atreus
    In his grip to kill them, and then again
    His fancy would seize some other of the chiefs.
    The man was wandering in diseased delusions;
    I pressed him, urged him into the fatal net.
    At last, when he was weary of the slaughter, 60
    He hobbled the cattle that were still alive,
    And the sheep, and brought them to his tent, thinking
    It was men he had captured and not poor horned beasts.
    And now he has them bound inside the lodge
    And is tormenting them. But I shall show you
    His madness in plain view. Take note of it;
    Then you can publish it to all the Greeks.

(Odysseus shrinks back.)

Get a grip on your nerves and wait. It's no disaster
To see the man. I'll turn his glance away.   70
He'll never see you or know your face. Halloo!
You there, who are binding fast your captives' arms
With fetters, come outside! Ajax! Come out!

Odysseus

Athena, what can you be thinking of?
Don't call him out!

Athena

Quiet, now! No cowardice!

Odysseus

No, no, for heaven's sake!
I'd very much rather he stayed inside.

Athena

What are you afraid of? He was only a man before.

Odysseus

Yes, but he was my enemy and still is.

Athena

But to laugh at your enemies—
What sweeter laughter can there be than that?

Odysseus

It's enough for me if he stays just where he is.   80

Athena

You're afraid, then, to see a madman face to face?

Odysseus

Certainly if he were sane, I should never shrink from him.

Athena

No need to do so now. He will stand near you,
And yet not see you.

Odysseus

How is that possible, if he sees with the same eyes still?

Athena

I can darken even the most brilliant vision.

Odysseus

I know that a god's contriving may do anything.

Athena

Be still, then, and remain right where you are.

Odysseus

If I must, I must. But I wish I were anywhere but here!

Athena

Ajax, I call you once again!
Is this how much you care for your old ally?   90

       (*Ajax enters through the principal door of the tent, carrying a
                       two-thonged leather whip.*)

Ajax

Hail, Athena! Daughter of Zeus,
Hail and welcome! How well you have stood by me!
I shall deck you with trophies all of gold
From the spoils of this hunting, in thanksgiving.

Athena

Excellent. But tell me, did you dip
Your blade well in the Greeks' blood?

Ajax

I think I may boast as much. I don't deny it.

Athena

Did you move your weaponed hand against the generals?

Ajax

I don't think they will slight Ajax again.

Athena

The men are dead, if I understand you correctly.

Ajax

Dead they are. Let them rob my armor now!   100

Athena

  Tell me, please, what happened to Laertes' son?
  He didn't escape you?

Ajax

  Oho, that villainous sneak! You want to know where *he* is?

Athena

  Yes. Your adversary, you know. Odysseus.

Ajax

  He's sitting there inside, my sweetest prisoner.
  I don't intend for him to die just yet.

Athena

  What are you going to do first?

Ajax

  First bind him to the pole that props my barrack.

Athena

  Poor miserable man! What treatment will you give him?

Ajax

  Crimson his back with this whip first, then kill him.   110

Athena

  Poor wretch! In pity don't mistreat him so!

Ajax

  Have your way, goddess, in all else, and welcome.
  But that man's punishment shall not be changed.

Athena

  Well, then, if your good pleasure wills it so,
  Do execution, carry out all you have in mind.

Ajax

  I must be at my work. Goddess, I grant you this:
  Stand always my ally as you have today.

                                                          (*Exit.*)

Athena

  Do you see, Odysseus, how great the gods' power is?

Who was more full of foresight than this man,
Or abler, do you think, to act with judgment?   120

Odysseus

None that I know of. Yet I pity
His wretchedness, though he is my enemy,
For the terrible yoke of blindness that is on him.
I think of him, yet also of myself;
For I see the true state of all us that live—
We are dim shapes, no more, and weightless shadow.

Athena

Look well at this, and speak no towering word
Yourself against the gods, nor walk too grandly
Because your hand is weightier than another's,
Or your great wealth deeper founded. One short day   130
Inclines the balance of all human things
To sink or rise again. Know that the gods
Love men of steady sense and hate the proud.

(Exeunt.)
(Enter the Chorus of Salaminian sailors.)

Chorus

Son of Telamon, lord of the firm floor
Of Salamis, where the sea chafes and swirls,
Ajax, my lord,
When you are fortunate, I too feel gladness;
But when the fury of Zeus or the virulent
Slur of the Greeks' slander
Strikes you, I shrink in fear, and my eye
Like a bird's, like a dove's, shows terror.   140
Now out of this fading night
Come huge oppressive rumors of dismay,
Wretched and shameful;
For you, they say, in the dark went striding out
Over the horse-delighting grassland,
Swinging your bright sword, slaughtering and wasting
All that remained of booty,

Flocks and herds belonging to the host.
Such tales as these, whisperings and fabrications,
Odysseus is supplying to every ear,
And many believe him. For as he speaks of you,   150
His words win credit, and each new hearer
More than the teller relishes his chance
To insult at your distress.
Strike at a great man, and you will not miss;
But if one should bend such slander at me,
None would believe him. Envy stalks
After magnates of wealth and power;
Yet humble men without their princes
Are a frail prop for a fortress. They
Should be dependent upon the great,   160
And the great be upheld by lesser ones.
But the shallow cannot be taught these things—
They raise instead an ignorant clamor;
And against it we have no defense, my lord,
But you. When once they are out of your sight,
They screech like a gaggle of angry birds;
But fear of the huge falcon,
All of a sudden, I think,
If you should only appear,   170
Would make them cower and be still.

 Strophe
Can it have been wild, bull-consorting Artemis
 That stirred you, evil Tale,
Mother of my disgrace, to move against the flocks?
 Was she angered perhaps for victory-dues unpaid,
 Or disappointed of rich captured arms,
 Or hunting recompense for a stag slain?
Or was it Enyalios, the bronze-cased Lord of War
 That blamed *our* lord's co-operant spear,
And spitefully paid him out in the night's error?   180

Antistrophe

For never, son of Telamon, of your own heart's prompting,
    Would you so far have strayed
To fall upon the flocks. Yet Frenzy comes
When the gods will. Apollo and Zeus forfend
    These tales be true that the Greeks are spreading!
        Yet if the high kings
    Or Sisyphus' execrated son
Weave with false art a suppositious tale, 190
        Guard us from that false speech—
Hide not, so, your face in your tent beside the sea.

Epode

Rise, up from the place
Where you sit so obdurate, forbearing to fight your cause,
    While ruin flares toward heaven,
    And your enemies' bold outrage
    Freshens through all the glades
In a blast of ringing laughter and hard spite.
    But I am fixed in my grief. 200

(Enter Tecmessa from the tent.)

Tecmessa

Mariners who serve with Ajax,
Our prince of the old and kingly line
Sprung from Athenian earth, we
Who care for him and his father's far-off home
Have cause indeed for grief;
For he, our great grim man of power, lies low,
And a troubling flood is on him.

Chorus

But what, succeeding to yesterday's
Load of wretchedness, has this night brought?
Tell us, daughter of Phrygian Teleutas; 210
For the valiant Ajax loves you,
And honors his spear-won bride—
Being near him, perhaps you have knowledge and can speak.

Tecmessa

But how shall I speak a thing that appalls my speech?
You shall hear too clearly of an accident
Awful as death.
Madness has seized our noble Ajax;
He has come to ignominy in the night.
What a sight is to be seen within the tent!
Victims, slain with his own hand, deep in blood,
As for an oracle, speakingly reveal him.   220

Chorus

  Strophe

You have vouched it true, then, that report of our fiery chief,
That tale we cannot bear, yet may not escape:
Huge it grows, and authoritative voices
Give it huge reinforcement. Oh, I fear
For that which is moving upon us. He will be done to death,
Our glorious prince, because
With frenzied hands and a dark sword he slew   230
Herds and their mounted guardians in a heap.

Tecmessa

Alas, then, it can only have been from there
That he brought those bound beasts home!
And some he slew on the tent's floor
Cleanly with a neck-cut; others he hacked asunder
With slashes at their ribs. But two special
White-footed rams he lifted up, shore off
One's head and the tip of its tongue, and cast them from him;
The other he bound upright against a pillar,   240
Seized a stout length of harness, made from it
A singing whip, two-thonged, to lash him with,
And, mid the blows, poured forth such awful curses
As no man, but some demon, must have taught him.

Chorus

  Antistrophe

Now is the time for a man to muffle his head

And over the land to urge his stealthy way,
Or else, sitting the thwarts to row,
To trust his life to a ship's swift course on the deep—   250
Such are the threats that the sons of Atreus, two in power,
Stir toward us. I am in dread to share
With him the blows and hurt of the killing stone;
For an awful thing to be near is the doom that holds him.

Tecmessa

No longer so. After the lightning
Flash and leap of the storm-wind,
He is calm. But now, being clear in mind,
He is freshly miserable. It is a painful thing
To look at your own trouble and know   260
That you yourself and no one else has made it.

Chorus

But still, if his fit is past, I should think he was lucky;
A seizure, once it is done with, matters less.

Tecmessa

If someone posed the question, which would you choose:
To grieve your friends while feeling joy yourself,
Or to be wretched with them, shares alike?

Chorus

The last, lady, is twice as bad a thing.

Tecmessa

We are ill no longer now, but merely ruined.

Chorus

What do you mean? I cannot understand you.   270

Tecmessa

Ajax, so long as the mad fit was on him,
Himself felt joy at all his wretchedness,
Though we, his sane companions, grieved indeed.
But now that he's recovered and breathes clear,
His own anguish totally masters him,

While we are no less wretched than before.
Is not this a redoubling of our grief?

Chorus

You are quite right. Lady, I wonder
If a fearful blow of God's anger may have hit him.
It is strange that he feels no happier sane than raving. 280

Tecmessa

Strange, perhaps. But the facts are as they are.

Chorus

How at the start did this catastrophe
Swoop down? Tell us: we share the pain of it.

Tecmessa

Indeed, you are partners and shall hear it all.
In the depth of night, after the evening flares
Had all gone out, Ajax, with sword in hand,
Went slowly groping toward the door, intent
Upon some pointless errand. I objected,
And said, "Ajax, what are you doing? Why
Do you stir? No messenger has summoned you: 290
You have heard no trumpet. Why, the whole army now's
    asleep!"
He answered briefly in a well-worn phrase,
"Woman, a woman's decency is silence."
I heard, and said no more; he issued forth alone.
I don't know what horrors occurred outside,
But when he came back in, he brought with him
A mass of hobbled bulls and shepherd dogs
And woolly captives. He struck the heads off some;
Others' he severed with an upward cut;
And some, held fast in bonds, he kept abusing
With words and blows, as though they were human beings—
And all the while he was vexing poor dumb beasts. 300
At length he darted out the door and spoke
Wild, rending words, directed toward some phantom,
Exulting with a harsh laugh *how he'd paid them,*
Odysseus and the sons of Atreus. Then

He sprang back in again, and somehow, slowly,
By painful stages came to his right mind.
And when he saw his dwelling full of Ruin,
He beat his head and bellowed. There he sat,
Wreckage himself among the wreck of corpses,
The sheep slaughtered; and in an anguished gripe
Of fist and fingernail he clutched his hair.   310
He sat so, without speaking, for some time;
Then finally spoke those fearful, threatening words—
What should befall me if I failed to say
What had befallen him: he asked me where he stood.
Friends, I was terrified by all he'd done,
And told him, simply, everything I knew.
Then he cried out—long wails of shattering pain,
Like none I ever heard from him before;
He always used to say such cries were base,
Marks of an abject spirit. His own way   320
Was not to cry aloud in his distress,
But low and muffled, like a roaring bull.
Now, though, quite overcome by his misfortune,
Refusing food and drink, he sits there motionless,
Relapsed among the beasts his iron brought down.
There are clear signs, too,
That he's aiming to do some dreadful thing; his words
And his lamentations both somehow suggest it.
Friends—this was the thing I came to ask of you—
Won't you come in and comfort him, if you can?
He is noble, and may listen to his friends.   330

Chorus
Honored Tecmessa, what a fearful frenzy,
By your account, his griefs have moved him to!

(*Ajax inside the tent gives a heavy groan, which rises
slowly almost to a shriek.*)

Tecmessa
Worse may be coming. Didn't you hear his voice,
Ajax', distorted in that ghastly cry?

(*Ajax groans again miserably.*)

Chorus

Either he still is mad, or else can't bear
The company his madness made around him.

Ajax (*within*)

Boy! Where is my child?

Tecmessa

Dear God! Eurysaces, it's you he's calling.   340
What can he want? Where are you? What shall I do?

Ajax (*within*)

Teucer! Where are you? Where is my brother Teucer?
Will that raid of his last forever? And I here perishing!

Chorus

No, he seems to be sane. Open the door.
Perhaps seeing someone, though it's only us,
May help him to compose himself.

Tecmessa (*opens the door, revealing Ajax sitting dejectedly in the
    middle of slaughtered bulls and sheep*)

There, now you see.
You can judge for yourself the state of his affairs,
And how the man is too.

Ajax

Ah!
Loved mariners, my only friends,
Still faithful in the old proved way,   350
Look at this swirling tide of grief
    And the storm of blood behind it,
    Coursing around and round me.

Chorus

Horrible!
Tecmessa, what you told us was too true—
Insanity stands here revealed indeed!

Ajax

> *Antistrophe*
> Ah!
> Stout hearts and skilful seamen,
> Strong hands to move the oar,
> I see no friend but you,
> No, none, to ease my pain. 360
> For God's sake, help me die!

Chorus

> Hush! Check those awful words!
> Don't seek a worse cure for an ill disease,
> And make your pain still heavier than it is.

Ajax

> *Strophe*
> Here I am, the bold, the valiant,
> Unflinching in the shock of war,
> A terrible threat to unsuspecting beasts.
> Oh! what a mockery I have come to! What indignity!

Tecmessa

> Ajax, my lord and master,
> I beg you not to say such things.

Ajax

> Go away! Take yourself out of my sight! 370

> (*He groans.*)

Chorus

> In God's name, be more gentle and more temperate.

Ajax

> How could I be so cursed?
> To let those precious villains out of my hand,
> And fall on goats and cattle,
> On crumpled horns and splendid flocks,
> Shedding their dark blood!

Chorus

> The thing is done. Why wail about it now?
> You cannot make it undone.

Ajax

   Antistrophe
  Ah, yes, son of Laertes
  Spying everywhere, always   380
  The tool of every mischief,
  Filthiest scoundrel of all the army,
  What a huge laugh you're laughing now, what gloating!

Chorus

  It is God's giving if we laugh or weep.

Ajax

  Ah, if I could just once catch sight of him!
  Crushed as I am, I'd . . .

Chorus (interrupting)

  My lord, no blustering words.
  Your situation's desperate; can't you see?

Ajax

  Zeus, father of my fathers,
  How can I strike them down,
  That devious, hateful rogue and the two joined kings,   390
  And last find death myself?

Tecmessa

  When you pray that prayer, why, pray for my death too;
  Why should I live when once my lord is dead?

Ajax

   Strophe
  O
  Darkness that is my light,
  Murk of the underworld, my only brightness,
  Oh, take me to yourself to be your dweller,
  Receive and keep me. I cannot look
  To any of the race of gods for help,
  Being no longer worthy,
  Nor yet to humankind.   400
  But the martial goddess, daughter of Zeus, cruelly works my ruin.

Where shall a man flee?
Where shall I turn for refuge?
All that I was has perished
With these poor creatures here,
And I abused by a fool's dream
Of stalk and capture. Friends, friends,
The massed army will take my life
With bloody insistent blows.

Tecmessa

What wretchedness, to hear a brave man speak   410
Such words as once he would not deign to use!

Ajax

   Antistrophe

O
Sounding straits of the sea
Caves by the sea's edge, meadows on the shore,
Long and long have you kept me here in Troyland;
But now I shall not revive again, never again—
A man of sense may know it.
Scamander, neighboring river, gentle to Greeks,   420
You shall no longer see this man,
Such a man (let me now speak my boast)
As Troy ne'er saw the like of, not in all
The warlike host that hither came from Greece.
But now in dishonor
I lie abject.

Chorus

I cannot bid you stifle such great griefs;
And yet it is agony to hear your grieving.

Ajax

Agony. Who would have thought my name and fortune   430
Could square so well together! My name is Ajax:
Agony is its meaning. And my fortunes
Are cause indeed for an agony of wailing,

Cause and enough twice over. How my father,
Fighting here under Ida long ago,
Won with his sword the loveliest prize of all
For valor, and sweet praise at his return;
But I, his son,
Coming in my turn with a force no less
To this same land of Troy, no less than he a champion,
Nor less deserving, yet am left an outcast,
Shamed by the Greeks, to perish as I do!   440
And yet I seem to know this simple truth:
If the bestowing of the famous armor
Had rested with Achilles while he lived,
To give them as a war-prize to the bravest,
No rival then would have filched them from my hands;
But now the sons of Atreus have contrived
That a man of most dishonest mind should have them,
Pushing my claims aside. And I say this,
That if my eyes and mind had not leapt whirling
Wide from my aim, those two would never again
Cheat anyone with their awards and ballots!
But, instead, the fierce-eyed, overpowering   450
Daughter of Zeus, just then as I was readying
My hand and plot against them, set me sprawling,
Distraught and frenzied, and I dipped my hands
In the blood of beasts like these. And now they are laughing
And triumph in their clear escape, which I
Never intended for them. But when God
Strikes harm, a worse man often foils his better.
And now, Ajax—what is to be done now?
I am hated by the gods, that's plain; the Greek camp hates me:
Troy and the ground I stand upon detest me.
Shall I go, then, from this place where the ships ride,   460
Desert the Atridae, and cross the Aegean to my home?
But when I'm there,
What countenance can I show my father Telamon?
How will he ever stand the sight of me

If I come before him naked, armed with no glory,
When he himself won chaplets of men's praise?
That won't bear thinking of. Well, then,
Shall I make a rush against the walls of Troy,
Join with them all in single combat, do
Some notable exploit, and find my death in it?
But that might give some comfort to the sons of Atreus.
No. I must find some better way entirely—   470
An enterprise which will prove to my old father
That the son of his loins is not by breed a weakling.
It's a contemptible thing to want to live forever
When a man's life gives him no relief from trouble.
What joy is there in a long file of days,
Edging you forward toward the goal of death,
Then back again a little? I wouldn't give much for a man
Who warms himself with the comfort of vain hopes.
Let a man nobly live or nobly die
If he *is* a nobleman: I have said what I had to say.   480

Chorus

Ajax, no one could ever call those words
Spurious or alien to you. They are your own heart's speech.
Pause, though, a moment; put aside these thoughts;
And give your friends a chance to win you over.

Tecmessa

Ajax, my master, life knows no harder thing
Than to be at the mercy of compelling fortune.
I, for example, was born of a free father;
If any man in Phrygia was lordly and prosperous, he was.
Now I'm a slave. Such, it seems, was the gods' will,
And the will of your strong hand. But since I've come   490
To share your bed with you, my thoughts are loyal
To you and yours. And I beg you
In the holy name of Zeus who guards your hearth-fire,
And by your bed, in which you have known peace with me,
Don't give me up to hear the harsh speech

Of your enemies and bow to it, their bondslave.
For this is certain: the day you die
And by your death desert me, that same day
Will see me outraged too, forcibly dragged
By the Greeks, together with your boy, to lead a slave's life.
And then some one of the lord class,   500
With a lashing word, will make his hateful comment:
"There she is, Ajax' woman;
He was the greatest man in the whole army.
How enviable her life was then, and now how slavish!"
Some speech in that style. And my ill fate
Will be driving me before it, but these words
Will be a reproach to you and all your race.
Ajax, revere your father; do not leave him
In the misery of his old age—and your mother,
Shareholder in many years, revere her too!
She prays the gods for your safe return, how often!
And last, dear lord, show pity to your child.   510
Robbed of his infant nurture, reft of you,
To live his life out under the rule of guardians
Not kind nor kindred—what a wretchedness
You by your death will deal to him and me!
And I no longer have anywhere to look for help,
If not to you. My country was destroyed
Utterly by your spear, and another fate
Brought down my mother and my father too,
To dwell in death with Hades. Then what fatherland
Shall I ever have but you? Or what prosperity?
You are my only safety. O my lord,
Remember even me. A man ought to remember   520
If he has experienced any gentle thing.
Kindness it is that brings forth kindness always.
But when a man forgets good done to him
And the recollection of it slips away,
How shall I any longer call him noble?

Chorus
Ajax, I wish you could have pity in your heart
As I do. For then you might approve her words.

Ajax
Well, she can certainly count on my approval
If only she sets her mind to do as I bid her.

Tecmessa
Dearest Ajax, I will be all obedience.

Ajax
Then bring me my child and let me see him.   530

Tecmessa
It was only because of my fears that I removed him.

Ajax
In all this terrible business? Or do I understand you?

Tecmessa
For fear the poor little one might come in your way and be killed.

Ajax
Yes, that would have been worthy of my evil genius.

Tecmessa
At all events I took care that it shouldn't happen.

Ajax
You did well and deserve credit for your foresight.

Tecmessa
Is there anything, then, you want me to do for you?

Ajax
Yes. Let me speak to my boy and see his face.

Tecmessa
He's not far off. The servants are looking after him.

Ajax
Why doesn't he come at once, then?   540

Tecmessa
Eurysaces! Your father is calling for you.

(To one of the servants inside.)
You bring him! you have him by the hand.

Ajax

Is he coming? Doesn't he hear your words?

(Enter, from the side door, a servant leading Eurysaces by the hand.)

Tecmessa

Here he is. See, the servant's bringing him.

Ajax

Lift him up, lift him to me. He won't be frightened,
Even by seeing this fresh-butchered gore,
Not if he really is my son. Break in
The colt straight off to his father's rugged ways;
Train him to have a nature like his sire.
My boy, have better luck than your father had,   550
Be like him in all else; and you will not be base.
You know, even now I somewhat envy you:
You have no sense of all this misery.
Not knowing anything's the sweetest life—
Ignorance is an evil free from pain—
Till the time comes when you learn of joy and grief.
And when you come to that,
Then you must show your father's enemies
What sort of a man you are, and what man's son.
Till then feed on light breezes, basking
In the tenderness of your young life, giving your mother joy.
For rest assured, the Greeks will not offer you outrage   560
Or hatefully insult you, even when we are parted.
I leave you a strong warden at the door,
Teucer. He will protect and rear you up
And stint you nothing, even though now he's far away,
Gone on a distant raid in enemy country.
—You, men at arms and seafarers, my followers,
I enjoin this act of kindness on you all:

Pass on my command to Teucer; bid him take
My boy here to my home, present him
To Telamon and my mother, Eriboea,
And let him tend and nourish their old age   570
With constancy, till at the last they find
Their dark apartments with the god below.
As for my arms—
I say no arbiter of the Greeks shall set them
As a prize of competition for the army;
Certainly my destroyer shall not. Rather
You, my boy, take from me this great weapon
From which you have your name, Eurysaces;
Hold and direct it by its stalwart strap,
This sevenfold-oxhide-thick unbreachable shield.
The rest of my armor shall be buried with me.
But there's enough. Come, take the child quickly;
Close up the house. And let there be no wailing
Here out of doors. Lord, what a plaintive creature   580
Womankind is! (*He goes inside.*) Make fast, and hurry!
No good physician quavers incantations
When the malady he's treating needs the knife.

Chorus

I'm terrified by your eager urgency,
And take no comfort in your whetted tongue.

Tecmessa

Ajax, my lord, what is your mind bent upon?

Ajax

Don't probe and question! It becomes you to submit.

Tecmessa

How my heart falters! Ajax, by your child
And by the gods I beg you, don't be our betrayer!

Ajax

You're growing tedious. Don't you know by now
That I owe the gods no service any more?   590

Tecmessa

What impious words!

Ajax

Reprove those who hear you.

Tecmessa

And will you not relent?

Ajax

You've said too much already.

Tecmessa

My lord, it is my fear that speaks!

Ajax (to the servants)

Shut the doors at once!

Tecmessa

In the gods' name, soften!

Ajax

You have a foolish thought
If you think at this late date to school my nature.

> (*The doors are shut; Tecmessa remains quietly crouching
> or kneeling beside them. A servant stands behind her,
> holding Eurysaces by the hand.*)

Chorus

Strophe

O splendid Salamis, my heart recalls,
Blest island, where you lie
At peace in the surf's pounding,
Radiant in all men's sight and prized forever.
But Time has grown old since I   600
Have kept this wretched bivouac under Ida,
Losing count of the months' lapse,
Feeling the slow abrasion;
And dark is my thought's forecast:
Shall I win, shall I yet come, shall my coming be
To the somber and detested house of Death?

Antistrophe
And now wretchedly I must face
A new bout, for Ajax, ill to cure,   610
Sits by, and holy madness is his consort.
You sent him forth, fair island, in a time long past,
A warrior brilliant among warriors. Now
He keeps his thoughts' flock in loneliness
And grieves his friends.
And the works of war that once his strong hands did
Are fallen, fallen,
Undear, unfriended by the friendless kings.   620

Strophe
I think, too,
Of his mother, with the white of age upon her:
Surely when the news of his mind's ravage
Is brought to her (O lamentable! lamentable!)
Not like the poor lorn nightingale
In a low sob will she utter her heart's anguish,
But high, rending strains will break from her,   630
The breast be beaten, and the tresses torn.

Antistrophe
Better if he
Were hidden in Hades, now his mind is gone;
For though his proud lineage
Excelled his warlike peers,
He keeps no more the steady heart we knew,
But ranges in extravagant madness. Wretched father!   640
What a hard word you must hear! Calamity
Fallen upon your son, such as no other
Of all his race has borne, but only he.

(*Enter Ajax from the tent with a sword in his hand.*)

Ajax
Strangely the long and countless drift of time
Brings all things forth from darkness into light,
Then covers them once more. Nothing so marvelous

That man can say it surely will not be—
Strong oath and iron intent come crashing down.
My mood, which just before was strong and rigid,   650
No dipped sword more so, now has lost its edge—
My speech is womanish for this woman's sake;
And pity touches me for wife and child,
Widowed and lost among my enemies.
But now I'm going to the bathing place
And meadows by the sea, to cleanse my stains,
In hope the goddess' wrath may pass from me.
And when I've found a place that's quite deserted,
I'll dig in the ground, and hide this sword of mine,
Hatefulest of weapons, out of sight. May Darkness
And Hades, God of Death, hold it in their safe keeping.   660
For never, since I took it as a gift
Which Hector, my great enemy, gave to me,
Have I known any kindness from the Greeks.
I think the ancient proverb speaks the truth:
An enemy's gift is ruinous and no gift.
Well, then,
From now on this will be my rule: Give way
To Heaven, and bow before the sons of Atreus.
They are our rulers, they must be obeyed.
I must give way, as all dread strengths give way,
In turn and deference. Winter's hard-packed snow
Cedes to the fruitful summer; stubborn night   670
At last removes, for day's white steeds to shine.
The dread blast of the gale slackens and gives
Peace to the sounding sea; and Sleep, strong jailer,
In time yields up his captive. Shall not I
Learn place and wisdom? Have I not learned this,
Only so much to hate my enemy
As though he might again become my friend,
And so much good to wish to do my friend,   680
As knowing he may yet become my foe?
Most men have found friendship a treacherous harbor.

Enough: this will be well.

You, my wife, go in

And fervently and continually pray the gods
To grant fulfilment of my soul's desire.
And you, my friends, heed my instructions too,
And when he comes, deliver this to Teucer:
Let him take care for me and thought for you.
Now I am going where my way must go;   690
Do as I bid you, and you yet may hear
That I, though wretched now, have found my safety.

(Ajax goes out through the wing; Tecmessa
and Eurysaces go into the tent.)

Chorus

   Strophe

I shudder and thrill with joy,
I leap and take wings—Lord Pan!
Come to me over the sea
From your huge, snow-buffeted mountain,
From the long, harsh ridge of Cyllênê.
I would dance, I am bent upon dancing!
Teach me (you are the gods' teacher
And yourself you need no teacher)
Wild, high, excited dances, Mysian, Cnosian—   700
I would dance, I am bent upon dancing!
And over the open sea
Come to me in the clear light,
Apollo, Lord of Delos—
Be with me in kindness always.

   Antistrophe

The harsh god has taken
His siege of grief from our eyes.
(I exult with love and with joy!)
Once again, Zeus,
King of the bright air, your perfect daylight
May bathe our skimming seacraft in its whiteness.

Ajax forgets his pain, 710
And now, with holy rite and due observance,
Once more knows reverent thoughts.
Great Time makes all things dim,
And nothing seems beyond the verge of speech,
Since Ajax has resolved
(Amazing!) his heart's fierceness and his stern
Strife with the sons of Atreus.

(*Enter a Messenger*)

Messenger

Friends, I would deliver this news first to you:
Teucer has just come back from rugged Mysia. 720
No sooner did he reach headquarters than
The whole Greek army gathered to abuse him.
They'd seen him coming quite a long way off
And, when he arrived, stood around him in a circle,
Jabbing at him with jeers from every side.
Called him the brother of a lunatic
And traitor to the army; threatened him
With stoning to a torn and bloody death.
So far they went that eager fingers then
Had plucked forth swords from scabbards, but the thing, 730
Just as it hurried toward its uttermost,
Grew quiet at the elders' peaceful words.
But where is Ajax? I must speak my charge,
And cannot do it but to my lord himself.

Chorus

He is not here. He went away just now;
His heart is changed, and bends to bear the yoke
Of a changed purpose.

Messenger

          May God help him then!
Perhaps the man that sent me was too slow
In sending, or I lingered on the way.

Chorus

What is so urgent? Why do you think you're late? 740

Messenger

    Teucer declared the man should not go out,
    But stay indoors, till he himself arrives.

Chorus

    He *has* gone out, though—seeking his truest good.
    He wants to be relieved of the gods' anger.

Messenger

    A very foolish and misguided thought,
    If Calchas can foresee events at all!

Chorus

    What are you saying? What can you know of it?

Messenger

    This much I know—I happened to be near:
    For Calchas rose and left the kingly circle   750
    And came to speak with Teucer privately
    Without the Atridae; gently he placed his hand
    In Teucer's own, and urged and pled with him
    To use all shifts to keep his brother safe
    Under his tent-roof, and confine him there
    Throughout the length of this now present day,
    If ever he wished to see him alive again.
    Only for this one day, the prophet said,
    Will the Goddess Athena vex him with her anger.
   "Wherever men forget their mere man's nature,
    Thinking a thought too high, they have no use
    Of their huge bulk and boldness, but they fall   760
    On most untoward disasters sent by Heaven.
    Ajax, even when he first set out from home,
    Proved himself foolish, when his father gave him
    His good advice at parting. 'Child,' he said,
   'Resolve to win, but always with God's help.'
    But Ajax answered with a senseless boast:
   'Father, with God's help even a worthless man
    Could triumph. I propose, without that help,
    To win my prize of fame.' In such a spirit

He boasted. And when once Athena stood 770
Beside him in the fight, urging him on
To strike the enemy with his deadly hand,
He answered then, that second time, with words
To shudder at, not speak: 'Goddess,' he said,
'Go stand beside the other Greeks; help them.
For where I bide, no enemy will break through.'
These were the graceless words which won for him
The goddess' wrath; they kept no human measure.
But if he lives this day out, then perhaps,
With God's help, we may be his saviors still."
This was the seer's message. Teucer rose 780
At once and sent me off, bearing you these
Instructions, with strict charge to keep them. But
If Ajax has deprived me of my hope,
His life is done. Else Calchas has no art.

Chorus

Tecmessa, I think you were born for every misery.
Come and attend to this man's fearful story.

                          (*As though to himself.*)
The razor grazes near, and I feel no comfort.

                    (*Enter Tecmessa, carrying Eurysaces.*)

Tecmessa

I have only just found respite from that other
Siege of calamities. What new alarm is this?

Chorus

Listen to the message this man has brought.
It concerns Ajax, and it sounds grim. 790

Tecmessa

Alas, what *is* your message? Not that we're ruined?

Messenger

As to your own case, I can't say. But if Ajax
Has left his tent, there is not much hope for him.

Tecmessa

But he *has* gone out. I tremble in suspense
To know your meaning.

Messenger

Teucer sends strict directions that Ajax
Must be kept under the cover of his tent
And not permitted to go out alone.

Tecmessa

But where *is* Teucer? And why does he say this?

Messenger

He has just returned. And he apprehends
That Ajax' going out will be his ruin.

Tecmessa

Heaven help us! Who was the man that told him this?   800

Messenger

Calchas the prophet. He warned us to be on our guard
All day, for it brings him either life or death.

Tecmessa

Alas, friends, stand between me and my doom!
Hurry, some of you, and bring Teucer quickly;
The rest divide—let one group search the eastward
And one the westward bendings of the shore,
To trace his dangerous path. I can see now
That I have been beguiled of his intent
And exiled from his kindness which I knew.
But oh! my child, what shall I do? Not stay,
But join the search as far as my strength supports me.   810
Come, let's be at the work! No time to linger,
If we aim to save a man that's bent on death.

Chorus

I am ready. More than my words shall show it.
You'll find me swift of foot and prompt in action.

*(Tecmessa leaves Eurysaces with the attendants and goes
hurriedly out. Meanwhile, the Chorus divides into
two equal semichoruses and exits through the
side entrances.)*

SCENE: *An empty place by the seashore. No scenery need be indicated
except some bushes, behind which Ajax' body will fall. His preparations, though, should be largely visible to the audience. Enter
Ajax.*

Ajax *(carefully fixes the sword in place, tamps down the ground, and feels
the edge of the blade)*

He's firm in the ground, my Slayer. And his cut
(If I have time even for this reflection)
Should now be deadliest. For, first, the sword
Was Hector's gift, a token of guest-friendship,
And he of all guest-friends my bitterest foe;
Here, too, it stands, lodged in this hostile ground
Of Troy, its edge made new with iron-devouring stone.   820
And, last, I've propped it, so, with careful handling,
To help me soon and kindly to my death.
This preparation I have made. And now,
Making my invocation, as is right,
I call first, Zeus, on you. Grant me a little thing:
Rouse up some messenger for me, to bear
The news of my disaster first to Teucer,
So that he first may gently lift me up
When I have fallen on this reeking sword.
I would not have some enemy spy me out
And cast me forth, a prize for birds and dogs.   830
Grant me, O Zeus, this one thing. And do you,
Hermes, Conductor to the Nether World,
Waft me with one swift unconvulsive leap
Upon this piercing blade. And you, Dread Furies—
You who are ever maidens and do watch
Above all fates and sufferings of men—

Come with long strides, my helpers; mark my end,
How Atreus' sons have brought me to my ruin,
And sweep upon them for their ruin too.
They see me falling now by my own hand; 840
So too by loved and kindred hand may they!
Go, swift and punishing Erinyes,
Taste the whole army's blood, and spare them nothing.
And you that drive your chariot up the steep
Of Heaven, Lord Helios—when you next shall see
My own dear country, check your golden reins,
And bring the tale of my distressful death
To my old father and to her that nursed me.
Poor mother! When she hears this wretched word, 850
How her grief's note will quaver through the town!
But I must leave this idle vein of weeping
And set about my business with some speed.
Strong God of Death, attend me now and come.
And yet I shall converse with you hereafter
And know you in the world below. But you,
Sweet gleam of daylight now before my eyes,
And Sun-God, splendid charioteer, I greet you
For this last time and never any more.
O radiance, O my home and hallowed ground
Of Salamis, and my father's hearth, farewell! 860
And glorious Athens, and my peers and kin
Nurtured with me, and here all springs and streams,
My nurses, you that wet the plains of Troy,
Farewell! This last word Ajax gives to you;
The rest he keeps, to speak among the dead.

(He falls on the sword and collapses behind the bushes.
Enter, from one wing, the first of the two divisions
of the Chorus.)

First Semichorus
Toil breeds toil upon toil,
Where, where have I not searched?

No place knows that I share its secret.
Listen! What noise was that?   870

> (*Enter, from the other wing, the other division*
> *of the Chorus.*)

Second Semichorus
Only us, your shipmates.

First Semichorus
What luck?

Second Semichorus
From the ships to westward we've scanned all the ground.

First Semichorus
And discovered . . . ?

Second Semichorus
Labor enough; no trace of him we seek.

First Semichorus
Nor yet on the path to eastward, facing the sunrise:
No sign of him at all.

> (*The two halves of the Chorus unite.*)

Chorus
What struggling fisherman
Of those that seek their haul
With labor in the hours of sleep;   880
What nymph of mountain side
Or seaward-rolling river
Might see the grim man
Wandering somewhere and cry out to me?
I wish one would! For surely
It's a hard thing that I must range and plod,
With never a fair course
To bring me near my goal;
But I cannot see the afflicted man's faint trace.   890

> (*Tecmessa has entered from the wing and reached the*
> *place where Ajax has fallen. She is still invisible,*
> *though, being masked by the bushes.*)

Tecmessa

Oh! No! No!

Chorus

Whose is that harsh cry bursting from the copse?

Tecmessa

Oh! Oh!

Chorus

It is she, I see her now, the poor captive wife,
Tecmessa. She is lost in lamentation.

Tecmessa

Friends, I am ruined, overwhelmed, undone.

Chorus

What is the matter?

Tecmessa

Here at my feet lies Ajax, newly slain.
His fallen body enfolds and hides the sword.

Chorus

Oh, now I shall not win home!   900
You have dealt me death, my lord,
Your poor unhappy shipmate.
—And I feel for her, poor wretched one, poor wife!

Tecmessa

He is dead, dead. We can only weep for him.

Chorus

Whose hand helped him to his fate?

Tecmessa

His own hand and act. It's plain to see.
This blade, packed in the ground,
On which he fell, declares it.

Chorus

How blind I was! And you bled alone, your friends not guarding!   910
I was all deaf and stupid, totally heedless.

Let me see him,
Rugged and ill-starred Ajax, where he lies.

Tecmessa

You *must* not see him! I will cover him
With this enfolding garment from all sight.

> (*She removes her own mantle, which should be ample*
> *and rectangular, and covers him.*)

Surely no one who loved him could endure
To see the foam at his nostrils and the spout
Of darkening blood from the wound his own hand made.
Alas, what shall I do? Which of your friends   920
Will bear you up? Where's Teucer? Oh, may he come in time
To give fit tendance to his fallen brother!
Ajax! To be so great, and suffer this!
Even your enemies, I think, might weep for you.

Chorus

You were bound, hard spirit,
Bound in the end (it is clear now)
To work the term of your luckless
Life's share of affliction, that vast journey.
What could they mean but that,
The groans your fierce heart uttered
By night and in the sunlight,   930
Fraught with hate
For the sons of Atreus,
Fraught with a mind for harm?
That time was to be a great
Inaugural time of sorrows
When the strife was set for soldiership
Over the priceless armor.

Tecmessa

Oh! The pain of it!

Chorus

A noble grief, I know, goes to the heart.

Tecmessa

Oh! Oh!

Chorus

I don't wonder, lady,
That you cry out, and again cry out, your grief,   940
Deprived so recently of one so dear.

Tecmessa

You may conjecture that;
I know and feel it all too certainly.

Chorus

That is true.

Tecmessa

Poor little one! What a yoke of servitude
We go to! What hard taskmasters!

Chorus

They are ruthless indeed, the two sons of Atreus,
If they do the unspeakable thing
You have spoken in your distress:
God forbid!

Tecmessa

Even in what we suffer I see the gods' hand.   950

Chorus

Yes, they have given an overload of grief.

Tecmessa

I think Pallas, the dreadful goddess, has bred
This pain, perhaps for her favorite, Odysseus.

Chorus

That waiting, laboring man,
How he insults in his black heart!
He mocks our madding griefs
With loud laughter, bitter to bear,
And the twin kings hear and join him.   960

Tecmessa

   Well, let them laugh their laughter and exult
   In Ajax' downfall. They didn't want him living;
   Perhaps, now he is dead, they will yearn for him,
   When the fighting presses. Ignorant men
   Don't know what good they hold in their hands until
   They've flung it away. His death was a bitterer thing to me
   Than sweet to them; but for himself a happiness.
   For he won his great desire, the death he looked for.
   Why should those others mock him any more?
   His death concerns the gods, not them at all.   970
   Let Odysseus think of this and make his empty insult.
   For them there is no Ajax; mine is gone,
   But not the grief and loss he leaves to me.

                        (Teucer is heard in the wing.)

Teucer

   O God! God!

Chorus

   Hush! For I think it's Teucer's voice I hear,
   And his cry goes straight to the mark of this disaster.

                            (Teucer enters.)

Teucer

   O my dear brother Ajax, have you come
   To grief, as this strong rumor says you have?

Chorus

   He is dead, Teucer. Know the simple truth.

Teucer

   Then my ill-luck is bearing heavily down!   980

Chorus

   It is true.

Teucer

        Miserable!

Chorus

You may well groan.

Teucer

                Rash and calamitous!

Chorus

Yes, Teucer.

Teucer

            The grief comes sharp. But where
Is the little one? Where in the whole width
Of Troyland shall I look for him?

Chorus

                    He is alone
By the tents.

Teucer (to Tecmessa)

Go quickly, then,
Quickly, and bring him here. Some enemy else
May snatch him, as one would a lion-whelp
Torn from its mother. Hurry and lose no time!
When a man lies dead and cannot help himself,
The world delights to mock and injure him.

                                (*Exit Tecmessa.*)

Chorus

Teucer, that was his last command to you,   990
To take care for his child, as you are doing.

Teucer

This sight of all sights that my eyes have seen
To me is harshest, and no other road,
Of all my feet have taken, so has grieved
My soul as this, dear Ajax, which I took
In haste to seek the truth and trace it home
When first I heard the news of your disaster.
It was sharp news, and sped through all the army
As if some God had sent it: you were dead.
And when I heard it, still a long way off,   1000

I groaned with inward misery; now I see;
It is true, and it destroys me.
Ah, me!
Come and uncover; let me see the worst.

(He uncovers the face of Ajax.)

Hard, bitter countenance, lines of fierce resolve,
How can I look at you? Oh, what a crop
Of anguish you have sown for me in death!
Where can I go? Who ever will receive me,
Now I have failed to help you in your need?
Old Telamon is your father, and mine too:
No doubt he'll welcome me and beam on me
When I come home without you. Very likely!   1010
He's not much given to smiling, even when things go well.
What will he not say? What reproach will he spare me?
Bastard and *gotten by the war-spear, coward,*
Nerveless deserter and *abandoner*—
Of you, dear Ajax! or perhaps suggest
I did it out of treachery, so that I
Might get your house and kingship by your death.
These will be that harsh old man's reproaches:
Age makes him morose and stirs him up
To causeless anger. In the end I'll be
Cast into exile and denied my country,
A slave in his account and not a freeman.   1020
At home those are my expectations; here in Troy
My enemies are numerous, my help small.
Such are the benefits your death has brought me.
What shall I do? How shall I disengage you,
Brother, from off this bitter, gleaming spike,
Your murderer, by whose cut you gasped your life out?
Do you see how in time Hector, though dead,
Was to destroy you? Only consider this
Amazing thing, the fortunes of two men:
The girdle Hector had as Ajax' gift
Was that which dragged him from the chariot rails,   1030

Clamping his flesh and grating him until
He swooned in death; this sword Hector gave Ajax,
Who perished on it with a death-fraught fall.
Did not a Fury beat this weapon out?
And was it not Aidoneus, that grim craftsman,
Who made that other one? In my opinion,
This was the gods' contrivance, like all other
Destinies of men, for the gods weave them all;
But if anyone should find my thought at fault,
Let him keep his opinion, and I mine.

Chorus

Cut short your speech, and quickly consider   1040
How best to hide him in some sort of grave,
And what you must say next. I see a man
Coming, our enemy, to laugh, I think,
Like one who means us harm, at our misfortunes.

Teucer

Which chief of the army is it that you see?

Chorus

Menelaus, the one we made this voyage to gratify.

Teucer

I see him now.
At closer range he's not hard to distinguish.

                    (*Enter Menelaus, attended by two heralds.*)

Menelaus

You, there! I tell you not to lift that corpse
Nor bury it, but leave it where it is.

Teucer

And why the expense of this somewhat grand announcement?

Menelaus

My pleasure, and the High Command's decree.   1050

Teucer

Perhaps you'd care to give some justification for it.

Menelaus

Listen, then.

When we brought Ajax here from Greece,
We thought he would be our ally and our friend:
On trial we've found him worse than any Trojan—
Plotting a murderous blow at the whole army,
A night attack, to nail us with his spear.
And unless some god had smothered that attempt,
We should have met the end that he has met,
Done to a helpless, miserable death,
And he be living still. But God changed   1060
His criminal heart to fall on sheep and cattle.
Therefore I say, no man exists on earth
Who shall have the power to give him burial,
But he shall be tossed forth
Somewhere on the pale sand, to feed the sea birds.
There it is, and I want no fire-breathing.
Maybe we couldn't rule him while he lived;
But now he is dead, we most assuredly will,
With a firm directing hand, whether you like it or not.
So long as he lived, he never would heed our words,   1070
Never. And yet it's a poor common soldier
That feels no duty to obey his betters.
Laws will never be rightly kept in a city
That knows no fear or reverence, and no army
Without its shield of fear can be well governed.
And even if a man rears a huge frame,
He had better know how small a cause can throw him.
When a man is moved by wholesome fear and shame,
You may know that combination makes for safety;   1080
But insubordination and the rule
Of do-as-you-like invariably, mark my words,
Sooner or later drive a city on
Before the gale into the sea's gulf.
Enact, I say, some salutary fear:
And let's not think we can do just what we please,

And then, when we grow vexatious, pay no fees.
There's turnabout in these things. A while ago
He was the hot aggressor; now it's I
Who entertain large ideas. And I give you notice,
Don't bury him. For you may find, if you do,
That you're apt to take a tombward fall yourself.   1090

Chorus

Menelaus, these are fine principles you've upreared;
Don't shame them now by outrage to the dead.

Teucer

Friends, I never shall be amazed again
To see a man of humble birth go wrong,
When those who claim the noblest birth of all
Utter such wrongful speech as you've just heard.
Come, tell me again: you say you brought this man
Here for the Greeks as an ally *you* enlisted?
Didn't he make the voyage here on his own,
As his own master? How, then, are you his general?   1100
What gives you title to command his people,
Who followed him from home? King of Sparta
You came, no general over us. You've no more claim
To marshal him than he has to drill you.
Why, you sailed here in a subordinate place,
Not lord of all, that you should ever claim
The right to captain Ajax! Rule your own;
Chastise their arrogant speech. But Ajax,
In spite of your prohibitions and your brother's,
I shall lay in his tomb, reverently and justly,
Regardless of your frowns. It wasn't at all   1110
For your wife's sake he made the expedition,
Like some poor, toiling subject; but for the oaths
Which he had sworn—no service due to you.
He took no stock of nobodies. Think this over,
And come then with more heralds at your back,

And maybe the general too. But I'll take no notice
Of your pother, so long as you're what you are.

Chorus

I can't approve such bold speech in misfortune;
Harsh words, however just they are, still rankle.

Menelaus

This bowman seems to think quite well of himself.   1120

Teucer

My archery is no contemptible science.

Menelaus

Think how he'd boast if he wore a warrior's armor!

Teucer

I'm a match light-armed for you in bronze, I think.

Menelaus

That tongue of yours! What a fierce heart it fosters!

Teucer

A man may have some boldness in the right.

Menelaus

So! It was right he should kill me and then prosper!

Teucer

Kill? Truly this *is* a miracle,
If you've been killed and still are living!

Menelaus

A god saved me; I was dead in *his* intention.

Teucer

Well, don't affront the gods, if the gods have saved you.

Menelaus

Could it be that I should fail to revere the gods' laws?   1130

Teucer

Yes, if you intervene
To interrupt the burial of the dead.

Menelaus

Of my own enemies! *They* must not be buried.

Teucer

Ajax opposed you, then, on the field of battle?

Menelaus

He hated me, as I did him. You knew that well.

Teucer

There was some reason for it:
You were found out procuring fraudulent votes.

Menelaus

Charge his defeat to the judges, not to me.

Teucer

You have a gift for suave and stealthy villainy.

Menelaus

Someone is going to smart for that speech.

Teucer

No worse, I judge, than the smart I shall inflict.

Menelaus

I tell you just one thing. This man must not be buried.   1140

Teucer

And this shall be your answer. He shall be
Buried at once.

Menelaus

I observed a man once of fast and saucy speech
Who had pressed sailors to make a voyage in a storm;
When the weather got really rough, you couldn't hear
Him piping anywhere: he hid himself in his cloak,
And anybody aboard could step on him at will.
And very possibly you and your reckless speech—
If a big whistling storm should suddenly come
Out of a little cloud—your clamorous uproar
Might be quenched in a very similar fashion.

Teucer

And I once saw a man inflated with foolishness,   1150
Who insulted the misfortunes of his neighbors.
And another man, closely resembling me,

Quite like me in temperament, gave him a straight look
And said to him, "Man, don't outrage the dead.
You certainly shall regret it if you do."
That was the advice he gave that worthless man.
I see him now, and he is, it seems to me,
You, and nobody else. Am I speaking in riddles?

Menelaus

I'm leaving. I shall only look absurd
To stay and chide you, when I might use force.   1160

(*Exit.*)

Teucer

Go, then. It does me little credit, either,
To listen to an empty man's loud talk.

Chorus

A great and wrathful contest is shaping.
Teucer, bestir yourself. Find him,
As quickly as you can, some hollow
Cavity in the earth, that shall become
His dank, capacious tomb, a signal
Reminder of him to men in after time.

Teucer

Here, just in time for that, his wife and child
Are coming, to perform with kindred touch
The service due his pitiable body.   1170

(*Enter Tecmessa with Eurysaces.*)

Come, little one, kneel down, as suppliants do,
Grasp your father, the creator of your life.
Hold in your hands this lock of mine

(*Cuts it, and puts it in the boy's hand.*)
and hers,

(*Cuts it, etc.*)

And this, a third, your own

(*Puts his hand on the boy's head and separates the lock
in readiness to cut it.*)

—a suppliant's treasure.
Keep your station, and make your supplication.
And if anyone in the army tries to wrest you
Forcibly from this corpse, may his corpse be
Thrown out unburied from his land and home,
Wretchedly, as he is a wretch, cut off
At the root with all his race, even as I
Have cut this lock of hair.

(Cuts it and gives it to Eurysaces.)

Take it, dear child, and guard it, and let no one   1180
Remove you, but cling fast, inclining over him.

(To the Chorus)

And you, don't huddle near like a crowd of women,
Instead of the men you are, but rally round
And help, till I come back, having provided
A tomb for him, though all the world gainsay me.

(Exit Teucer.)

Chorus
  Strophe
  Which year, I wonder, shall be my long toil's last,
  And when shall the battered count of them all be full?
  They bring upon me a ceaseless curse of spear-sped
  Trouble over the length and breadth of Troy,   1190
  A grief and a shame to all Greek men.

  Antistrophe
  Whoever it was that first revealed to Hellas
  Their common scourge, detested arms and war,
  I curse him. Would the large air first had taken him
  Or else the impartial house of Death. Generations
  Of toil be made for us. Ah,
  There indeed was a harrier of men!

  Strophe
  It was he that denied my share
  In the sweet companionship   1200

Of garland and deep cup;
And miserly he grudged me
The flute's soft lovely clamor
And a pleasant bed in the night,
And love, love he abridged and interdicted.
Ah, me! I languish, so. None cares
That my locks are damp with the thick continual dew
Which is all my thought of Troy.   1210

Antistrophe
And he, valorous Ajax,
Who was once my ward and cover
From every flying shaft
And dread in the hours of night,
Now is handed over to his harsh daemon.
What joy, then, is left to me?
Oh, if somehow I might find myself
Rounding a wood-topped bulwark of the sea,
Sunium's level tip where the surf washes,
And make my salutation   1220
To holy Athens!

                            (*Enter Teucer hastily.*)

Teucer
I hurried back when I saw the commander-in-chief,
Agamemnon, approaching. And here he is;
I think he will give his hateful lips full freedom.

                    (*Enter Agamemnon with retinue.*)

Agamemnon
You, there! Are you the one they tell me of,
Who has made bold to yawp these powerful speeches,
Unpunished, so far, against me? You,
The son of a captive slave-woman! What if your mother
Had been a princess? *Then* I think you'd strut,   1230
Then you'd talk big! Why, as it is, being
Nothing yourself, you have risen up to protect
That man who now is nothing, and have sworn
That I am not the general nor the admiral

Either of the Achaeans or of you,
Since Ajax, as you say, came under his own command!
These are quite some taunts to hear from a slave.
And what is the man on whose behalf you've bawled
These very ambitious claims? Where did he go,
Or stand in battle, where I did not too?
Was he the one real man in the whole Greek army?   1240
Ah! that contest for Achilles' armor!
We shall regret the day we published it
If every moment we must be defamed
And slandered by this Teucer, if you please!
Who can't accept the court's majority verdict,
Defeated as he is, or yield to it,
No! but you losers pelt us still with slanders,
And seek to wound us with your crafty plots.
Yet where such reckless courses have their head,
No law can stand unshaken, not when we
Must shove the lawful victors from their place,
And give precedence to the ranks behind.
This must be curbed. It's not a man's great frame   1250
Or breadth of shoulders makes his manhood count:
A man of sense has always the advantage.
A very little whip can serve to guide
A hulking ox straight forward on his road.
And I fancy something of that medicine
Is coming for you, unless you get some sense!
That man is dead, now—just a shadow;
And yet you seem to count on *him* to protect
Your sauciness! I say, learn moderation!
Think of your slave's birth; bring someone else,   1260
A freeman, here to plead your case before me.
I'm disinclined to hear more words from you,
Being not much versed in your barbarian speech.

Chorus

I wish you both might learn a moderate mind!
That is the best I have to say to you.

Teucer

Alas! How fugitive is the gratitude
Men owe the dead, how soon shown to deceive!
This man has no trifling remembrance,
Ajax, of you, though oftentimes for him
You risked your life and bore the stress of war.
All that is gone now, easily tossed away.
You, who just now spoke that long, foolish speech,
Can't you remember any more at all
How you were penned once close behind your picket,
And all but ruined in the rout of war   1270
With flames licking the ships' quarter-decks
Already, and Hector high in the air, leaping
Over the fosse to board, but Ajax came,
Alone, to save you? Who fended off *that* ruin?
Wasn't it he, the very man you now   1280
Declare fought nowhere but where you fought too?
What do you say? Did he deal fairly then?
And when that other time he closed alone
In single fight with Hector, not conscripted,
But chosen when each champion put his lot
Into the crested helmet—Ajax then
Put in no shirking lot among the rest,
No clod of moist earth, no! but one to skip
Lightly, first and victorious, from the helm.
It was he that did those things, and I stood by him:
The slave, yes! the barbarian mother's son!
Wretched man, why do you light upon *that* taunt?   1290
Aren't you aware that your own grandfather,
Old Pelops, was a barbarous Phrygian? Or
That Atreus, yes, your actual *father*, set
Before his brother a most unholy dish
Of his own sons' flesh? And you yourself
Had a Cretan for your mother, in whose bed
An interloping foreigner was discovered,
And she consigned, and by her parent's order,

To drown among the fishes of the deep.
These are your origins. Can you censure mine?
Telamon was my father, and he won
My mother as his valorous prize of war.   1300
She was a princess by her birth, the child
Of King Laomedon, and Heracles
Distinguished her to be my father's gift.
Two royal races gave me to the world.
How shall I shame my kin if I defend them
In their adversity, when you with shameless words
Would fling them out unburied? Listen to this:
If you should venture to cast Ajax out,
You must cast out the three of us as well,
Together in one heap with him. I make my choice
To stand in public and to die for him,   1310
Rather than for your wife—or was it your brother's wife?
So! Think of your own case, and not merely mine;
For if you vex me, you may wish you had been
A coward, rather than too bold with me.

                                          (*Enter Odysseus.*)

Chorus

You arrive, my lord Odysseus, just in time,
If you have come to make not strife but peace.

Odysseus

What is this, gentlemen? For quite some distance
I could hear the sons of Atreus raising their voices
Over this valiant corpse.

Agamemnon

                    Indeed we were.
Hadn't we just been hearing infamous language,   1320
My lord Odysseus, from this fellow here?

Odysseus

What language do you complain of? If he gave
Insult for insult, I could pardon him.

Agamemnon

    I gave him ugly words:
    It was an ugly wrong he offered me.

Odysseus

    What did he do to injure you?

Agamemnon

                    He said
    He would not leave that corpse unburied, but
    Declared he'd bury it in spite of me.

Odysseus

    Agamemnon, may a friend speak truth to you,
    And still enjoy your friendship as before?

Agamemnon

    Speak. I would be foolish to resent your words;   1330
    You are my truest friend in the whole army.

Odysseus

    Then listen. Don't cast out this brave man's body
    Unburied; don't in the gods' name be so hard.
    Vindictiveness should not so govern you
    As to make you trample on the right. I too
    Found this man hateful once, beyond the rest
    Of all my fellow soldiers, since the time
    I won Achilles' armor. Nevertheless,
    In spite of his enmity, I cannot wish
    To pay him with dishonor, or refuse
    To recognize in him the bravest man   1340
    Of all that came to Troy, except Achilles.
    It would be wrong to do him injury;
    In acting so, you'd not be injuring him—
    Rather the gods' laws. It's a foul thing to hurt
    A valiant man in death, though he *was* your enemy.

Agamemnon

    Do you, Odysseus, take his part against me?

Odysseus
  I do.
  I hated him while it was fair to hate.

Agamemnon
  But now he is dead,
  Shouldn't you rightly trample on his corpse?

Odysseus
  Forbear, my lord, to seek unworthy triumphs.

Agamemnon
  Reverence doesn't come easily to a prince.   1350

Odysseus
  Regard for a friend's advice is not so difficult.

Agamemnon
  A good man should defer to his superiors.

Odysseus
  No more, now.
  You win the victory when you yield to friends.

Agamemnon
  Think what a man you're interceding for!

Odysseus
  My enemy, it's true. But he was noble.

Agamemnon
  Do you intend pity to a corpse you hate?

Odysseus
  His greatness weighs more than my hate with me.

Agamemnon
  Men who act so are changeable and unsteady.

Odysseus
  Men's minds are given to change in hate and friendship.

Agamemnon
  Do you, then, recommend such changeable friends?   1360

Odysseus

I cannot recommend a rigid spirit.

Agamemnon

You'll make me look a coward in this transaction.

Odysseus

Generous, though, as all the Greeks will say.

Agamemnon

You want me, then, to let this corpse be buried?

Odysseus

Yes. For I too shall come to that necessity.

Agamemnon

In everything, I see, men labor for themselves.

Odysseus

For whom should I rather labor than myself?

Agamemnon

Let this be called your doing, and not mine.

Odysseus

However you do it, you will deserve praise.

Agamemnon

Understand my position. I would do   1370
This and much more at your request. But as for him,
Whether on earth or in the underworld,
I hate him. You may do whatever you wish.

                              (*Exit Agamemnon with his retinue.*)

Chorus

Whoever fails to recognize your wisdom
And value it, Odysseus, is a fool.

Odysseus

And now I have a promise,
Teucer, to make to you. From now on, I
Shall be as much your friend as I was once
Your enemy; and I should like to join

In the burial of your dead—doing with you
That labor, and omitting none of it,
Which men should give the noblest of their fellows.   1380

Teucer

Noble Odysseus, I can only praise you.
How greatly you deceived my expectations!
For though you hated him worst of the Argives,
You alone came to help, and did not wish,
Because you lived, to outrage him in death.
That wit-struck general did otherwise—
He and his noxious brother—and decreed
That Ajax' corpse should rot without a tomb.
Therefore, may Zeus who rules on high Olympus,
Remembering Furies, and avenging Justice   1390
Destroy them miserably, just as they
Sought to work outrage and abomination
On my dear brother's body. Son of Laertes,
I feel some hesitation at your offer
And fear I cannot let you touch the corpse:
That might offend the dead. But bear your part
In all the rest, and if you wish to bring
Any others of the army, they shall be welcome.
I'll see to all the rest. But you, Odysseus,
Are written in our hearts a nobleman.

Odysseus

I could have wished to help.   1400
But if your preference is otherwise,
I shall respect your wish and take my leave.

                                        (*Exit Odysseus.*)

Teucer

Shoulder the work. Delay
Has grown too long already.
Some of you hurry and dig
The hollow trench; others
Set the tall cauldron

Amid the surrounding flames
To ready the holy bath;
And one troop bring from within the tent
His glorious suit of armor.

Now you, my boy,
Take hold with your little strength   1410
Upon your father's body,
And help in tenderness to lift him up;
For still the warm conduits
Spout forth his life's dark force.
Come now, come, everyone
That claims to be his friend,
Begin, proceed, and bear him up,
This man of perfect excellence—
No nobler one has ever been than he:
I speak of Ajax, while he lived.

(*The cortege forms.*)

Chorus

What men have seen they know;
But what shall come hereafter
No man before the event can see,
Nor what end waits for him.   1420

(*Exeunt, following the body.*)

THE
WOMEN OF
TRACHIS

Translated and with an Introduction by

MICHAEL JAMESON

INTRODUCTION TO *THE WOMEN OF TRACHIS*

Heracles was rarely the subject of tragedy, although the most popular hero of Greek mythology. In the theater he was more commonly seen in satyr plays and comedy, and, indeed, this is an indication of his great appeal: he was both god and man, hero and buffoon. At times he appeared as a rescuer to conclude a play in which he was not the central character (in Aeschylus' lost *Prometheus Unbound*, in Euripides' *Alcestis*, in Sophocles' *Philoctetes*), but he is not tragic at such times or in the triumphant accomplishment of his labors but at the moment of his solitary defeat. Sophocles and Euripides (in his *Heracles*) each took for his plot one of his two defeats, while ignoring the other—his agony in the poisoned shirt and his homicidal madness against his wife and children. It may be that a single, terrible defeat is necessary to the career of one who is Everyman on a heroic scale and that the poisoned shirt and the madness are "doublets," coming from different versions of his life, concerning two different wives who are only later combined into a single account. Modern research suggests that at least two heroes have merged to form the classical Heracles—the one from Tiryns, the other from Thebes.

Our play contains the first sure reference to Heracles' decision to be burned alive on the pyre, although two divergent traditions about his end are as early as Homer and Hesiod: the one, that, great as he was, even the son of Zeus had to die like any other man; the other, that, after battling Death in various guises, he wins immortality among the gods on Olympus. In later times this latter is the dominant version, and the pyre which destroys his mortal body is the means of his ascent, as in Seneca's *Hercules Oetaeus*. The story of the pyre cannot be original with Sophocles, for we see it on Attic vases beginning in the early part of the century, and it seems always to have been connected with his becoming a god. Why, then, does

Sophocles avoid all reference to the final resolution of the hero's agony? For Heracles here expects death, and there is not the slightest hint of apotheosis, although it is explicit in the poet's *Philoctetes*. To find an answer, we must see the place of the last scene in the play, assuming that it is an integral part of the whole and not a conventional appendage dictated by mythology.

At the beginning Deianira tells us: "Now he wins through to the end of all his labors / and now I am more than ever afraid" (ll. 36–37), and soon after she reports a prophecy to her son Hyllus: "It said that either he would come to his life's end / or have by now, and for the rest of his time, / a happy life, once he had carried out this task" (ll. 79–81). So the play begins with his wife's anxiety over Heracles' last labors, which will mean the "end" (*telos*) for him and for her, in all its ambiguity; and it is the working-out of this end through a series of revelations constantly coming closer to the full truth that is the action of the play. When Heracles realizes that his end has come and has added further strokes to complete his fate, he closes the action with the order that he be carried out to the pyre to be burned alive: "The true / respite from suffering is this—my final end" (ll. 1255–56). It is this, the discovery of the end of Heracles, that gives the play its unity; for clearly, as the action is not centered on a single character, it does not have the obvious unity of an *Oedipus the King*, nor can it be made into such a play by ignoring either Heracles or Deianira and regarding the remaining character as the true hero. The title we have, avoiding both the principals, should be a warning. And once we allow that the subject of the play is larger than the tragedy of either character and inextricably involves both, we cannot stop short of the total action; to see the play, for instance, as an exposition of the destructive power of love makes a mere "afterpiece" of the last scene, where Heracles learns the truth and acts upon it. Rather, this is the play's climax as well as its conclusion.

The movement of the play as a series of revelations is expressed in action and imagery and is underscored in language through the prominent use in the Greek of the root of *phainein* ("reveal") and of its synonyms and opposites (there is a similar emphasis on *telos*, "end," and its derivatives). In imagery the contrast of the dark, secret, night-time, and deadly with the bright and clear, with sun, fire, and lightning, culminates in the black, dead enemies (the Hydra's poison, Nessus' gift) that defeat Heracles, and the fire with which in turn he will vanquish them and himself. In action, the expected appearance of Heracles, seemingly assured, is replaced by the silent mystery of Iole and the concealment of Lichas, which, when exposed, are followed by the secrecy of Deianira and of Nessus, revealed to Deianira by the sunlight on the tuft of wool, to the world by the altar fire at Cenaeum; the full revelation of his end to Heracles and of his further decision coincides with a new discovery— the revelation of Hyllus' character as a son worthy of his father.

There is also revelation of the divine agency behind the events: Lichas calls his false story of why Heracles has been absent so long "a tale where it is seen Zeus did the work" (l. 251, *praktōr phanei*); later, when the truth is out, "that silent / handmaiden, Cyprian Aphrodite / is revealed; this is her work" (ll. 859–61, *phanera . . . ephanē praktōr*); but in the end, when all is seen to agree with Zeus's oracles, "there is / nothing here which is not Zeus" (ll. 1277–78). Through the oracles mentioned at the beginning and near the end, we see that the events leading up to Heracles' defeat are part of the external, inevitable pattern against which the suffering and the actions of the characters must be seen. What happens when Heracles understands this pattern, being in accord with it and yet beyond it, may be the most important part of the play. As far as the characters, or we, can see, the Gods do not care. The meaning and worth of men's actions are what they make of them. We may remember now that "Sophocles claimed he depicted men as they ought to be, Euripides as they are" (Aristotle *Poetics* xxv. 11). If Euripides' characters were closer to reality, Sophocles' own were larger than life, on a heroic scale. How do his characters here fit his own description?

Deianira is easily the more sympathetic character for the modern reader, and many have been tempted to read the play as her tragedy. We see in the beginning her early fear of marriage and of lust, symbolized for her by the monstrous Acheloüs and then by Nessus; strictly outside the action, they are kept before us by her own and the chorus' reminiscence. For the end of Heracles' toils means her husband at rest at home and the end of violence and fear. No sooner has all this been realized, as it seems, than violence and lust burst into her own house and her own bed. Here we first see her stature in her kindness and her restraint after she knows who Iole is, in her refusal to hurt or even blame her husband or the girl. (Throughout there may well be a contrast intended with Aeschylus' Clytemnestra in the *Agamemnon.*) She resorts to a love charm with reluctance and misgivings, for they were unbecoming a great lady and notoriously dangerous. We feel that she was incredibly foolish to trust a gift from Nessus, and soon she thinks so too, and yet we may fail to appreciate how plausible is his magic: the blood of Nessus is to her vile and repulsive, no less so because of the vaguely apprehended effect of the Hydra's poison, but it is precisely from the vile and repulsive that the most potent magic comes. Furthermore, Nessus and the centaurs in general were an incarnation of the erotic (as his attempt on her confirms—the poet's taste seems to have suppressed a peculiarly appropriate ingredient of the charm found in the tradition, the centaur's semen). What better source for a love charm to turn back toward his wife the lust of Heracles, "all desire when the beast's / inducements, all dipped in persuasion, have melted him" (ll. 661–62)? When she is told of the deadly effect of the poison and is cursed by her son, she leaves without a word to justify herself and, re-enacting the central ritual of her life, she makes the bed of Heracles for the last time and kills herself upon it. "How could any woman bring her hands to this?" (l. 898) the Chorus asks, for this is not the hanging of Jocasta or Antigone but the more masculine self-destruction with the sword. A woman, ordinary in her devotion to her marriage and family, shows her extraordinary nobility and strength at the time of her utter disaster.

But, for the Greeks, Heracles has even more of the heroic properties. No man has done more or suffered more. This is not to say that he is likable or, in the sickness of his passion, admirable. Nonetheless, for Deianira and Hyllus, when they think of her losing such a husband, he is "the best of all men" (ll. 177, 811–12). There is no idea of his being punished for his immorality, nor is there any attempt to soften the impact of his enormous faults. Everything about him is larger than life. When his violent lust is revealed, it is not treated as showing him to be any less of a hero but as evidence of the super-human power of the one foe that has overcome him. Love is seen as a sickness, and the poison, intended as a drug, a remedy, brings about another sickness that can be cured only by suicidal fire. "I ask you to be my healer, / the only physician who can cure my suffer-ing," he begs his son (ll. 1208–9). But this last sickness, the working of the poison, is also conceived of as a beast, the last of all that he has faced (cf. ll. 987, 1009 f., 1028 ff., 1053 ff.), and in the poet's language the other beasts are linked together to form a composite enemy that gains its late revenge. In this play, Heracles is more the beast-slayer than the savior of mankind, and it is in this role that, before he knows the truth, he thinks to punish Deianira. There is no point in reprov-ing him in his ignorance and his horrible pain for this desire. Is any other reaction conceivable for one who knows only what he knows, who is in his pain, and, most important, has led his life? ". . . alive / I punished the evil and I punish them in death" (ll. 1110–11). Nor need we reprove or gloss over his failure to forgive her when he knows she was innocent. The knowledge that the poison came from Nessus puts everything in a new light. Before, though he prayed for death, he had not, it would seem, admitted to himself that his end had come. Now he knows, and he turns to face it. His end is not to be avoided, but his agony remains, and he treats it as a sickness and as a beast. He had said that this "flowering of madness" was "inexorable" (*akēlēton*, l. 999, that is, "not to be charmed away"). "Is there any singer of spells, / any craftsman surgeon who can / exorcise this curse, but Zeus?" (ll. 1000–1002). Now, calmly, forcing his will on his son, he applies the measures he had called for in his delirium: the fire and the sword he had used in his purification, purging the earth of beasts (ll. 1013 ff.), he turns on himself, resuming the role he has played all his life.

One cannot doubt that the audience as a whole would have thought beyond to the apotheosis, but, by suppressing all mention of elevation to the Gods through fire and by not motivating the fire through an oracle, the poet focuses attention on the thing chosen—the fire itself as destroying and purifying—and on the act of choosing. Heracles suffers and acts not with the promise of immortality but with the firm expectation of death, and it is this which gives meaning to his choice. The hero who has wept and wailed, shamefully vanquished by a woman and his dead enemies, returns to the attack, even as Oedipus puts out his eyes, Ajax yields, only to choose suicide, and Antigone, buried alive, kills herself. Heracles tells his "tough soul," ". . . make an end / of this unwanted, welcome task" (ll. 1259 ff.). He makes his end his own.

Appropriately, it is Hyllus who closes the play, for it is through him that we have felt the emotional impact of the long last scene—Heracles, however stunning his actions, is hardly enough like us now for sympathy. When Hyllus accused his mother, we wanted to cry out, "She did not mean to . . ." and almost at once, with her death, his contrition acknowledges, as it were, that we were right. Now the new blows are felt through our sympathy with him. He must restrain his half-crazed father in his ghastly agony, he must brave a murderous anger to tell him the truth, and he must burn, or all but burn, his father alive and marry the woman he thinks of as his parents' murderer. The dramatic power of the scene needs no comment, but we should also see that thus he ends the chain of violent love by accepting a marriage that appalls him, assuming his father's mantle where alone his father had not triumphed through courage and endurance.

Finally, what of Zeus and the Gods who have shown so little compassion in "all that's happened; they / who are called our fathers, who begot us, / can look upon such suffering" (ll. 1266–69)? For Sophocles, in this play at least, the Gods are "the way things are"—the invincible power of love, the predicted and inevitable end; they form the immovable background to human suffering and heroism. The action of the play insists that this is so, that there is what we might call an "inhuman" design, but it is more concerned with what, this being so, Deianira, Heracles, and Hyllus do and suffer and with the way in which, whatever their weakness, they show how men ought to be.

The Date

The date of the play is not known. Internal evidence has led to widely different conclusions, but a comparison with certain features of Euripides' *Medea* (431 B.C.) and *Heracles* (420–419 B.C.?) seems to help in placing it in the twenties of the fifth century. The date is of interest primarily for the study of Sophocles' development and for possible relations with the work of Euripides. The play is utterly apolitical. It was, then, probably written after *Ajax* and *Antigone*, close to *Oedipus the King*, when the poet was past sixty, and with *Electra* (probably) and *Philoctetes* and *Oedipus at Colonus* certainly still to come.

A Note on the Text

For the most part I have translated the text of A. C. Pearson ("Oxford Classical Texts" [Oxford, 1923]); at a few points I have agreed with R. C. Jebb (*The Trachiniae*, Part V of *Sophocles, The Plays and Fragments* [Cambridge, 1892]) as against Pearson, especially in lines 207, 328, 526, 660, 837, 905, 1084, 1186, and 1191; more rarely I have departed from the interpretation of a word or phrase preferred by Jebb in his commentary, especially in lines 35, 101, 216, 231, 250, 309, 886, and 1010. In lines 100–102 the "seanarrows" probably refer to the Bosphorus and Hellespont, the "twin continents" to Europe and Africa at the Pillars of Heracles (Gibraltar); this agrees with H. Lloyd-Jones, *Classical Quarterly*, XLVIII (1954), 91–92. Finally, with Wilamowitz, I add τέλος in line 528, and at line 857 I read Herwerden's ἅ τ'ὀλεθρίαν for τότε θοάν. I do not attempt any justification, since this is not the place and since, in any case, the choices have been much influenced by the exigencies of making a translation.

THE WOMEN OF TRACHIS

Deianira, Wife of Heracles

Nurse

Hyllus, Son of Heracles and Deianira

Chorus, Women of Trachis, Friends of Deianira

A Messenger

Lichas, Herald of Heracles

Captive Women of Oechalia, Including the Young Iole (all silent parts)

An Old Man

Heracles

Bearers and Attendants of Heracles (silent parts)

THE WOMEN OF TRACHIS

SCENE: *Trachis, before the house of Heracles and Deianira. Deianira and the Nurse enter from the house.*

Deianira

It was long ago that someone first said:
You cannot know a man's life before the man
has died, then only can you call it good or bad.
But I know mine before I've come to Death's house
and I can tell that mine is heavy and sorrowful.   5
While I still lived in Pleuron, with Oeneus my father,
I conceived an agonizing fear of marriage.
No other Aetolian woman ever felt such fear,
for my suitor was the river Acheloüs,
who used to come to ask my father for my hand,   10
taking three forms—first, clearly a bull, and then
a serpent with shimmering coils, then a man's body
but a bull's face, and from his clump of beard
whole torrents of water splashed like a fountain.
I had to think this suitor would be my husband   15
and in my unhappiness I constantly prayed for death
before I should ever come to *his* marriage bed.

But, after a time, to my joy there came
the famous Heracles, son of Alcmena and Zeus.
In close combat with Acheloüs, he won the contest   20
and set me free. I do not speak of the manner
of their struggles, for I do not know. Someone
who watched the spectacle unafraid could tell.
I sank down, overwhelmed with terror lest
my beauty should somehow bring me pain. Zeus of the contests   25
made the end good—if it has been good.

Chosen partner for the bed of Heracles,
I nurse fear after fear, always worrying
over him. I have a constant relay of troubles;
some each night dispels—each night brings others on.   30
We have had children now, whom he sees at times,
like a farmer working an outlying field,
who sees it only when he sows and when he reaps.
This has been his life, that only brings him home
to send him out again, to serve some man or other.   35

Now he wins through to the end of all his labors,
and now I find I am more than ever afraid.
Ever since he killed the mighty Iphitus,
we, his family, live here in Trachis, a stranger's guests,
forced to leave our home. But no one seems to know   40
where Heracles himself can be. I only know
he's gone and left with me a sharp pain for him.
I am almost sure that he is in some trouble.
It has not been a short time—first a year,
by now still more, and there has been no word of him.   45
Yes, this tablet he left behind makes me think
it must surely be some terrible trouble. Often
I pray the Gods I do not have it for my sorrow.

Nurse

Deianira, my mistress, many times before
I have watched as you wept and sobbed, bewailing   50
your absent Heracles, and I said nothing. But now
I wonder—if it is proper that the free should learn
from the thoughts of slaves and I give you advice—
how is it that your family abounds with sons, and yet
you send no one to inquire for your husband?   55
Hyllus, especially, it would be natural to send
if he is at all concerned for his father's safety.
See, here he is, running to the house,
so if what I have said seems of any value,
you can use the boy and follow my advice.   60

(Hyllus enters from the wings.)

Deianira

O my child, my son, even the low-born throw
a lucky cast when they speak well. This woman is
a slave, but what she says is worthy of the free.

Hyllus

What is it she said? Tell me, Mother, if you may.

Deianira

With your father abroad so long, it does not   65
look well that you have made no inquiry for him.

Hyllus

But I know where he is, if I can believe what I hear.

Deianira

My child, have you heard in what country he stays?

Hyllus

All this past year, in all its length of time
they say he was in service to a Lydian woman.   70

Deianira

If he could really endure that, then anything
might be said of him.

Hyllus

               He is free now, I hear.

Deianira

Then where is he now? Is he alive or dead?

Hyllus

They say he is in Euboea, where he campaigns against
the city of Eurytus, unless he is still preparing.   75

Deianira

Did you know, my child, that it was about
this very place he left me a true prophecy?

Hyllus

What prophecy, Mother? I knew nothing about this.

Deianira

 It said that either he would come to his life's end
 or have by now, and for the rest of his time,   80
 a happy life, once he had carried out this task.
 Child, his future lies in the balance. Surely, then,
 you will go to help him, since we are only safe   83
 if he can save himself. His ruin is ours.   85

Hyllus

 I shall go, Mother, and had I known the contents
 of this oracle before, I would have been there
 long ago. As it was, my father's usual
 good luck kept me from worrying and being too fearful.
 Now that I know of it, I shall not stop until   90
 I have learned the whole truth about his fate.

Deianira

 Go now, my son. There is always some advantage
 in learning good news, even if one learns it late.

    (*Hyllus leaves by one of the side entrances; the Chorus
         enters, speaking, by the other.*)

Chorus

 Shimmering night as she lies despoiled brings you
 to birth at dawn, lays you to bed ablaze—   95
 O Sun, Sun! I beg you,
 tell me of Alcmena's child.
 Where, where is Heracles?
 All afire with the brilliance of lightning, tell me!
 —is he in the sea-narrows,   100
 or does he rest against the twin
 continents? Your sight is the strongest.

 With longing in her heart for him, I learn
 that Deianira, over whom men fought,
 like some unhappy bird,   105
 never lays to bed her longing,
 her eyes tearless, but
 nurses fear that well remembers her husband's

journey, worn upon her troubled
husbandless bed, miserable,   110
with expectation of misfortune.

As many waves under
the untiring south wind or north
may be seen on the wide
ocean coming on   115
and going by, so he, the descendant
of Cadmus is twisted, but on life's
next toilsome surge, as on the Cretan
deep, he will be elevated.
Some god always pulls him   120
safely back from the house of Death.

             (*The Chorus turns toward Deianira.*)

Therefore, I reprove you,
respectfully, but still
dissenting. You should not let
all expectation of good   125
be worn away. Nothing painless
has the all-accomplishing King
dispensed for mortal men. But
grief and joy come circling
to all, like the turning paths   130
of the Bear among the stars.

The shimmering night does not stay
for men, nor does calamity,
nor wealth, but swiftly they are gone,
and to another man it comes
to know joy and its loss.   135
Therefore, I bid even you, O Queen, always
hold fast to this knowledge in your expectations.
When has Zeus been so careless of his children?   140

            (*Deianira comes forward and speaks.*)

Deianira

  You are here, I suppose, because you have heard

of my suffering. May you never learn
by your own suffering how my heart is torn.
You do not know now. So the young thing
grows in her own places; the heat of the sun-god   145
does not confound her, nor does the rain, nor any wind.
Pleasurably she enjoys an untroubled life
until the time she is no longer called a maiden
but woman, and takes her share of worry in the night,
fearful for her husband or for her children. Then,   150
by looking at her own experience, she comes
to understand the troubles with which I am weighed down.

Many sufferings have made me weep before.
But I shall tell you of one unlike all the rest.
When King Heracles set off from home on his   155
last journey, he left an old tablet in the house,
on which some signs had been inscribed. Never before
could he bring himself to speak to me of this,
though he went out to many contests; he used to go
as if for some great achievement, not to die.   160
This once, as though he were no longer living, he told me
what property from our marriage I should take and how
he wished the portions of ancestral land divided
among the children, first fixing the time at three months
after he had been away from here one year: 165
then he would either die exactly at this time,
or, by getting past this time limit, he would
in the future live a life without grief.
He said that this was fated by the Gods to be
the final limit of the labors of Heracles,   170
as once at Dodona he heard the ancient oak
declare on the lips of the twin Doves, the priestesses.
The period of their prediction exactly coincides
with the present time, when all must come true;
so that I leap up from pleasant sleep in fright,   175
my friends, terrified to think that I may have to live
deprived of the one man who is the finest of all.

Chorus

    Peace—speak words of good omen. I see a man
    with laurel on his head who comes to speak to you.

                         (A messenger enters from the side in a great hurry,
                                    full of his important news.)

Messenger

    O Deianira, my mistress, I am the first messenger   180
    to free you from your uncertainty. You should know
    that Alcmena's son lives and is victorious
    and brings from battle first-fruits for the gods of the land.

Deianira

    What did you say, old man? What are you telling me?

Messenger

    Soon there shall come to your halls that most enviable man,   185
    your husband, appearing in his conquering might.

Deianira

    Who told you this? Some townsman or a stranger?

Messenger

    This is what Lichas, the herald, proclaims to many
    in the meadow where the cattle pasture. I heard him
    and rushed off, that, as the first to bring the news, I might   190
    profit from your gratitude and gain your favor.

Deianira

    Why is he not here himself if all is well?

Messenger

    He is not free to move as he would like, lady.
    Around him in a circle stand all the people of Malis
    and question him. He is not able to take a step.   195
    Everyone is curious and wants to know all
    and will not let him go until he's heard him to
    his heart's content. So though *he* does not want to, he stays
    with those who want him. You will see him soon in person.

Deianira

    O Zeus, master of the unharvested meadow of Oeta,   200
    though it has been long, you have given us joy.

Cry out, O you women who are within the house
and you who are without—now that the unhoped-for sunshine
of this news has risen high, we pluck its gladness.

Chorus   205
Let there be joyous shouting, and jubilation around the hearth,
for soon this house will win a husband; and let the clamor
of men within it go in chorus to honor Apollo,
who wears the fine quiver, our defender. Together
raise on high the paean, paean, O maidens,   210
and shout aloud the name of his sister,
Artemis Ortygia, deer-hunter, who holds the twin torches,
and of the nymphs our neighbors.   215
I take it up, I shall not
push the flute aside, you master of my heart.
See how it excites me—
Euoi!—
the ivy that lately set the bacchants whirling in rivalry.   220
Oh, Oh, Paean! See, see, dear lady,
you are face to face with it now,
it is clear to look upon.

      (*Enter Lichas, Heracles' envoy, followed by a group
          of captive women, among them Iole.*)

Deianira
I do see the group that comes to us, dear women.   225
The sight did not slip past my sentinel eyes.
I proclaim our welcome to the herald, here after
a long time—if the news he brings is welcome.

Lichas
Our coming *is* good, lady, and good, too, our message,
based on accomplished fact. When a man prospers,   230
his profit must be to earn an excellent report.

Deianira
O kindest of men, tell me first what I want first
to hear: Shall I have Heracles alive?

Lichas

  I can tell you that I left him not only alive
  but strong and flourishing and unburdened by disease.   235

Deianira

  Where? In a Greek or in a foreign land? Tell me.

Lichas

  On a shore of Euboea, where he marks out altars
  and tributes of the land's harvest for Cenaean Zeus.

Deianira

  Is he fulfilling a vow or obeying an oracle?

Lichas

  A vow he took while he tried with his spear to overthrow   240
  the country of these women whom you see before you.

Deianira

  And by the gods, who are they, and who is their master?
  They are pitiable, if their misfortune does not deceive me.

Lichas

  He selected them when he sacked the city of Eurytus
  as possessions for himself and a choice gift for the Gods.   245

Deianira

  Was it against this city, then, that he was gone
  an unforeseeable time, days beyond number?

Lichas

  No, most of this time he was kept in Lydia,
  and, as he himself declares, he was not free
  but a bought slave. (One should not hesitate, lady,   250
  to tell a tale where it is seen Zeus did the work.)
  He was sold to Omphale, the foreign queen,
  and served her a full year, as he says himself,
  and was so stung by this disgrace he had to bear
  that he set himself an oath and swore that he   255
  would live to see the author of his suffering,
  along with wife and child, all in slavery.

These were not empty words, but when he was pure again,
he raised an army of strangers and came against the city
of Eurytus, who alone of mortals was   260
responsible, he claimed, for what he had suffered.
Heracles had come to his house and to his hearth
as an old friend. But Eurytus thundered greatly against him
like the sea and spoke with great malice in his heart:
Let Heracles have in his hands, he said, inescapable arrows.   265
In the bow's test *his* sons left Heracles behind,
as for speech—Heracles was a free man's slave,
a broken thing! Then he got him drunk at the banquet
and threw him out of the house. It was this that galled;
and when one day Iphitus came to the hill of Tiryns,   270
searching for the tracks of horses that had strayed,
the moment his eyes looked one way, his mind on something else,
Heracles hurled him from the top of that flat bastion.
But the King was angry at this act of his,
he who is the father of all, Zeus Olympian,   275
and had him sold and sent out of the country and did not relent,
since this was the only man he had ever killed
by guile. If he had taken vengeance openly,
Zeus surely would have pardoned his rightful victory.
The Gods like foul play no better than do men.   280
They who were so arrogant with their vicious tongues,
they themselves all are inhabitants of Hell,
while their city is enslaved. The women you see
come to you, finding, in place of prosperity,
an unenviable existence. These were your husband's wishes   285
which he commanded and I, faithful to him, fulfil.
You may be sure that he himself will come as soon
as he has made the holy sacrifice to Zeus,
God of his fathers, for his conquest. Of much news
happily reported, this must be the sweetest to hear.   290

Chorus

O Queen, now your delight is clear, both for what
has come about already, and what you have heard promised.

Deianira

  Yes, I should have every right to rejoice
  when I hear the news of my husband's great success.
  Surely my joy must keep pace with his good fortune.   295
  Still, if one gives it much thought, one knows a feeling
  of dread for the man who prospers so, lest he fall.
  For a terrible sense of pity came over me,
  my friends, when I saw these ill-fated women
  wandering homeless, fatherless, in a foreign land.   300
  Before they were, perhaps, the daughters of free men,
  but now they shall have to pass their lives as slaves.

  O Zeus, who turns the tide of battle, grant that I
  may never see you come like this against *my* children,
  and if you will come, at least not while I am alive.   305
  This is the fear I feel when I look at them.

                   (Deianira comes close to Iole.)
  O unfortunate girl, tell me who you are.
  Are you married? Are you a mother? To judge by your looks,
  you have never known treatment like this, but you
  are someone noble. Lichas, whose daughter is this girl?   310
  Who was her mother, and who was the father that begat her?
  Speak out, for on seeing her I pitied her most
  among these women, since only she knows how to feel.

Lichas

  What do *I* know? Why do you question me? Perhaps
  in birth she is not among the humblest of that land.   315

Deianira

  Not of royal birth? Had Eurytus a daughter?

Lichas

  I do not know. I made no long interrogation.

Deianira

  Did you not learn her name from one of her companions?

Lichas

  No, I did not. I performed my task in silence.

Deianira

Then do tell us yourself, my poor child, for it   320
would be a great shame not to know who *you* are.

Lichas

It will be quite unlike her manner up to now
if she begins to speak, I can assure you, since
she has not said a single thing, not one word yet.
She suffers constantly the weight of her misfortune   325
like pangs of labor, weeping and miserable, from the time
she left her wind-blown fatherland. Truly, it is her
bad luck that she cannot speak, but pardon her.

Deianira

Then let her be, and let her go into the house
however she please. She should not have further grief   330
on my account to add to her present unhappiness.
What she has already is enough. Let us all
enter the house so you may hasten wherever you wish
to go and I may see to the preparations within.

> (*Deianira turns to lead Lichas and the captive women into the
> house; the Messenger, who had stayed to one side while
> Lichas spoke with Deianira, approaches and
> detains her while the others pass indoors.*)

Messenger

Wait! Stay a moment here that you may learn,   335
without these others, who they are that you lead inside,
and, since you have heard nothing at all, you may discover
what you must. For of all this I have knowledge.

Deianira

What do you want? Why have you stopped me from going in?

Messenger

Stay and hear me. The earlier message you had from me   340
was no waste of time, nor, I think, will this be.

Deianira

Should we call the others back, or do you wish
to speak only to me and to my friends here?

Messenger

    To you and your friends I may speak—leave the others.

Deianira

    They are gone now, so please give me an explanation.   345

Messenger

    Nothing that man has just been telling you was spoken
    in strict honesty. Either he is a liar now,
    or he was no honest messenger before.

Deianira

    What are you saying? Tell me clearly everything
    you know. I cannot understand what you have said.   350

Messenger

    I myself heard this man say—and many men
    were present who can bear me out—that for the sake
    of this girl Heracles destroyed Eurytus
    and his high-towered Oechalia; and, of the Gods, it was
    Love alone who bewitched him into this violence—   355
    not his laborious service in Lydia for Omphale,
    nor the fact that Iphitus was hurled to his death—
    it was Love, whom he brushes aside in this new version.
    But the truth is that when he could not persuade the father
    to give the child to him for his secret bed,   360
    he fabricated a petty complaint, an excuse
    to campaign against the girl's country, and sacked   362/364
    the city. And now, as you see, he is coming home   365
    and has sent her here, not without a reason, lady,
    and not to be a slave. You must not expect that!
    It would not be likely if he is inflamed with desire.
    So I thought it best to reveal the whole affair
    to you, my mistress, just as I happened to hear it from him,   370
    and there were many others listening to this same story
    in the public gathering of the men of Trachis who can
    refute him as well as I. If what I say is unkind,
    I am sorry, but still I have told the strict truth.

Deianira

Oh! Oh! What has happened to me? I have   375
welcomed a secret enemy under my roof.
Oh, I am miserable, miserable! How truly nameless
is she, as the man who brought her swore to me—
a girl so brilliant in her looks and in her birth!

Messenger

Yes, she had Eurytus for her father and was called   380
Iole, but of course *he* could tell you nothing
of her origin since he had never asked!

Chorus

Damn all scoundrels, but damn him most of all
who practices a secret, degrading villainy.

Deianira

What shall I do? I must ask you, for the story   385
which has now come out leaves me utterly stunned.

Chorus

Go and talk to Lichas. Perhaps he would speak out
if you insisted on knowing, whether he liked it or not.

Deianira

I shall go. Your advice is not unreasonable.

Messenger

Shall I wait meanwhile? What do you wish me to do?   390

Deianira

Stay, for I see the man has started from the house
of his own accord, without my summoning him.

(*Lichas enters from the house.*)

Lichas

Lady, what should I say when I come to Heracles?
Give me instructions, for, as you see, I am on my way.

Deianira

How quickly you are rushing off when you were   395
so long in coming, before we have even talked again.

Lichas

If there is anything you wish to ask me, I am at your service.

Deianira

Will I be able to trust in the truth of what you say?

Lichas

Yes—great Zeus be my witness!—as far as my knowledge goes.

Deianira

Tell me, then, who is the woman you brought with you?   400

Lichas

A Euboean. But I do not know her parents.

Messenger

You there! Look here! To whom do you think you are talking?

Lichas

And you—what do you mean asking such a question?

Messenger

You would be well advised to try to answer me.

Lichas

I speak to her who commands, Deianira, daughter   405
of Oeneus and the consort of Heracles, if my eyes
do not deceive me—it is my *mistress* that I address.

Messenger

There it is, the very thing I wanted to hear.
You say she is your mistress?

Lichas

                    It is the honest truth.

Messenger

Well, then, what do you think should be your punishment   410
if you are discovered to have been dishonest with her?

Lichas

What do you mean "dishonest"? What are these tricky riddles?

Messenger

No riddles at all! You are the one who is being tricky.

Lichas

  I am leaving. I have been a fool to listen so long.

Messenger

  Not yet, not before you answer a few questions.   415

Lichas

  Say what you want. You'll not be at a loss for words.

Messenger

  That captive girl whom you brought to the house, you know
  whom I mean?

Lichas

          I do, but why do you ask about her?

Messenger

  You look at her with no sign of recognition,
  but did you not say she was Iole, the daughter of Eurytus?   420

Lichas

  Where on earth did I say so? Who is going to come
  and testify that he was there and heard me talk?

Messenger

  You spoke before many of the townspeople. A large crowd
  in the public place of Trachis heard you say this.

Lichas

  Oh, yes—
  They may have said they heard me. But to repeat an impression   425
  is not the same as giving an accurate account.

Messenger

  Impression, indeed! Did you not state under oath that you
  were bringing this girl as a consort for Heracles?

Lichas

  I said that? By the Gods, explain to me,
  dear mistress—this stranger here, who on earth is he?   430

Messenger

  A man who was there and heard you say her city was

completely crushed through desire for her; no woman
of Lydia destroyed it, but his clear love for her.

Lichas

Please have this fellow leave. No sensible person,
mistress, wastes his time exchanging words with a madman.   435

Deianira

By Zeus who flashes lightning over the topmost glen
of Oeta, do not cheat me of the truth! Speak,
and you will find that I am not a spiteful woman
nor one who does not know how it is with man—
we cannot always enjoy a constant happiness.   440
How foolish one would be to climb into the ring
with Love and try to trade blows with him, like a boxer.
For he rules even the Gods as he pleases, and
he rules me—why not another woman like me?
You see that I would be altogether mad   445
to blame my husband, because he suffers from this sickness,
or that woman. She has been guilty of nothing shameful,
and she has done no harm to me. No, it is
inconceivable. If you have learned to lie from him,
then you are not learning honest lessons. If you school   450
yourself in this fashion, you succeed only
in seeming dishonest when you are trying to be decent.
Tell me the whole truth. To gain the reputation
of a liar is utter dishonor for a free man.
You cannot think that I will not hear. There are   455
many men to whom you have spoken, and they will tell me.

                    (Deianira pauses, but Lichas remains silent.)
Are you afraid of hurting me? You are wrong.
The only thing that could hurt would be not to know.
Where is the danger in knowing? One man and many women—
Heracles has had other women before.   460
Never yet has one of them earned insults
from me, or spiteful talk, nor will she, even
if she is utterly absorbed in her passion,

for I pitied her deeply when I saw her because
her own beauty has destroyed her life, and, against her will,   465
this unfortunate girl has sacked and enslaved the land
of her fathers. Now let all this flow away
on the wind. To you I have this to say: You may
be dishonest with others, but never lie to me.

Chorus

Obey her. What she says is good. You will have   470
no cause to complain later, and you will gain our thanks.

Lichas

Well, dear mistress, I realize that you are not
unreasonable. You see things as we mortals must.
So I shall tell you the whole truth. I shall not hide it.
It is just as this man said. A terrible longing   475
ran through Heracles—and it *was* for this girl.
Because of her, Oechalia, the land of her fathers,
was overthrown by his spear with great destruction.
None of this did he tell me to hide, I must say
in fairness to him; none of this did he ever deny.   480
I myself, O my mistress, was fearful lest I
should cause pain in your breast by these words of mine.
It was I who erred, if you would call this error.
But since, as it turns out, you know the whole story,
for your own sake as much as for his, be kind   485
to the woman and show that the words you spoke to her
before you knew were said in all sincerity.
Against all else he has won by sheer strength; but by
this love for her he has been completely vanquished.

Deianira

Those are my feelings too, and so too shall I act.   490
You may be sure I shall not choose to add to my
afflictions hopeless resistance to the Gods. Now let us
go into the house. I have messages for you
to carry, and there are gifts to match the gifts you brought—
these too you must take. It would not be right to leave   495
empty-handed when you came so well provided.

(Deianira and Lichas and perhaps the Messenger,
who must be rewarded, enter the house.)

Chorus

Strong is the victory the Cyprian Goddess always wins.
I pass by
the Gods; I would not tell how Zeus was tricked by her;   500
nor Hades, who lives in the night;
nor Poseidon, the shaker of the earth.
But for our lady's hand
who were the two valiant contenders in courtship?
Who were they who came out to struggle in bouts that were   505
all blows and all dust?

One was a strong river with the looks of a high-horned
four-footed bull,
Acheloüs from Oeniadae; the other   510
came from the Thebes of Bacchus,
shaking his back-sprung bow, his spears and club
—the son of Zeus. They came
together then in the middle, desiring
her bed. Alone, in the middle with them, their referee,   515
Cypris, goddess of love's bed.

Then there was thudding of fists and clang of bows
and confusion of bulls' horns;
and there was contorted grappling,   520
and there were deadly blows from butting heads
and groaning on both sides.
But the tender girl with the lovely
eyes sat far from them on a hillside,
waiting for the one who would be her husband.   525
So the struggle raged, as I have told it;
but the bride over whom they fought
awaited the end pitiably.
And then she was gone from her mother,
like a calf that is lost.   530

(Deianira comes out from the house.)

Deianira

    Dear friends, while our visitor is in the house
talking to the captured girls before he leaves,
I have come out to you, unobserved. I want
to tell you the work my hands have done, but also to have
your sympathy as I cry out for all I suffer.   535
For here I have taken on a girl—no,
I can think that no longer—a married woman, as
a ship's master takes on cargo, goods that outrage my heart.
So now the two of us lie under the one sheet
waiting for his embrace. This is the gift my brave   540
and faithful Heracles sends home to his dear wife
to compensate for his long absence! And yet, when he
is sick as he so often is with this same sickness,
I am incapable of anger. But to live
in the same house with her, to share the same marriage,   545
that is something else. What woman could stand that?
For I see her youth is coming to full bloom
while mine is fading. The eyes of men love to pluck
the blossoms; from the faded flowers they turn away.
And this is why I am afraid that he may   550
be called my husband but be the younger woman's man.
But no sensible woman, as I've said before,
should let herself give way to rage. I shall tell you,
dear friends, the solution I have to bring myself relief.

    I have had hidden in a copper urn   555
for many years the gift of a centaur, long ago.
While I was still a child, I took it from the wounds
of the hairy-chested Nessus as he was dying.
He used to ferry people, for a fee, across
the deep flood of the Evenus, in his arms   560
with no oars to drive him over nor ships' sails.
I too was carried on his shoulders when my father
sent me to follow Heracles for the first time

as his wife. When I was halfway across
his hands touched me lustfully. I cried out and at once   565
the son of Zeus turned around, raised his hands,
and shot a feathered arrow through his chest; into
his lungs it hissed. The beast spoke his last words to me
as he died: "Daughter of old Oeneus,
if you listen to me, you shall have great profit   570
from my ferrying, since you are the last I have brought across.
If you take in your hands this blood, clotted in
my wounds, wherever it is black with the bile
of the Hydra, the monstrous serpent of Lerna, in which
he dipped his arrows, you will have a charm over   575
the heart of Heracles, so he will never look
at another woman and love her more than you."
I have thought of this, my friends, for since his death
I have kept it in the house, tightly closed.
I followed all instructions he gave me while he still lived   580
and dipped this robe in the charm. Now it is all done.

I am not a woman who tries to be—and may
I never learn to be—bad and bold. I hate
women who are. But if somehow by these charms,
these spells I lay on Heracles, I can defeat   585
the girl—well, the move is made, unless you think
I am acting rashly. If so, I shall stop.

Chorus

If there is reason for confidence in these measures,
you do not seem to us to have acted badly.

Deianira

I have this much confidence only: there seem to be   590
good prospects, but I have never brought them to the test.

Chorus

One can only tell from action. Whatever you think,
you have no way of judging before you try it out.

Deianira

    Well, we shall know soon. I see the messenger
    coming out of doors, and he will be going shortly. 595
    Only be discreet. In darkness one may be
    ashamed of what one does, without the shame of disgrace.

                              (Lichas comes out from the house.)

Lichas

    What would you wish me to do? Command me, O daughter of
      Oeneus.
    I have already stayed too long, and now I am late.

Deianira

    Lichas, this is the very thing I have looked after 600
    while you were talking to the foreign women inside.
    Here is a gift made by my own hands for you
    to take to my husband—this long, fine-woven robe.
    When you give it to him, you must tell him that it
    should touch the skin of no man before it touches his, 605
    nor should he let the light of the sun look upon it,
    nor any holy inclosure, nor the gleam from a hearth,
    until he himself stands, conspicuous before all,
    and shows it to the Gods on a day of bull-slaughtering.
    For this was my vow: if I should ever see or hear 610
    that he was coming safe to his home, in all piety
    I would dress him in this robe to appear before
    the Gods to make new sacrifice in new clothing.
    And you shall carry a token of this vow which he
    will understand from the familiar encircled print 615
    of my seal.
            Go now, and as a messenger
    be sure to keep the rule not to exceed your orders.
    In this way, with thanks both from my husband and
    from me, you will earn our double gratitude.

Lichas

    If I, the messenger, practice this art of Hermes 620
    soundly, I shall never fail in serving you.

I shall present this chest exactly as it is,
and in explanation I shall repeat your words.

Deianira

Then you should be going now. You understand
completely how everything is here in this house. 625

Lichas

I understand, and I shall report that all is well.

Deianira

And, of course, since you saw it, you know the girl's
reception—you know I received her as a friend.

Lichas

Yes, I do, and I am astonished and delighted.

Deianira

What else is there to tell him? For I am afraid 630
you would be talking too soon of my longing for him
before I know if *he* feels longing for me.

(*Exit Lichas through a side entrance; Deianira enters the house.*)

Chorus

Safe harbors, hot-springs among
the rocks, the high cliffs of Oeta—
all you who live by these and by the inmost reaches 635
of the sea in Malis,
the coast of the Maid who shoots the golden shaft,
and there at the Gates,
the famous gatherings of the Greeks—

Soon again the lovely cries 640
of the flute will rise among you;
now it will not ring in disagreeable clamor
but like the lyre, music
for the gods. The son of Zeus and Alcmena
hurries to his home 645
bearing the prizes of all valor.

Gone from the city completely,
we missed him, waiting a long twelve months, while he
was on the sea, but we knew
nothing, and his loving wife 650
all lamentation always, sadly, most
sadly, broke her heart.
But now Ares, God of War,
stung to madness, dispels her day of troubles.

Oh let him come, let him come, 655
and his ship of many oars; let it
not stop before he ends his journey
at this city, leaving the island
hearth where, they say, he makes sacrifice.
Let him come from there 660
all desire when the beast's
inducements, all dipped in persuasion, have melted him.

(*Deianira comes out from the house.*)

Deianira

O my friends, I am afraid! Can it be
I have gone too far in all I have just done?

Chorus

What is the matter, Deianira, child of Oeneus? 665

Deianira

I don't know. I have a foreboding that I'll be shown
to have done great harm when I hoped to do good.

Chorus

Surely you do not mean your gift to Heracles?

Deianira

Yes, yes. Now I see that one should never
plunge eagerly into anything obscure. 670

Chorus

Explain the cause of your fear, if it can be explained.

Deianira

Something has happened which, if I tell you, my friends,
will seem a marvel such as you never thought to hear.
Just now, when I anointed the robe I sent to be
my husband's vestment, I used a tuft of fleecy white wool.   675
This piece has disappeared, devoured by nothing in
the house but destroyed by itself, eaten away
and crumbled completely to dust. I want to tell you this
in detail, so you may know the whole story.

I neglected none of the instructions that beast   680
the centaur explained to me, lying in agony
with the sharp arrowhead in his side. I kept them
like an inscription on bronze that cannot be washed away.
And I only did what I was told to do—
I must keep this drug away from fire and always   685
deep in the house where no warm ray of light may touch it
until I should want to apply it freshly smeared.
And this is what I did. Now, when it had to do its work,
at home, inside the house, secretly I smeared it on
some wool, a scrap I pulled from one of the household sheep,   690
and then I folded my gift and put it in a chest
before the sun could shine on it, as you saw.

But when I go in again, I see something
unspeakable, incomprehensible to human reason.
Somehow I had happened to throw the ball of wool,   695
which I had used to smear the robe, into the full heat
of the sun's rays, and, as it became warm,
it all ran together, a confused mass, and crumbled
to bits on the ground, looking most like the dust one sees
eaten away in the cutting of a piece of wood.   700
Like this it lies where it fell. But from the earth
on which it rests, clotted foam boils up
like the rich liquid of the blue-green fruit
from the vines of Dionysus, poured on the earth.

And now I do not know what to think. I see 705
myself as someone who has done a terrible thing.
From what possible motive, in return for what,
could the dying beast have shown me kindness, when he
was dying because of me? No, he beguiled me,
only to destroy the man who shot him. But I 710
have come to understand now when it is too late.
I alone, unless my fears are fanciful,
I, his unhappy wife, shall destroy him.
I know that arrow which struck Nessus injured even
Chiron, who was a god, and all animals, 715
whatever it touches, it kills. This same poison which seeped,
black and bloody, from the wounds of Nessus, how can
it fail to kill Heracles too? At least, this is
my fear. And yet I have made a decision: if he goes down,
under the same blow I will die with him. 720
I could not bear to live and hear myself called evil
when my only wish is to be truly good.

Chorus
Terrible results are appalling, but one
should not expect the worst before anything has happened.

Deianira
When the plans themselves are bad, there can be 725
no expectations that leave any place for courage.

Chorus
But whenever we trip up unwillingly,
the anger felt is tempered, and so it should be with you.

Deianira
You may talk like this, since you have no share
in the wrong; you have no burden all your own. 730

Chorus
Better to be silent now—say nothing more,
if you do not want to tell it to your son.
The one who went away to search for his father is here.

(Hyllus enters from the side.)

Hyllus

Mother! I wish I could have found you not as you are
but no longer alive, or safe but someone else's   735
mother, or somehow changed and with a better heart
than now. Three ways—Oh, for any one of them!

Deianira

My son, what has happened that I should be so hateful?

Hyllus

What has happened? Your husband, my father—
do you hear me?—you have killed him.   740

Deianira

No, no, my child! What have you blurted out?

Hyllus

Only what cannot fail to be. Once a thing
is seen, who can cause it never to have been?

Deianira

How could you say it? Who on earth told you
that I did this awful crime you charge me with?   745

Hyllus

I saw my father's heavy fall with my own eyes
myself; I did not hear of it from anyone.

Deianira

Where did you come upon him? Were you at his side?

Hyllus

If you must hear, then I must talk and tell you all.
When he sacked the famous city of Eurytus,   750
he marched away with the trophies and the first-fruits of victory.
On a wave-beaten shore of Euboea there is
a point called Cenaeum, where he marked out altars
and a whole precinct for Zeus, god of our fathers.
There I first saw him, glad after my longing.   755
He was about to make great slaughter for sacrifice

when his own herald Lichas arrived from our home,
bringing with him that gift of yours, the deadly robe.
He clothed himself in it just as you had instructed
and killed first his bulls, twelve perfect victims,   760
the pick of the booty; then he brought the number to
one hundred, driving a mixed herd to the altar.
And at first the poor wretch, his mind at ease,
rejoicing in his handsome dress, prayed to the Gods.
But as the flame from the juicy pine-wood fire   765
blazed high and bloody from the solemn rites,
the sweat broke out on his skin; the robe enfolded him
around his limbs, joined tightly to his sides
like the work of a sculptor. Spasms of pain
bit into his bones. Then like the vicious, murderous   770
viper's poison, it began to consume him.

Now he shouted for that unfortunate Lichas, who was
in no way guilty of your crime, demanding
to know the plot behind his bringing him this robe.
Unlucky man, he knew nothing and said it was   775
a gift from you alone, just as you had sent it.
And at that moment, as Heracles listened to his answer,
a piercing, tearing pain clutched at his lungs; he caught
Lichas by the foot where the ankle turns
and threw him against a wave-beaten rock that juts from the sea.   780
It pressed the pale brains out through his hair,
and, split full on, skull and blood mixed and spread.
All the people there cried out in horror for
the one man in his suffering, the other dead.
No one had the courage to come to Heracles.   785
He would be wrenched now to the ground, now in the air,
crying, shrieking. All around the rocks echoed,
the mountain headlands of Locris, the high cliffs of Euboea.
When he gave up at last, after throwing himself
miserably again and again to the earth, crying   790

and groaning again and again, damning the mismating
in your wretched bed, the whole marriage that he
had won from Oeneus, only to befoul his life,
he raised his eyes, distorted, from the dark smoke
that hung around him and saw me in the great crowd, 795
tears pouring down my face, and, looking at me, called:
"My son, come to me! Do not run from me
in my pain, even if you must die with me.
Take me away! Above all else I ask you to put me
in a place where no man can look at me. 800
If you have pity, at least carry me out of this land
as soon as you can, that I may not die here."
These were his orders; we placed him in the middle of
a boat and with difficulty landed him here,
howling in spasms of pain. You shall be seeing him 805
at once, still alive or dead only now.

Mother, this is what you have planned and done to my father,
and you are caught. For this, Justice who punishes
and the Fury will requite you. If it is right
for a son, I curse you, and it *is* right, since you 810
have given me the right by killing the best of all men
on earth, such as you shall never see again.

(*Deianira moves away and leaves by the side.*)

Chorus (*to Deianira*)
Why do you go off in silence? Surely you see
that by silence you join your accuser and accuse yourself?

Hyllus
Let her go, and I hope a fair wind blows 815
to carry her far out of my sight. For why should she
maintain the pointless dignity of the name
of mother when she acts in no way like a mother?
No, let her go—goodbye to her. And the delight
she gave my father, may she find the same herself. 820

(*Hyllus enters the house.*)

Chorus

   See, maidens, how, suddenly, it has closed
   with us, the prophetic word spoken
   with foreknowledge long ago, that said
   when the year of the twelfth plowing came to an end,
   then it would bring an end for the true-born son of Zeus   825
   to his relay of toils. And now, surely,
   at the right time, it all comes home.
   How can he who no longer sees
   still have, still, toilsome
   servitude, when he is dead?   830

   If there clings to him in a murderous cloud
   the centaur's treacherous, sure trap
   and his sides are soaked with venom
   that Death begat and the shimmering serpent bred,
   how shall he see another sun after today's   835
   when the Hydra, horrible and monstrous, has
   soaked in? From the black-maned beast's
   treacherous words there comes to torture him
   a murderous confusion,
   sharp points brought to burning heat.   840

   She, poor woman, knew nothing of this
   but, seeing great injury for her home
   from a new marriage swiftly approaching,
   applied her remedy;   845
   but what came from another's will, a fatal meeting,
   truly, lost, she laments,
   truly, she weeps a pale,
   foaming flood of tears. Doom
   as it advances makes clear before
   it comes a great disaster from treachery.   850

   A spring of tears burst open.
   Such sickness, alas, has poured upon him, suffering
   to pity as never yet came upon the hero

from his enemies.   855
Woe for the dark head of the front-fighting spear
that won in battle this
fatal bride from steep
Oechalia. But that silent
handmaiden, Cyprian Aphrodite,   860
is revealed; it is her work.

(*Wailing is heard inside the house.*)

Chorus (*the women speak separately throughout this scene*)
Can I be mistaken? Do I hear something,
a cry of grief surging now through the house?

What can I say?   865
The sound is all too clear. They are shrieking for
misfortune inside. The house suffers a new blow.

(*The Nurse comes out of the house.*)

And see
this old woman who is coming toward us, to tell us
something, see how sad she is and how she frowns.   870

Nurse
O maidens, that gift she sent to Heracles,
truly it was the beginning of great sorrow for us.

Chorus
What new calamity have you to tell us, old woman?

Nurse
Deianira, motionless, has moved away
to start upon the very last of all her journeys.   875

Chorus
No, you cannot mean she is dead?

Nurse
                                            You know all.

Chorus
Then she is dead, the poor woman?

Nurse
                                            I tell you again, she is.

Chorus

Gone, poor thing! Can you tell us how she died?

Nurse

Horrible, the way it happened!

Chorus

Tell us, woman,

the fate she met   880

Nurse

She destroyed herself.

Chorus

Was her mind in a passion or sick?

Nurse

The weapon's cruel point
killed her.

Chorus

How could she think of
death on top of death   885
and end her life all alone?

Nurse

The grim steel cut her.

Chorus

And helpless did you see her awful act?

Nurse

Yes, I saw it. For I was standing near her there.

Chorus

Oh, what was it? How? Tell us.   890

Nurse

She herself by herself set her hand to it.

Chorus

What are you saying?

Nurse

The clear truth.

Chorus

    That bride, newly come,
    has borne, has borne a mighty
    Fury for this house.   895

Nurse

    Yes, and if you had been near and had seen
    what Deianira did, still more would you pity.

Chorus

    How could any woman bring her hands to this?

Nurse

    Yes, it was terrible. You will learn everything
    and bear me witness. When she went into the house, alone,   900
    and saw her son in the courtyard, arranging a cushioned bed
    to take with him as he went back to meet his father,
    she hid herself where no one might look at her and groaned,
    falling against the altars, that now they would be
    deserted; and whenever she touched some household thing   905
    she used to use before, the poor creature would weep.
    Here and there, from room to room, she kept turning,
    and if she saw some servant of the household who was
    dear to her, she would look at her sadly and weep,
    and she would call out loud to her fate and to   910
    her house that would have no children any more.

    Then she stops all this, and suddenly I see her
    rushing into the bedchamber of Heracles,
    and secretly, from the shadows, I keep watch
    over her. I see the woman casting sheets   915
    and spreading them upon the bed of Heracles.
    Then, as soon as she had finished, she leapt up
    and sat there in the middle of her marriage bed,
    and, bursting into torrents of hot tears, she said:
    "O my bed, O my bridal chamber, farewell   920
    now forever, for never again will you take me
    to lie as a wife between these sheets of yours."

She says nothing more, but with a violent sweep
of her arm unfastens her gown where a pin
of beaten gold lies above her breast. She had   925
uncovered her whole side and her left arm.
And I go running off with all the strength I have
and tell her son what his mother is planning to do.
But in the time I have been rushing there and back
we see that she has cut her side to the liver   930
and the seat of life with a double-bladed sword.
Her son shrieked, for he realized, poor boy,
that in his anger he had forced her to this act.
He had just learned from people in the house that she
had done unwittingly the will of the beast.   935

Then the miserable boy abandoned himself utterly
to sobs and mourning for his mother; he threw himself
upon her lips and there, pressing his side to hers,
he lay and groaned over and over that he
had struck her thoughtlessly with a cruel accusation,   940
weeping because at one moment he was doubly
orphaned for all his life, losing his father and her.

> (*The Nurse throws open the doors of the house, revealing
> Hyllus and the body of Deianira,
> lying on a couch.*)

This is the way things are within. If anyone
counts upon one day ahead or even more,
he does not think. For there can be no tomorrow   945
until we have safely passed the day that is with us still.

> (*The Nurse enters the house.*)

Chorus
    Which shall I lament first?
    Which is the more final disaster?
    In my distress I cannot tell.
    The one we can see in the house,   950

the other besets us in our thoughts—
to have and to await are the same.

Oh for a strong blast
of fair wind coming to my hearth
to carry me away from this place   955
that I may not die of fright
when I no more than look
at Zeus's valiant son.
They say he is coming to the house
in unassuageable pain,   960
a wonder beyond telling.

(Men enter from the side, carrying Heracles in a litter,
accompanied by an old man; Hyllus enters from
the house, closing the doors after him.)

Near, then, not distant
is he for whom I cried, like the shrill
nightingale. Here strangers are approaching.   965
How are they carrying him? As though
mourning for a friend,
their steps are slow, soundless.
Ah! He is carried without a word.
Am I to think that he
is dead or only asleep?   970

Hyllus

O my father!
O my sorrow! What is left
for me? How can I help?

Old Man

Be silent, child, do not excite
the wild pain that makes him savage.   975
He still lives, though fallen. You must
bite your lips.

Hyllus

        What? Alive?

Old Man

    Do not wake him, held fast in sleep.
    Do not excite, do not set stirring
    that awful returning   980
    sickness.

Hyllus

          But it drives me mad,
    so helpless under an immense weight!

Heracles

    O Zeus,
    what land have I come to? Among what men
    do I lie worn out by these   985
    unceasing pains? O my agony!
    The filthy thing eats me again.

Old Man

    Now do you see how much better it was
    to hide your sorrow in silence, nor shatter
    sleep from his head   990
    and eyes?

Hyllus

          No, I cannot stand it
    when I see him in this suffering.

Heracles

    O altar steps of Cenaeum, is this
    all the thanks you win me for all
    the sacrifice I made on you?   995
    Torture, torture is all Zeus gives me!
    I wish I had never seen your altar
    with these poor eyes that must face now
    this inexorable flowering of madness.
    Is there any singer of spells,   1000
    any craftsman surgeon who can
    exorcise this curse, but Zeus?
    Even to see him would be a wonder!

(The bearers set the litter down.)

Oh! Let me be. Let
me sleep in my misery,   1005
let me sleep my last sleep.

Where are you touching me? Where are you laying me?
You are killing me, killing me.
You have prodded awake what slumbered.

It has caught me. Oh! It comes on again.   1010
O most ungrateful of the Greeks, where are all you
for whom I destroyed myself purging so many beasts
from all the seas and woods? Now when *I* am sick,
will no one turn the beneficial fire, the sword on me?

Oh! Why will no one   1015
come and cut away
my head from my abominable body.

(The Old Man tries to restrain and support Heracles.)

Old Man

Come, you are the man's son. The task is more
than my strength can manage. You must help. Your strength
can easily do more for him than I.

Hyllus

                          I touch him,   1020
but to make him unconscious of pain, that is beyond
my power or any man's. Such is the will of Zeus.

Heracles

My son, my son! where are you? Help me, here,
here, lift me up. Oh! Oh! My fate!   1025

It lunges, lunges again, the vile thing
is destroying me—
savage, unapproachable sickness.   1030

O Pallas! It is torturing me again. O my son,
pity me who begot you, draw the sword—no one   1035

will blame you—strike me in the breast, heal the pain
with which your godless mother has made me rage. Oh
to see her fallen, felled by this death she deals me!   1040

Sweet Hades, kinsman, brother of Zeus, lull me to sleep,
to sleep; with quick death end my agony.

Chorus

My friends, I hear and shudder at the king's misfortunes—
so great a man, hounded by such suffering.   1045

Heracles

Many are the toils for these hands, this back,
that I have had, hot and painful even to tell of.
But neither the wife of Zeus nor hateful Eurystheus
has ever condemned me to such agony as this
that the false-faced daughter of Oeneus has fastened   1050
upon my shoulders, a woven, encircling net
of the Furies, by which I am utterly destroyed.
It clings to my sides, it has eaten away
my inmost flesh; it lives with me and empties the channels
of my lungs, and already it has drunk up   1055
my fresh blood, and my whole body is
completely killed, conquered by these unspeakable fetters.
Neither the spear of battle, nor the army of
the earth-born Giants, nor the violence of beasts,
nor Greece, nor any place of barbarous tongue, not all   1060
the lands I came to purify could ever do this.
A woman, a female, in no way like a man,
she alone without even a sword has brought me down.

O my son, now truly be my true-born son
and do not pay more respect to the name of mother.   1065
Bring her from the house with your own hands and put
her in my hands, that woman who bore you, that I may know
clearly whether it pains you more to see *my* body
mutilated or *hers* when it is justly tortured.
Come, my child, dare to do this. Pity me,   1070

for I seem pitiful to many others, crying
and sobbing like a girl, and no one could ever say
that he had seen this man act like that before.
Always without a groan I followed my painful course.
Now in my misery I am discovered a woman.   1075

Come close to me now, stand by your father and
look well at my misfortune, see what I suffer.
I shall take off the coverings and show you. Look,
all of you, do you behold this poor body?
Can you see how miserable, how pitiful I am?   1080

Oh, oh, the pain!
That malignant tearing scorches me again,
it shoots through my sides, it *will* have me struggle,
it will not let me be—miserable, devouring sickness.
O King Hades, receive me!   1085
O flash of Zeus, strike!
Drive against me, O King, hurl down the bolt
of lightning, Father. Now it feeds on me again,
it has sprung out, it blooms. O my hands, my hands,
O my back, my chest, O my poor arms, see   1090
what has become of you from what you once were.
The lion that prowled the land of Nemea, that scourge of herds-
    men,
that unapproachable, intractable creature,
with your strength once you overpowered it,
and the serpent of Lerna and that galloping army   1095
of double-bodied, hostile beasts, violent, lawless,
supremely strong, and the boar of Erymanthus,
and under the earth the hell hound with three heads,
irresistible monster, the awful Echidna's whelp,
and guarding the golden apples the dragon at the end of the
    earth—   1100
and I have had my taste of ten thousand other toils,
but these hands let no one set his trophies over me.

Now look at me, torn to shreds, my limbs unhinged,
a miserable ruin sacked by invisible disaster, I
who am called the son of the most noble mother,   1105
I who claim to be begotten of Zeus in the heavens.
But I tell you this, even if I am nothing,
nothing that can even crawl, even so—
only let her come who has done this to me—
these hands will teach her, and she can tell the world: alive   1110
I punished the evil, and I punish them in death.

Chorus
    O unhappy Greece, I can see how great
    a mourning you shall have if you lose this man.

Hyllus
    Father, since you let me speak to you now,
    let me have silence while I speak, though you are sick.   1115
    I ask only for what is right. Give me yourself
    without this grim anger which stings you to such fury.
    Otherwise you cannot know how mistaken
    is the pleasure your fury craves, the pain it feels.

Heracles
    Say what you want and be done with it. I am too sick—   1120
    I can make no sense at all of your riddles.

Hyllus
    It is about my mother that I come to speak,
    about her present state and her unwilling error.

Heracles
    Damn you! How dare you speak of her again, the mother
    Who is a father's murderer—and in my hearing?   1125

Hyllus
    Her state is such that one should not keep silent.

Heracles
    No, no silence for the crime she has committed!

Hyllus
    Nor for what she has done today, you will admit.

Heracles

   Speak, but beware. Do not disgrace yourself.

Hyllus

   I shall speak. She is dead. She has just been killed.   1130

Heracles

   By whom? I cannot believe it. It is too bitter news.

Hyllus

   She is dead by her own hand and by no other.

Heracles

   Ah! She's dead too soon. She should have died by mine.

Hyllus

   Even your fury would turn aside if you knew all.

Heracles

   A strange beginning, but go on—what do you mean?   1135

Hyllus

   In all that she did wrong she had intended good.

Heracles

   Good? Does she do good when she kills your father?

Hyllus

   It was a charm for love she wanted to put on you
   that failed—when she saw that marriage in her house.

Heracles

   Who in Trachis knows such deadly drugs as this?   1140

Hyllus

   Nessus the centaur long ago persuaded her
   to excite your desire with this fatal charm.

Heracles

   Woe, woe is me! This is my miserable end.
   Lost! I am lost! I see the light no longer.
   Ah! Now I know the doom that is upon me.   1145
   Come, my child. You no longer have a father.
   Call together all my children, your brothers,

and call the unhappy Alcmena who was the bride of Zeus
to her cost. You shall learn from me with my
last words all the prophecies I know.   1150

Hyllus

But your mother is not here. It happens that
she is living now at Tiryns on the sea,
and of your children she has taken some with her
to care for, and others, I must tell you, are living in Thebes.
But all of us who are here—if there is anything,   1155
Father, we must do, we shall listen and serve you.

Heracles

Then hear your task. You have come to that point
where you must show the sort of man you are that you
are called my son. Long ago my father revealed
to me that I should die by nothing that draws breath   1160
but by someone dead, an inhabitant of Hell.
This was that beast, the centaur, who has in death killed me
alive, even as it had been divinely revealed.
Now I shall show you how more recent prophecies
agree with this exactly and give support to the old.   1165
I went to the grove of the mountain-dwelling Selli who sleep
upon the ground and I copied down the words
from my father's oak that speaks with many tongues,
which told me that, at this present, living time,
release from all the toils imposed on me would be   1170
complete. And I thought that then I would be happy.
But it only meant that I would die then.
For the dead there are no more toils. My son,
since all this is coming true so clearly, you must
be ready to stand by my side in the fight, and you must not   1175
hesitate till I am forced to use sharp words.
On your own, agree to act with me; discover
yourself the finest rule—obedience to your father.

Hyllus

Father, I am alarmed to see where your words lead,
but I shall obey you in whatever you decide.   1180

Heracles

You must give me your right hand first of all.

Hyllus

Will you tell me why you must have this strong pledge?

Heracles

Quickly, give me your hand. Do not disobey me.

Hyllus

Here, I reach my hand. I shall deny you nothing.

Heracles

Swear now by the head of Zeus who begot me.   1185

Hyllus

Swear to do what? Will you tell me that?

Heracles

Swear to fulfil completely the task I give to you.

Hyllus

I do swear, and I take my oath on Zeus.

Heracles

And pray for punishment if you break your oath.

Hyllus

I pray, though I shall keep my oath and not be punished.   1190

Heracles

You know that high crag of Zeus on Mount Oeta?

Hyllus

Yes. I have often stood there to sacrifice.

Heracles

Then you must take my body up there, with your
own hands and with the help of any friends you wish,
and you must fell a great forest of deep-rooted oak,   1195
and many trees of the lusty wild olive

you must cut down as well, and put my body on them,
and then take the flaming brand of a pine torch
and burn. Let me have no tears, no mourning. Do
your job without lamentation, without tears,   1200
if you are your father's son, or even below
I shall wait for you, a crushing curse forever.

Hyllus

Oh! What are you saying? What have you forced me to do?

Heracles

What must be done. If you do not do it, then be
another man's son—do not call yourself mine.   1205

Hyllus

Father, Father, how can you? You are asking me
to be your murderer, polluted with your blood.

Heracles

No, I am not. I ask you to be my healer,
the only physician who can cure my suffering.

Hyllus

How would I cure your body by setting it on fire?   1210

Heracles

If that frightens you, do the rest at least.

Hyllus

I shall carry you there—that I could not begrudge you.

Heracles

And you will complete the pyre as I told you?

Hyllus

So long as I do not touch it with my own hands.
Everything else I shall do. You can be sure of me.   1215

Heracles

Even that much is enough. Now after your other
great kindness, do me this one small favor.

Hyllus

No matter how great a favor it is, it shall be done.

Heracles

You know, of course, the girl who is the daughter of Eurytus?

Hyllus

It is Iole you mean, I suppose.   1220

Heracles

I see you know her. This, then, is what I tell you to do,
my son. When I die, if you wish to be pious
and remember the oaths you have sworn to your father,
you must take this girl as your wife, and do not
disobey me. No other man but you must ever   1225
have her who has lain with me at my side. You,
my son, must engage yourself to her bed.
Obey. Although you listen to me in greater matters,
disobedience in lesser things wipes out the favor.

Hyllus

Ah! It is wrong to argue with a sick man,   1230
yet how can one stand to see him with such thoughts as these?

Heracles

You speak as if you would do none of the things I ask.

Hyllus

How could anyone when she alone shares
the blame for my mother's death and your condition?
How could anyone choose to do that, unless   1235
avenging fiends had made his mind sick? Better
for me, too, to die than live with my worst enemy.

Heracles

I see the man will not give me my due, though I
am dying; but I tell you, if you disobey
my commands, the curse of the Gods will be waiting for you.   1240

Hyllus

Oh! Soon, I can see, you will show how sick you are.

Heracles

You! You rouse my agony from its sleep.

Hyllus
So wretched, so helpless am I, no matter where I turn.

Heracles
Because you do not choose to listen to your father.

Hyllus
But shall I listen, Father, and learn impiety?   1245

Heracles
It is no impiety if you give my heart pleasure.

Hyllus
Do you command me and make it right for me to do this?

Heracles
I do command you, and I call the Gods to witness.

Hyllus
I shall do it then, and I shall not forswear
since you have shown the Gods it is your will. No one   1250
could think me wrong in obeying you, Father.

Heracles
In the end you act well. Now make your mercy
follow swift upon your words. Put me on
the pyre before another tearing, stinging blow
can strike. Come, hurry. Lift me up. The true   1255
respite from suffering is this—my final end.

Hyllus
Nothing can prevent its full accomplishment
for you, since you command and compel me, Father.

Heracles
Come then, O my tough soul,
before this sickness is stirred again,   1260
set a steel bit in my mouth,
hold back the shriek, and make an end
of this unwanted, welcome task.

(*The bearers raise the litter and leave by the side,
followed by Hyllus and the Chorus.*)

Hyllus

   Raise him, my helpers. From you let me have
   much compassion now for what I do.   1265
   You see how little compassion the Gods
   have shown in all that's happened; they
   who are called our fathers, who begot us,
   can look upon such suffering.
   No one can foresee what is to come.   1270
   What is here now is pitiful for us
   and shameful for the Gods;
   but of all men it is hardest for him
   who is the victim of this disaster.

               (Hyllus turns to the leader of the Chorus.)
   Maiden, come from the house with us.   1275
   You have seen a terrible death
   and agonies, many and strange, and there is
   nothing here which is not Zeus.
                                 (Exeunt.)

ELECTRA

Translated and with an Introduction by

DAVID GRENE

INTRODUCTION TO THE
ELECTRA

Iт is often said by classical scholars that, of the three dramatic treatments of the Orestes legend which we possess in the Greek tragedies, that of Sophocles stands closest to the Homeric account. Homer introduces the story of Orestes several times in the *Odyssey* and always for its exemplary effect. The return of Orestes and the punishment of Aegisthus, and only incidentally Clytemnestra, is mentioned as a warning of what will happen to the suitors when Odysseus comes home. Homer shows no awareness of the brutality of the murder of the mother by her son or of any of the consequences, religious or sociological, which interest both Aeschylus and Euripides later. The whole is a saga of successful revenge. It is worth noticing, of course, that Homer introduces the incident as an *example* of what may happen when Odysseus comes home. He is not giving us his speculations on matricide. Still, even at that, it is perhaps curious that the revenge taken, including the killing of Clytemnestra, can be treated with such clarity of moral judgment in favor of the killers.

In outline Sophocles appears to handle the story as Homer does, as a revenge theme, with no divine or other sanctions invoked against the murderers. But it is difficult to believe that Sophocles' interpretation should be taken on so simple a level. Almost forty-five years before the Sophoclean play, Aeschylus had written the *Oresteia*, which treated the legend with exactly the questions in mind that Homer had omitted. The *Oresteia* was a great popular success. It is extremely unlikely that Sophocles later could have reverted to the older and simpler explanation of the story without submitting a new interpretation of his own. The latter is, in fact, what he did.

He certainly did write with the Homeric out ие in mind. For instance, in Aeschylus the responsibility for goading Orestes to kill both Aegisthus and Clytemnestra is Apollo's, and consequently the purification, with all its attendant complications and conflict, belongs to Apollo. Sophocles minimized Apollo's role, mentioning him only a few times in the play as the author of indefinitely favorable oracles. The question of the purification or of Orestes' madness after the killing of his mother does not arise. But Sophocles has used the very flatness of the Homeric version to emphasize the unspoken questions which are in the mind of his fifth-century audience. If this is simply a story of murder and the settlement of a family feud, including the killing of a mother by her son, we are given a special Sophoclean portrait of the figures involved—mother, daughter, son, and Aegisthus, but especially Electra, the elder daughter.

For the play is rightly called after Electra. All the other people are included, principally, so that we should know more about her when we see her dealing with them—the savage, yet frightened, mother; the cautious and rather colorless Orestes; the timid, sensible, and unattractive sister; and the vulgar and bullying Aegisthus. Everyone acts as the foil of Electra. Everyone brings out another shade in the character previously missing. Electra makes no soliloquies to reveal herself as she does in Euripides. She is herself, in relation to others. She seems hardly to exist as a person except as a combination of reactions to others' deeds and words. Her father's death, her mother's enmity, her sister's passiveness, her brother's delay, Aegisthus' tyranny—these are her life. She says again and again that they are the causes for her being what she is.

Furthermore, Sophocles shows us Electra in reaction to happenings that in fact never took place. The disguised Paedagogus gives a vivid account of a chariot race in which Orestes is killed, the whole story being false. Orestes arrives, disguised, accompanied by the urn which supposedly contains his own ashes. Both of these are remarkable incidents as we have them in the play. The chariot race which occupies nearly 200 lines, or almost one-seventh of the entire piece, is based partly on that described in the *Iliad*, Book xxiii. It may also be based partly on some famous contemporary chariot race in which the audience would be interested and of which we know nothing. But the more exciting the account, the more it engaged the audience's attention, the greater, surely, must have been the jolt when it was realized that the description corresponded to no dramatic reality.

The terrible grief felt by Electra when she saw the urn believed to contain her brother's ashes must have awakened a jarring emotion in the audience, who knew that he was not dead, and some resentment at Orestes for standing by his sister and not telling her. These things are too gross to be explained away by any contrast between the Athenian audience's expectation and those of the theater of our own time. I think we are meant to see Electra not as a real person in her own right but as a mass of responses to other persons and their deeds and words, whether true or false. It is hard to imagine her loving someone understandingly, as Tecmessa and Deianeira did. Husband-less, childless, as she describes herself, cut off from father and mother and sister, she moves in an atmosphere of hate and hysteria provoked by facts and lies indiscriminately.

If we still think that Electra is justified by Sophocles, let us notice that she directs Aegisthus' body to be thrown to the dogs. This is, as all Greek students know, an outrage on religion and human decency, as the fifth century understood it, and is described as such by Sophocles himself in the *Ajax* and the *Antigone*. It happened at times, it is true, during the Peloponnesian War, and it is always regarded as barbaric.

No, this is no justification of Electra. Sophocles is often concerned with the power of hate—in the *Ajax*, the *Trachiniae*, the *Philoctetes*, and the *Oedipus at Colonus*. The *Electra* is a play about the power of hate and misery bred in a particular personality which finally seems to lose the natural power to create. The girl cannot live spontaneously. Her life is a series of responses—of hate for ill treatment, of love and hope for the fulfilment of revenge. The events of the years gone by shape everything else, to the elimination of any sense of the immediate present, except as the continuation of the past. The *Electra* is perhaps the best-constructed and most unpleasant play that Sophocles wrote. The tightness and cogency of the plot go together with the absence of nobility and magnitude in the chief character in a way which never occurred again in the extant plays. For sheer clarity and power, its author probably never improved on it.

ELECTRA

CHARACTERS

Paedagogus, the Old Servant Who Looked after Orestes when a Boy

Orestes, Son of Agamemnon, Murdered King of Mycenae

Electra, Daughter of Agamemnon

Chorus of Women of Mycenae

Chrysothemis, Sister of Electra

Clytemnestra, Widow of Agamemnon and Wife of Aegisthus

Aegisthus, Usurping King of Mycenae

ELECTRA

SCENE: *Before the royal palace in Mycenae.*

Paedagogus

Son of Agamemnon, once general at Troy,
now you are here, now you can see it all,
all that your heart has always longed for.
This is old Argos of your yearning, the grove
of Inachus' gadfly-haunted daughter.
And here, Orestes, is the Lycean market place
of the wolf-killing God. Here on the left
the famous temple of Hera. Where we have come now,
believe your eyes, see golden Mycenae,
and here the death-heavy house of the Pelopidae.   10

Once on a time, your father's murder fresh,
I took you from this house, received you from the hand
of your sister, whose blood and father were yours.
I saved you then. I have raised you from that day
to this moment of your manhood to be the avenger
of that father done to death. Orestes, now,
and you, Pylades, dearest friend, take counsel
quickly on what to do. Already the sunlight,
brightening, stirs dawning bird song into clearness,
and the black, kindly night of stars is gone.
Before a man leaves his house, sets foot on the path,   20
let us hold our parley. We are where
we must not shrink. It is high time for action.

Orestes

Dearest of servants:
very plain are the signs you show of your nobility
toward me. It is so with a horse of breeding.
Even in old age, hard conditions
do not break his spirit. His ears are still erect.

So it is with you. You urge me, and yourself
follow among the first. Therefore, I will make plain
all my determinations. Give keen ear   30
to what I say, and where I miss the mark
of what I should, correct me.

When I came to Pytho's place of prophecy
to learn to win revenge
for my father's murder on those that did that murder,
Phoebus spoke to me the words I tell you now:
"Take not spear nor shield nor host;
go yourself, and craft of hand
be yours to kill, with justice but with stealth."
Now we have heard the oracle together.
Go you into this house when occasion calls you.
Know all that is done there, and, knowing, report   40
clear news to us. You are old. It's a long time.
They will never know you. They will not suspect you
with your gray silver hair. Here is your story.
You are a stranger coming from Phanoteus,
their Phocian friend, the greatest of their allies.
Tell them a sudden accident befell
Orestes, and he's dead. Swear it on oath.
Say in the Pythian games he was rolled
out of his chariot at high speed.
That is your story now.   50

We shall go first to my father's grave
and crown it, as he bade us, with libations
and with cuttings from my thick, luxuriant hair.
And then we shall come here again
and in our hands a carved bronze-sided urn,
the urn that you know I hid here in the bushes.
By these means we shall bring the pleasant news
with our tale of lies, that here is my body,
quite gone to ashes, charred and burned, before them.

For why should it irk me if I die in word
but in deed come through alive and win my glory?   60
To my thinking, no word is base when spoken with profit.
Before now I have seen wise men often
dying empty deaths as far as words reported them,
and then, when they have come to their homes again,
they have been honored more, even to the skies.
So in my case I venture to predict
that I who die according to this rumor
shall, like a blazing star, glare on my foes again.

Land of my father, Gods of my country,
welcome me, grant me success in my coming,
and you, too, house of my father;
as your purifier I have come,
in justice sent by the Gods.   70
Do not send me dishonored out of this country,
but rich from of old time, restorer of my house.
This is all that I have to say. Old man,
let it be yours to go and mind your task.
We two must go away. It is seasonable,
and seasonableness is greatest master of every act.

Electra (*from inside the house cries out*)
  Ah! Ah!

Paedagogus
  Inside the house some one of the servants,
  I think, is crying.

Orestes
  Might it not be   80
  unfortunate Electra? Do you want us
  to stay here and to listen to her cries?

Paedagogus
  No. Nothing must come before we try
  to carry out what Loxias has bidden us.
  From there we must make our beginning,

pouring the lustral offerings for your father.
For that, I think, will bring us victory,
and mastery in our enterprise.

(*Orestes and his friends withdraw; Electra emerges.*)

Electra
O Holy Light
and air, copartner with light in earth's possession,
how many keening dirges,
how many plangent strokes
laid on the breast till the breast was bloody,   90
have you heard from me
when the darkling night withdrew?
And again in the house of my misery
my bed is witness to my all-night sorrowing
dirges for my unhappy father.
Him in the land of the foreigner
no murderous god of battles entertained.
But my mother and the man who shared her bed,
Aegisthus, split his head with a murderous ax,
like woodsmen with an oak tree.
For all this no pity was given him,   100
by any but me, no pity for your death,
father, so pitiful, so cruel.
But, for my part, I
will never cease my dirges and sorrowful laments,
as long as I have eyes to see
the twinkling light of the stars and this daylight.
So long, like a nightingale, robbed of her young,
here before the doors of what was my father's house
I shall cry out my sorrow for all the world to hear.

House of the Death God, house of Persephone,   110
Hermes of the Underworld, holy Curse,
Furies the Dread Ones, children of the Gods,
all ye who look upon those who die unjustly,
all ye who look upon the theft of a wife's love,

come all and help take vengeance for my father,
for my father's murder!
And send me my brother to my aid.
For alone to bear the burden I am no longer strong enough,
the burden of the grief that weighs against me.   120

Chorus

 Electra, child of the wretchedest of mothers,
 why with ceaseless lament do you waste away
 sorrowing for one long dead,
 Agamemnon, godlessly trapped
 by deceits of your treacherous mother,
 betrayed by her evil hand?
 May evil be the end
 of him that contrived the deed,
 if I may lawfully say it!

Electra

 True-hearted girls,
 you have come to console me in my troubles.   130
 I know, I understand what you say,
 nothing of it escapes me.
 But, all the same, I will not
 leave my mourning for my poor father.
 You whose love responds to mine in all ways,
 suffer me my madness,
 I entreat you.

Chorus

 But from the all-receptive lake
 of Death you shall not raise him,
 groan and pray as you will.
 If past the bounds of sense you dwell in grief   140
 that is cureless, with sorrow unending,
 you will only destroy yourself,
 in a matter where the evil knows no deliverance.
 It is only your discomfort.
 Why do you seek it?

Electra

    Simple indeed is the one
    that forgets parents pitifully dead.
    Suited rather to my heart
    the bird of mourning
    that "Itys, Itys" ever does lament,
    the bird of crazy sorrow, Zeus's messenger.
    And Niobe, that suffered all, you, too,   150
    I count God
    who weeps perpetually
    in her rocky grave.

Chorus

    Not alone to you, my child,
    this burden of grief has come.
    You exceed in your feeling far
    those of your kin and blood.
    See the life of Chrysothemis
    and Iphianassa,
    and that one whose manhood grows in secret,
    sorrowing, a prince,   160
    whom one day this famed land of noble Mycenae
    shall welcome back, if God will bless his coming,
    Orestes.

Electra

    I have awaited him always
    sadly, unweariedly,
    till I'm past childbearing,
    till I am past marriage,
    always to my own ruin.
    Wet with tears, I endure
    an unending doom of misfortune.
    But he has forgotten
    what he has suffered, what he has known.
    What message comes from him to me
    that is not again belied?   170

Yes, he is always longing to come,
but he does not choose to come, for all his longing.

Chorus

> Take heart, take heart, my child.
> Still great above is Zeus,
> who oversees all things in sovereign power.
> Confide to him your overbitter wrath.
> Chafe not overmuch against
> the foes you hate, nor yet forget them quite,
> for Time is a kindly God.
> For neither he that lives
> by Crisa's cattle-grazing shore,   180
> the son of Agamemnon, will be heedless,
> nor the God that rules by Acheron's waters.

Electra

> But for me already the most of my life
> has gone by without hope.
> And I have no strength any more.
> I am one wasted in childlessness,
> with no loving husband for champion.
> Like some dishonored foreigner,
> I tenant my father's house in these ugly rags   190
> and stand at a scanty table.

Chorus

> Pitiful was the cry at the homecoming,
> and pitiful, when on your father on his couch
> the sharp biting stroke of the brazen ax
> was driven home.
> Craft was the contriver, passion the killer,
> dreadfully begetting between them a Shape,
> dreadful, whether divine or human,
> was he that did this.   200

Electra

> That day of all days that have ever been
> most deeply my enemy.

O night, horrible burden
of that unspeakable banquet.
Shameful death that my father saw
dealt him by the hands of the two,
hands that took my own life captive,
betrayed, destroyed me utterly.
For these deeds may God in his greatness,
the Olympian one, grant punishment to match them.   210
And may they have no profit of their glory
who brought these actions to accomplishment.

Chorus

    Take heed you do not speak too far.
    Do you not see from what
    acts of yours you suffer as you do?
    To destruction self-inflicted
    you fall so shamefully.
    You have won for yourself
    superfluity of misfortune,
    breeding wars in your sullen soul
    evermore. You cannot fight
    such conflicts hand to hand, with mighty princes.   220

Electra

    Terrors compelled me,
    to terrors I was driven.
    I know it, I know my own spirit.
    With terrors around me, I will not hold back
    these mad cries of misery, so long as I live.
    For who, dear girls, who that thought right
    would believe there were suitable comforting
    words for me?
    Forbear, forbear, my comforters.
    These ills of mine shall be called cureless   230
    and never shall I give over my sorrow,
    and the number of my dirges none shall tell.

Chorus
>But only in good will to you I speak
>like some loyal mother, entreating
>not to breed sorrow from sorrow.

Electra
>What is the natural measure of my sorrow?
>Come, how when the dead are in question,
>can it be honorable to forget?
>In what human being is this instinctive?
>Never may I have honor of such,
>nor, if I dwell with any good thing,   240
>may I live at ease, by restraining
>the wings of shrill lament to my father's dishonor.
>For if he that is dead
>is earth and nothing,
>poorly lying,
>and they shall never in their turn
>pay death for death in justice,
>then shall all shame be dead
>and all men's piety.   250

Chorus
>My child, it was with both our interests at heart
>I came, both yours and mine. If what I say
>is wrong, have your own way. We will obey you.

Electra
>Women, I am ashamed if I appear
>to you too much the mourner with constant dirges.
>What I do, I must do. Pardon me. I ask you
>how else would any well-bred girl behave
>that saw her father's wrongs, as I have seen these,
>by day and night, always, on the increase
>and never a check?   260
>First there's my mother, yes, my mother, now become
>all hatred. Then in the house I live with those
>who murdered my father. I am their subject, and

whether I eat or go without depends
on them.
     What sort of days do you imagine
I spend, watching Aegisthus sitting
on my father's throne, watching him wear
my father's self-same robes, watching him
at the hearth where he killed him, pouring libations?   270
Watching the ultimate act of insult,
my father's murderer in my father's bed
with my wretched mother—if mother I should call her,
this woman that sleeps with him.
She is so daring that she paramours
this foul, polluted creature and fears no Fury.
No, as though laughing at what was done,
she has found out the day on which she killed
my father in her treachery, and on that day
has set a dancing festival and sacrifices   280
sheep, in monthly ritual, "to the Gods that saved her."
So within that house I see, to my wretchedness,
the accursed feast named in his honor.
I see it, moan, and waste away, lament—
but only to myself. I may not even cry
as much as my heart would have me.
For this woman, all nobility in words,
abuses me: "You hateful thing, God-hated,
are you the only one whose father is dead?
Is there no one else of human kind in mourning?   290
My curse upon you! May the Gods below
grant you from your present sorrows no release!"
Such is the tone of her insults, unless she hears
from someone of Orestes' coming. Then
she grows really wild and stands beside me shrieking:
"Are you too not responsible for this?
Is not this your doing, you who stole
Orestes from these hands of mine, conveying him
away? But you may be sure you will pay for it

and pay enough." She howls so, and nearby her
is her distinguished bridegroom, saying the same,   300
that utter dastard, mischief complete,
who makes his wars with women.
But I am waiting for Orestes' coming,
waiting forever for the one who will stop
all our wrongs. I wait and wait and die.
For his eternal going-to-do-something
destroys my hopes, possible and impossible.

In such a state, my friends, one cannot
be moderate and restrained nor pious either.
Evil is all around me, evil
is what I am compelled to practice.

Chorus
    Tell me, as you talk like this, is Aegisthus here,   310
    or is he gone from home?

Electra
    Certainly, he's gone.
    Do not imagine, if he were near, that I
    would wander outside. Now he is on his estate.

Chorus
    If so, I can talk with you with better heart.

Electra
    For the present, he is away. What do you want?

Chorus
    Tell me: what of your brother? Is he really coming
    or hesitating? That is what I want to know.

Electra
    He says he is—but does nothing of what he says.

Chorus
    A man often hesitates when he does a big thing.   320

Electra
    I did not hesitate when rescuing him.

Chorus

    Be easy.
    He's a true gentleman and will help his friends.

Electra

    I believe in him, or else had not lived so long.

Chorus

    Say no more now. I see your sister,
    blood of your blood, of the same father and mother,
    Chrysothemis, in her hands burial offerings,
    the usual sacrifice to the Gods below.

                  (Enter Chrysothemis, Electra's sister.)

Chrysothemis

    What have you come to say out of doors,
    sister? Will you never learn, in all this time,   330
    not to give way to your empty anger?
    Yet this much I know, and know my own heart, too,
    that I am sick at what I see, so that
    if I had strength, I would let them know how I feel.
    But under pain of punishment, I think,
    I must make my voyage with lowered sails,
    that I may not seem to do something and then prove
    ineffectual. But justice, justice,
    is not on my side but on yours. If I am
    to live and not as a prisoner, I must
    in all things listen to my lords.   340

Electra

    It is strange indeed that you who were born
    of our father should forget him
    and heed your mother. All these warnings
    of me you have learned from her. Nothing is your own.
    Now you must make your choice, one way or the other,
    either to be a fool
    or sensible—and to forget your friends.
    Here you are saying: "If I had the strength,

I would show my hatred of them!" You who, when I
did everything to take vengeance for my father,
never did a thing to help—yes, discouraged the doer.   350
Is not this cowardice on top of baseness?
Tell me, or let me tell you, what benefit
I would achieve by giving up my mourning?
Do I not live? Yes, I know, badly, but
for me enough. And I hurt them
and so give honor to the dead, if there is, there
in that other world, anything that brings pleasure.
But you who hate, you tell me, hate in word only
but in fact live with our father's murderers.

I tell you: never, not though they brought me your gifts
in which you now feel pride, would I yield to them.   360
Have your rich table and your abundant life.
All the food I need is the quiet of my conscience.
I do not want to win your honor.
nor would you if you were sound of mind. Now, when you could
be called the daughter of the best of fathers,
be called your mother's. Thus to most people prove base,
traitor to your dead father and your friends.

Chorus
     No anger, I entreat you. In the words of both
     there is value for both, if you, Electra, can   370
     follow her advice and she take yours.

Chrysothemis
     O ladies, I am used to her and her words.
     I never would have mentioned this, had not
     I learned of the greatest of misfortunes coming
     her way to put a stop to her long mourning.

Electra
     Tell me of your terror. If you can speak to me
     of something worse than this condition of mine,
     I'll not refuse it still.

Chrysothemis

Well, I shall tell you.
From what I learned—and if you don't give over
your present mourning—they will send you where
never a gleam of sun shall visit you.
You shall live out your life in an underground cave
and there bewail sorrows of the world outside.
With this in mind, reflect. And do not blame me
later when you are suffering.
Now is a good time to take thought.

Electra

So this is what they have decided to do with me.

Chrysothemis

Yes, this exactly, when Aegisthus comes home.

Electra

As far as this goes, let him come home soon.

Chrysothemis

Why such a prayer for evil, my poor darling?

Electra

That he may come—if he will do what you say.

Chrysothemis

Hoping that *what* may happen you? Are you crazy?

Electra

That I may get away from you all, as far as I can.

Chrysothemis

Have you no care of this, your present life?

Electra

Mine is indeed a fine life, to be envied.

Chrysothemis

It might be, if you could learn common sense.

Electra

Do not teach me falseness to those I love.

380

390

Chrysothemis

That, that is not what I teach, but to yield to authority.

Electra

Practice your flattery. This is not my way.

Chrysothemis

It is a good thing, though, not to fall through stupidity.

Electra

I shall fall, if I must, revenging my father.

Chrysothemis

My father will have pardon for me, I know.

400

Electra

These are words that the base may praise.

Chrysothemis

You will not heed me then? You will not agree?

Electra

No, certainly.
May I not yet be so empty-witted.

Chrysothemis

Then I must go on the errand I was bid.

Electra

Where are you going? To whom
bringing burnt offering?

Chrysothemis

My mother sent me with offerings for father's grave.

Electra

What are you saying? To her greatest enemy?

Chrysothemis

"Whom she has killed"—you would add.

Electra

Which of her friends persuaded her? Who thought of this?

Chrysothemis

    I think it was night terrors drove her to it.   410

Electra

    Gods of my father, now or never stand my friends!

Chrysothemis

    Why do "night terrors" make you confident?

Electra

    I'll tell you that when you tell me the dream.

Chrysothemis

    I cannot tell you much, only a little.

Electra

    Tell me it, all the same. Often this little
    has made or ruined men.

Chrysothemis

    There is a story that she saw my father,
    the father that was yours and mine, again
    coming to life, once more to live with her.
    He took and at the hearth planted the scepter   420
    which once he bore and now Aegisthus bears,
    and up from out the scepter foliage sprang
    luxuriantly, and shaded all the land
    of this Mycenae. This is what I heard
    from someone present when she told the Sun
    the nature of her dreams.

                        But beyond this
    I know no more, only that she sends me
    because of her fear. And, by the Gods, I pray you,
    the Gods that live in this country, listen to me
    and do not fall out of stupidity.
    For if you should reject me, she will come
    again to harry you with punishment.   430

Electra

    My dear one, not a morsel that you hold
    allow to touch that grave, no, nothing.

It would not be God's law nor pious that you
should offer to my father sacrifices
and lustral offerings from that enemy woman.
Throw them to the winds! Or hide them in deep hollowed
earth, somewhere where no particle of them
may ever reach my father where he lies.
But let them be stored up for her as treasures
below, against the day when *she* shall die.
I tell you, if she were not the most brazen   440
of all of womankind, would she have dared
to pour these enemy libations
over the body of the man she killed?
Consider if you think that the dead man,
as he lies in his grave, will welcome kindly
these offerings from her by whom he was robbed
of life and honor? By whom, mutilated?
And for her purification she wiped
the blood stains on his head? Can you believe
that these will prove for her a quittance offering?
No, no. You let them be. You cut a lock
out of your own hair, from the fringe and mine,
mine, too, his wretched daughter's. Such a small offering,   450
yet all I have! Give it to him, this lustrous
lock of hair, and here, my girdle, unadorned.
Kneel then and pray that from that nether world
he may come, a friendly spirit, to our help
against his enemies. Pray that the boy Orestes
may live to fight and win against his enemies,
may live to set his foot upon them.
                                        And so
in days to come we shall be able to dress
this grave with richer hands than we can now.
I think, oh yes, I think that it was he
that thought to send this evil-boding dream   460
to her.

    Yet, sister, do yourself this service

and help me, too, and help the dearest of all,
our common father, that lies dead in the underworld.

Chorus

The girl speaks well. And you, my dear,
if you are wise, will follow her advice.

Chrysothemis

I will do it. It is not reasonable for us two
to squabble about what is just. We must haste to do something.
But, my friends, if I attempt this, I must have your silence.
If my mother hears of this, I am sure I shall rue   470
indeed the attempt I shall make.

Chorus

If I am not a distracted prophet
and lacking in skill of judgment,
Justice foreshadowing the event
shall come, in her hands a just victory.
Yes, she will come, my child, in vengeance
and soon.
Of that I was confident
when I lately heard,   480
of this dream of sweet savor.
Your father, the king of the Greeks,
has never forgotten,
nor the ax of old,
bronze-shod, double-toothed,
which did him to death
in shame and baseness.

There shall come many-footed, many-handed,
hidden in dreadful ambush,   490
the bronze-shod Fury.
Wicked indeed were they who were seized
with a passion for a forbidden bed,
for a marriage accursed, stained with murder.
In the light of this, I am very sure

that never, never shall we see
such a portent draw near without hurt
to doers and partners in crime.
There are no prophecies for mortal men
in dreadful dreams and soothsayings
if this night vision come not,   500
well and truly to fulfilment.

Horsemanship of Pelops of old,
loaded with disaster,
how deadly you have proved
to this land!
For since the day that Myrtilus
fell asleep, sunk in the sea,
wrecked utterly with the unhappy
wreck of his golden carriage,   510
for never a moment since
has destruction and ruin
ever left this house.

(Queen Clytemnestra enters from the palace.)

Clytemnestra

It seems you are loose again, wandering about.
Aegisthus isn't here, who always restrains you
from going abroad and disgracing your family.
But now that he is away you pay no heed
to me, although there's many a one you have told   520
at length how brutally and how unjustly
I lord it over you, insulting
you and yours.
                    There is no insolence in myself,
but being abused by you so constantly
I give abuse again.
                    Your father, yes,
always your father. Nothing else is your pretext—
the death he got from me. From me. I know it,
well. There is no denial in me. Justice,

Justice it was that took him, not I alone.
You would have served the cause of Justice if
you had been right-minded.
For this your father whom you always mourn,   530
alone of all the Greeks, had the brutality
to sacrifice your sister to the Gods,
although he had not toiled for her as I did,
the mother that bore her, he the begetter only.
Tell me, now, why he sacrificed her. Was it
for the sake of the Greeks?

They had no share in my daughter to let them kill her.
Was it for Menelaus' sake, his brother,
that he killed my child? And shall he not then pay for it?
Had not this Menelaus two children who
ought to have died rather than mine? It was their parents   540
for whose sake all the Greeks set sail for Troy.
Or had the God of Death some longing to feast
on my children rather than hers? Or had
that accursed father lost the love of mine
and felt it still for Menelaus' children?
This was the act of a father thoughtless
or with bad thoughts. That is how I see it
even if you differ with me.
                              The dead girl,
if she could speak, would bear me out.
I am not dismayed by all that has happened.
If you think me wicked, keep your righteous judgment   550
and blame your neighbors.

Electra
    This is one time you will not be able to say
    that the abuse I receive from you was provoked
    by something painful on my side.
                              But if
    you will allow me I will speak truthfully
    on behalf of the dead man and my dead sister.

Clytemnestra

    Of course, I allow you. If you had always begun
    our conversations so, you would not have been
    so painful to listen to.

Electra

                I will tell you, then.
    You say you killed my father. What claim more shameful
    than that, whether with justice or without it?   560
    But I'll maintain that it was not with justice
    you killed him, but the seduction of that bad man,
    with whom you now are living, drew you to it.
    Ask Artemis the Huntress what made her hold
    the many winds in check at Aulis. Or
    I'll tell you this. *You* dare not learn from her.

    My father, as I hear, when at his sport,
    started from his feet a horned dappled stag
    within the Goddess' sanctuary. He
    let fly and hit the deer and uttered some boast
    about his killing of it. The daughter of Leto   570
    was angry at this and therefore stayed the Greeks
    in order that my father, to compensate
    for the beast killed, might sacrifice his daughter.

    Thus was her sacrifice—no other deliverance
    for the army either homeward or toward Ilium.
    He struggled and fought against it. Finally,
    constrained, he killed her—not for Menelaus.
    But if—I will plead in your own words—he had done so
    for his brother's sake, is that any reason
    why he should die at your hands? By what law?
    If this is the law you lay down for men, take heed   580
    you do not lay down for yourself ruin and repentance.
    If we shall kill one in another's requital,
    you would be the first to die, if you met with justice.

No. Think if the whole is not a mere excuse.
Please tell me for what cause you now commit
the ugliest of acts—in sleeping with him,
the murderer with whom you first conspired
to kill my father, and breed children to him, and
your former honorable children born   590
of honorable wedlock you drive out.
What grounds for praise shall I find in this? Will you say
that this, too, is retribution for your daughter?
If you say it, still your act is scandalous.
It isn't decent to marry with your enemies
even for a daughter's sake.
                    But I may not
even rebuke you! What you always say
is that it is my mother I am reviling.
Mother! I do not count you mother of mine,
but rather a mistress. My life is wretched
because I live with multitudes of sufferings,
inflicted by yourself and your bedfellow.   600
But the other, he is away, he has escaped
your hand, though barely. Sad Orestes now
wears out his life in misery and exile.
Many a time you have accused me
of rearing him to be your murderer.
I would have done it if I could. Know that.
As far as that goes, you may publicly
proclaim me what you like—traitor, reviler,
a creature full of shamelessness.
                      If I am
naturally skilled as such, I do no shame
to the nature of the mother that brought me forth.

Chorus

    I see she is angry, but whether it is in justice,   610
    I no longer see how I shall think of that.

Clytemnestra

What need have *I* of thought in her regard
who so insults her mother, when a grown woman?
Don't you think she will go to any lengths, so shameless
as she is?

Electra

You may be sure I am ashamed,
although you do not think it. I know why
I act so wrongly, so unlike myself.
The hate you feel for me and what you do
compel me against my will to act as I do.   620
For ugly deeds are taught by ugly deeds.

Clytemnestra

O vile and shameless, I and my words and deeds
give you too much talk.

Electra

It is you who talk, not I. It is your deeds,
and it is deeds invent the words.

Clytemnestra

Now by the Lady Artemis you shall not escape
the results of your behavior, when Aegisthus comes.

Electra

You see? You let me say what I please, and then
you are outraged. You do not know how to listen.

Clytemnestra

Hold your peace at least. Allow me sacrifice,   630
since I have permitted you to say all you will.

Electra

I allow you, yes, I bid you, sacrifice.
Do not blame my lips; for I will say no more.

Clytemnestra (to the maid)

Come, do you lift them up, the offerings

of all the fruits of earth, that to this King here
I may offer my prayers for freedom from my fears.

(She speaks to the image of Apollo.)

Phoebus Protector, hear me, as I am,
although the word I speak is muted. Not among friends
is it spoken, nor may I unfold the whole
to the light while this girl stands beside me,   640
lest with her chattering tongue, wagging in malice,
she sow in all the city bad reports.
Yet hear me as I speak. So I will put it:
the dreams of double meaning I have seen
within this night, for them, Lycaean King,
grant what is good in them prosperous issue
but what is ill, turn it again upon
those that do us ill.
If there are some that from my present wealth
plot to expel me with their stratagems,
do not permit them. Let me live out my life,   650
just as my life is now, to the end uninjured,
controlling the house of Atreus and the throne,
living with those I love as I do now,
the good days on our side, and with such children
as do not hate me nor cause bitter pain.
These are my prayers, Lycaean Apollo, hear them
graciously. Grant to all of us what we ask.
For all the rest, although I am silent,
I know you are a God and know it all.
It is natural that the children of Zeus see all.

(Enter Paedagogus.)

Paedagogus

    Foreign ladies, how may I know for certain,   660
    is this the palace of the King Aegisthus?

Chorus

    This is it, sir. Your own guess is correct.

Paedagogus

    Would I then be right in thinking this lady
    his wife? She has indeed a royal look.

Chorus

    Quite right. Here she is for you, herself.

Paedagogus

    Greetings, your Majesty. I come with news,
    pleasant news for you and Aegisthus and your friends.

Clytemnestra

    I welcome what you have said. I would like first
    to know who sent you here.

Paedagogus

                    The Phocian,
    Phanoteus, charging me with a grave business.   670

Clytemnestra

    What is it, sir? Please tell me. I know well
    you come from a friend and will speak friendly words.

Paedagogus

    Orestes is dead. There it is, in one short word.

Electra

    O God, O God! This is the day I die.

Clytemnestra

    What is this you say, sir, what? Don't listen to her.

Paedagogus

    What I said and say now is "Orestes is dead."

Electra

    God help me, I am dead—I cannot live now.

Clytemnestra

    Leave her to herself. Sir, will you tell me the truth,
    in what way did he meet his death?

Paedagogus

                    This
    I was sent to tell, and I will tell you it all.   680

He went to the glorious gathering that Greece holds
in honor of the Delphic Games, and when
he heard the herald's shrill proclamation
for the first contest—it was a running race—
he entered glorious, all men's eyes upon him.
His running was as good as his appearance.
He won the race and came out covered with honor.
There is much I could tell you, but I must tell it briefly.   690
I do not know a man of such achievement
or prowess. Know this one thing. In all the contests
the marshals announced, he won the prize, was cheered,
proclaimed the victor as "Argive by birth,
by name Orestes, son of the general
Agamemnon who once gathered the great Greek host."
So much for that. But when a God sends mischief,
not even the strong man may escape.
                                        Orestes,
when, the next day, at sunset, there was a race
for chariot teams, entered with many contestants.   700
There was one Achaean, one from Sparta, two
Libyans, masters in driving racing teams.
Orestes was the fifth among them. He
had as his team Thessalian mares. The sixth
was an Aetolian with young sorrel horses.
The seventh was a Magnesian, and the eighth
an Aenean, by race, with a white team.
The ninth competitor came from God-built Athens,
and then a Boeotian, ten chariots in all.
They stood in their allotted stations where   710
the appointed judges placed them. At the signal,
a brazen trumpet, they were off. The drivers
cheered their horses on, their hands vibrating the reins,
all together. All the course was filled
with the noise of rattling chariots. Clouds of dust
rose up. The mass of drivers, huddled together,
did not spare the goad as each one struggled

to put the nave of his wheel or the snorting mouths
of his horses past his rival, wheels and backs
of the foremost drivers all beslobbered with foam,   720
as the breath of the teams behind beat on them.
So far all chariots were uninjured. Then
the Aenean's hard-mouthed colts got out of hand
and bolted as they finished the sixth lap
and turned into the seventh. There they crashed
head on with the Barcaean. After that,
from this one accident, team crashed team
and overset each other. All the plain
of Crisa was full of wrecks. But the man from Athens,   730
a clever driver, saw what was happening, pulled
his horses out of the way and held them in check,
letting past the disordered mass of teams in the middle.
Orestes had been driving last and holding
his horses back, putting his trust in the finish.
But when he saw the Athenian left alone,
he sent a shrill cry through his good horses' ears
and set to catch him. The two drove level,
the poles were even. First one, now the other,
would push his horses' heads in front.   740
Orestes always drove tight at the corners
barely grazing the edge of the post with his wheel,
loosing his hold of the trace horse on his right
while he checked the near horse. In his other laps
the poor young man and his horses had come through safe.
But this time he let go of the left rein
as the horse was turning. Unaware, he struck the edge
of the pillar and broke his axle in the center.
He was himself thrown from the rails of the chariot
and tangled in the reins. As he fell, the horses
bolted wildly to the middle of the course.
When the crowd saw him fallen from his car,
they shuddered. "How young he was," "How gallant his deeds,"   750
and "How sadly he has ended," as they saw him

thrown earthward now, and then, tossing his legs
to the sky—until at last the grooms
with difficulty stopped the runaway team
and freed him, but so covered with blood that no one
of his friends could recognize the unhappy corpse.
They burned him on the pyre. Then men of Phocis
chosen for the task have brought here in a small urn
the lamentable ashes—all that is left
of this great frame, that he may have his grave   760
here in his father's country.
                              That is my story,
bitter as stories go, but for us who saw it,
greatest of all ill luck these eyes beheld.

Chorus
    Woe, woe. The ancient family
    of our lords has perished, it seems, root and branch.

Clytemnestra
    Zeus, what shall I say? Shall I say "good luck"
    or "terrible, but for the best"? Indeed,
    my state is terrible if I must save
    my life by the misfortunes of myself.

Paedagogus
    My lady, why does this story make you dejected?

Clytemnestra
    Mother and child! It is a strange relation.   770
    A mother cannot hate the child she bore
    even when injured by it.

Paedagogus
    Our coming here, it seems, then is to no purpose.

Clytemnestra
    Not to no purpose. How can you say "no purpose"?—
    if you have come with certain proofs of death
    of one who from my soul was sprung,
    but severed himself from my breast, from my nurture, who

became an exile and a foreigner;
who when he quitted this land, never saw me again;
who charged me with his father's murder, threatened
terrors against me. Neither night nor day   780
could I find solace in sleep. Time, supervisor,
conducted me to inevitable death.
But now, with this one day I am freed from fear
of her and him. She was the greater evil;
she lived with me, constantly draining
the very blood of life—now perhaps I'll have peace
from her threats. The light of day will come again.

Electra

My God! My God! Now must I mourn indeed
your death, Orestes, when your mother here
pours insults on you, dead. Can this be right?   790

Clytemnestra

Not right for you. But he is right as he is.

Electra

Hear, Nemesis, of the man that lately died!

Clytemnestra

She has heard those she should and done all well.

Electra

Insult us now. For now the luck is yours.

Clytemnestra

Will you not stop this, you and Orestes both?

Electra

We are stopped indeed. We cannot make you stop.

Clytemnestra (to the messenger)

Your coming will be worth much, sir, if you
have stopped my daughter's never ceasing clamor.

Paedagogus (with a feint at departure)

Well, I will go now, if all this is settled.

Clytemnestra

O no! I should do wrong to myself and to   800
the friend who sent you if I let you go.
Please go inside. Leave her out here to wail
the misfortunes of herself and those she loves.

(Clytemnestra and the assumed messenger go into the house.)

Electra

There's an unhappy mother for you! See
how agonized, how bitter, were the tears,
how terribly she sorrowed for her son
that met the death you heard of! No, I tell you,
she parted from us laughing. O my God!
Orestes darling, your death is my death.
By your passing you have torn away from my heart
whatever solitary hope still lingered   810
that you would live and come some day to avenge
your father and my miserable self.
But now where should I turn? I am alone,
having lost both you and my father. Back again
to be a slave among those I hate most
of all the world, my father's murderers!
Is this what is right for me?
                        No, this I will not—
live with them any more. Here, at the gate
I will abandon myself to waste away
this life of mine, unloved. If they're displeased,
let someone kill me, someone that lives within.   820
Death is a favor to me, life an agony.
I have no wish for life.

Chorus

Where are Zeus's thunderbolts?
Where is the glowing sun?
If they see this and hide it
and hold their peace?

Electra (cries out)
  Oh!

Chorus
  Why do you cry, child?

Electra (cries again)
  Oh!

Chorus
  Speak no great word.   830

Electra
  You will destroy me.

Chorus
  How?

Electra
  If you suggest a hope
  when all is plain, when they are all gone
  to the house of Death, and when I waste
  my life away, you tread me further down.

Chorus
  King Amphiaraus, as I know,
  was caught in woman's golden snares
  and now beneath the earth
  reigns over all the spirits there.

Electra
  Oh! Oh!   840

Chorus
  Alas indeed, for pitiably

Electra
                          he died.

Chorus
  Yes.

Electra
  I know, I know. For him in sorrow
  there came a deliverer.

None such for me. For one there was,
but he is gone, ravished by death.

Chorus

Unhappy girl, unhappiness is yours!

Electra

I bear you witness with full knowledge.   850
Knowledge too full, bred of a life,
the crowded months surging with horrors
many and dreadful!

Chorus

We know what you mean.

Electra

So do not then, I pray you,
divert my thoughts to where . . .

Chorus

What do you mean?

Electra

. . . there is no hope, no kinsfolk,
and none among the nobles that will help.

Chorus

Death is the common lot of death-born men.   860

Electra

Yes, but to meet it so,
as he did, poor darling,
tangled in the leather reins,
among the wild competing hoofs.

Chorus

None can guess whence death will come.

Electra

True indeed. He is now a stranger
that was hidden in earth, by no hand of mine,
knew no grave I gave him,
knew no keening from me.   870

(Enter Chrysothemis.)

Chrysothemis
My darling,
I am so glad, I have run here in haste,
regardless of propriety. I bring you
happiness and a relief from all
the troubles you have had and sorrowed for.

Electra
Where could you find a cure—and who are you
to find it—for my troubles which know no cure?

Chrysothemis
We have Orestes here among us—that is
my news for you—as plain as you see myself.

Electra
Are you mad, poor girl, or can it be you laugh
at what are your own troubles as well as mine?   880

Chrysothemis
I swear by our father's hearth. It is not in mockery
I speak. He is here in person with us.

Electra
                              Ah!
Wretched girl! Who told you this that you believed him,
too credulous?

Chrysothemis
                    My own eyes were the evidence
for what I saw, and no one else.

Electra
                              Poor thing!
Poor thing! What proof was there to see? What did you
see that has set your heart incurably
afire?

Chrysothemis
            I pray you, hear me by the Gods,
and having heard me, call me sane or foolish.   890

Electra

Tell me, then, if the story gives you pleasure.

Chrysothemis

Yes, I will tell you all I saw.
When I came to our father's ancient grave,
I saw that from the very top of the mound
newly spilled rills of milk were flowing. Round
the coffin was a wreath of all the flowers
that grow. I saw in wonder, looked about
for someone who would be near me. When I saw
that all was quiet, I approached the grave.   900
At the top of the pyre there was a lock of hair;
as soon as I saw that, something jumped within me
at the familiar sight. I know I saw
the token of my dearest, loved Orestes.
I took it in my hands, never saying a word
for fear of saying what would be ill-omened,
but with my joy my eyes were filled with tears.
Both then and now I know with certainty
this offering could come from him alone.
Whom else could this concern, save you and me?
I did not do it, I know, and neither did you.   910
How could you? For you cannot leave this house,
even to pray, but they will punish you for it.
Nor can it be our mother. She is not inclined
to do such things, nor, doing them, to be secret.
These offerings at the grave must be Orestes'.
Darling, take heart. It is not always the same
Genius that stands by the same people. Till now
he was hateful to us. But now perhaps
this day will seal the promise of much good.

Electra

Oh, how I have been pitying you for your folly!

Chrysothemis

What is this? Do I not say what is to your liking?   920

Electra

You do not know where you are, nor where your thoughts are.

Chrysothemis

Why should I not have knowledge of what I saw?

Electra

He is dead, my dear. Your rescue at his hands
is dead along with him. Look to him no more.

Chrysothemis

Alas! From whom on earth did you hear this?

Electra

From one that was near to him, when he was dying.

Chrysothemis

Where is he then? I am lost in wonderment.

Electra

In the house. He is our mother's welcome guest.

Chrysothemis

Alas again! But who then would have placed   930
these many offerings on our father's tomb?

Electra

I think perhaps that someone put them there
as a remembrance of the dead Orestes.

Chrysothemis

Unlucky I! I was so happy coming,
hurrying to bring my news to you, not knowing
what misery we were plunged in. Now when I've come,
I find both our old sorrow and the new.

Electra

That is how you see it. But now listen to me,
and you can relieve the suffering that weighs on us.

Chrysothemis

How can I bring the dead to life again?   940

Electra

This is not what I mean. I am no such fool.

Chrysothemis

    What do you bid me do, of which I am capable?

Electra

    To have the courage to follow my counsel.

Chrysothemis

    If I can help at all, I will not refuse.

Electra

    Look: there is no success without hardship.

Chrysothemis

    I see. As far as my strength goes, I will help.

Electra

    Hear me tell you, then, the plans that I have laid.
    Friends to stand by and help us we have none—
    nowhere—you know that quite as well as I.
    Death has taken them and robbed us. We alone,   950
    the two of us, are left.
    While I still heard my brother flourished,
    alive, I had my hopes he would still come,
    some day, to avenge the murder of his father.
    But now that he's no more, I look to you,
    that you should not draw back from helping me,
    your true-born sister, kill our father's murderer
    that killed him with his own hand—Aegisthus.
    There is nothing I should now conceal from you.
    What are you waiting for, that you are hesitant?
    What hope do you look to, that is still standing?
    Now you must sorrow for the loss of fortune   960
    that was our father's. Now you must grieve
    that you have already so many years
    without a marriage and a husband. Do not
    hope you will get them now. For Aegisthus
    is not such a fool to suffer to grow up
    children of you and me, clearly to harm him.
    But if you follow my plans,

first, you will win from that dead father, gone
to the underworld, and from our brother with him,
the recognition of your piety.
And, secondly, as you were born to freedom,   970
so in the days to come you will be called free
and find a marriage worthy of you; for all
love to look to the noble.
Do you not see how great a reputation
you will win yourself and me by doing this?
For who of citizens and foreigners
that sees us will not welcome us with praise:
"These are two sisters, friends. Look on them well.
They saved their father's house when their foes
were riding high, stood champions against murder,
sparing not to risk their lives upon the venture.   980
Therefore, we all should love them, all revere them,
and all at feasts and public ceremonies
honor these two girls for their bravery."

This is what everyone will say of us,
in life and death, to our undying fame.
My dear one, hear me. Take sides with your father
and with your brother. Give me deliverance
from what I suffer. Deliver yourself, knowing this:
life on base terms, for the nobly born, is base.

Chorus
   In such concerns forethought is an ally   990
    to the one that gives, and her that gets advice.

Chrysothemis
   Ladies, before she spoke, if she had good sense,
   she would have held to prudence, as she has not.

                                               (To Electra.)

   To what can you look to give you confidence
   to arm yourself and call on me to help?
   Can you not see? You are a woman—no man.

Your physical strength is less than is your enemies'!
Their Genius, day by day, grows luckier
while ours declines and comes to nothingness.   1000
Who is there, plotting to kill such a man
as this Aegisthus, would come off unhurt?
We two are now in trouble. Look to it that
we do not get ourselves trouble still worse
if someone hears what you have said.
There is no gain for us, not the slightest help,
to win a noble reputation if
the way to it lies by dishonorable death.
For death is not the worst but when one wants
to die and cannot even have that death.
I beg of you, before you utterly
destroy us and exterminate our family,   1010
check your temper. All that you have said to me
shall be, for my part, unspoken, unfulfilled.
Be sensible, you, and, at long last, being weaker,
learn to give in to those that have the strength.

Chorus

Give heed to her. No greater gain for man
than the possession of a sensible mind!

Electra

You have said nothing unexpected. Well
I knew you would reject what I proposed.
The deed must then be done by my own hand
alone. For I will not leave it unfulfilled.   1020

Chrysothemis

Ah!
I would you had felt so when our father died.
You would have carried all before you.

Electra

I was the same in nature, weaker in judgment.

Chrysothemis

Practice to keep that judgment through your life.

Electra

That is advice which means you will not help me.

Chrysothemis

Yes—for the effort itself implies disaster.

Electra

I envy you your "judgment," hate your cowardice.

Chrysothemis

I will be equally patient when you praise me.

Electra

That you will never experience from me.

Chrysothemis

There's a long future to determine that.   1030

Electra

Begone; for there's no help in you for me.

Chrysothemis

There is, but there's no learning it in you.

Electra

Go and tell all this story to your mother.

Chrysothemis

On my side there is no such hatred as that.

Electra

Understand, at least, how you dishonor me.

Chrysothemis

There is no dishonor, only forethought for you.

Electra

Must I then follow *your* conception of justice?

Chrysothemis

You will think it *ours*, when you come to your senses.

Electra

It is terrible to speak well and be wrong.

Chrysothemis

A very proper description of yourself.   1040

Electra

What! Do you not think that I say what I do with justice?

Chrysothemis

There are times when even justice brings harm with it.

Electra

These are laws by which I would not wish to live.

Chrysothemis

If you made your attempt, you would find that I was right.

Electra

Yes, I will make it. You will not frighten me.

Chrysothemis

Are you sure now? You will not think again?

Electra

No enemy is worse than bad advice.

Chrysothemis

You cannot agree with any of what I say?

Electra

I have made my mind up—and not of yesterday.

Chrysothemis

I will go away then. You cannot bring yourself   1050
to find my words right, nor I your disposition.

Electra

Go then. I will never call you back,
not though you long for it. It would be utter
folly to make so hopeless an attempt.

Chrysothemis

Well, if you think that you are right, go on
thinking so. When you are deep in trouble, then
you may agree with what I said.

Chorus

We see above our heads the birds,
true in their wisdom,

caring for the livelihood   1060
of those that gave them life and sustenance.
Why do we not pay our debts so?
By Zeus of the Lightning Bolt,
by Themis, Dweller in Heaven,
not long shall they go unpunished.
O Voice that goes to the dead below,
carry piteous accents,
to the Atridae in the underworld,
and tell of wrongs untouched
by joy of the dance.

Tell them that now their house is sick,   1070
tell them that their two children
fight and struggle, that they cannot
any more live in harmony together.
Electra, betrayed, alone,
is down in the waves of sorrow,
constantly bewailing her father's fate,
like the nightingale lamenting.
She takes no thought of death;
she is ready to leave the light
if only she can kill
the two Furies of her house.
Was there ever one so noble   1080
born of a noble house?

None of the good will choose to live
basely, if so living
they cloud their renown and die nameless.
O my child, my child, even so you
have chosen the common lot of mourning,
have rejected dishonor,
to win at once two reputations
as wise and best of daughters.

I pray that your life may be lifted high   1090

over your foes,
in wealth and power as much as now
you lie beneath their hand.
For I have found you in distress
but winning the highest prize
by piety toward Zeus
for observance of nature's greatest laws.

Orestes (*disguised as a Phocian countryman*)
I wonder, ladies, if we were directed right
and have come to the destination that we sought?

Chorus
What do you seek? And what do you want here?   1100

Orestes
I have asked all the way here where Aegisthus lives.

Chorus
You have arrived and need not blame your guides.

Orestes
Would some one of you be so kind to tell
the household we have come, a welcome company?

Chorus
This lady, nearest you, will bear the message.

Orestes
Then, lady, will you signify within
that certain men of Phocis seek Aegisthus.

Electra
O God, O God, are these the certain proofs
you bring of rumors we had before you came?

Orestes
I do not know about rumor. Old Strophius sent me   1110
here to bring news about Orestes.

Electra
What is it, sir? How fear steals over me!

Orestes

> We have the small remains of him in this urn,
> this little urn you see us carrying.

Electra

> Alas, Alas! This is it indeed, all clear.
> Here is my sorrow visible, before me.

Orestes

> If you are one that sorrows for Orestes
> and his troubles, know this urn contains his body.

Electra

> Sir, give it to me, by the Gods. If he
> is hidden in this urn—give it into my hands,   1120
> that I may keen and cry lament together
> for myself and all my race with these ashes here.

Orestes (speaking to his men)

> Bring it and give it to her, whoever she is.
> It is not in enmity she asks for it.
> One of his friends perhaps, or of his blood.

Electra (speaking to the urn)

> Oh, all there is for memory of my love,
> my most loved in the world, all that is left
> of live Orestes, oh, how differently
> from how I sent you forth, how differently
> from what I hoped, do I receive you home.
> Now all I hold is nothingness,
> but you were brilliant when I sent you forth.   1130
> Would that you had left life before I sent you
> abroad to a foreign country, when I stole you
> with these two hands, saved you from being murdered.
> Then on that very day you would have died,
> have lain there and have found your share,
> your common portion, of your father's grave.
> Now far from home, an exile, on alien soil

without your sister near, you died unhappily.
I did not, to my sorrow, wash you with
the hands that loved you, did not lift you up,
as was my right, a weight of misery,   1140
to the fierce blaze of the pyre. The hands of strangers
gave you due rites, and so you come again,
a tiny weight inclosed in tiny vessel.
Alas for all my nursing of old days,
so constant—all for nothing—which I gave you;
my joy was in the trouble of it. For never
were you your mother's love as much as mine.
None was your nurse but I within that household.
You called me always "sister." Now in one day
all that is gone—for you are dead. All, all
you have snatched with you in your going, like   1150
a hurricane. Our father is dead and gone.
I am dead in you; and you are dead yourself.
Our enemies laugh. Frantic with joy, she grows,
mother, no mother, whom you promised me,
in secret messages so often, you
would come to punish. This, all this, the Genius,
the unlucky Genius of yourself and me,
has stolen away and sent you back to me,
instead of the form I loved, only your dust
and idle shade. Alas! Alas!

      (*She takes up an attitude of formalized mourning by the urn.*)
O body pitiable! Alas!   1160
O saddest journey that you went, my love,
and so have ended me! Alas!
O brother, loved one, you have ended me.
Therefore, receive me to your habitation,
nothing to nothing, that with you below
I may dwell from now on. When you were on earth,
I shared all with you equally. Now I claim
in death no less to share a grave with you.
The dead, I see, no longer suffer pain.   1170

Chorus

> Think, Electra, your father was mortal,
> and mortal was Orestes. Do not sorrow too much.
> This is a debt that all of us must pay.

Orestes

> Ah!
> What shall I say? What words can I use, perplexed?
> I am no longer master of my tongue.

Electra

> What ails you? What is the meaning of your words?

Orestes

> Is this the distinguished beauty, Electra?

Electra

> Yes.
>
> A miserable enough Electra, truly.

Orestes

> Alas for this most lamentable event!

Electra

> Is it for me, sir, you are sorrowing?   1180

Orestes

> Form cruelly and godlessly abused!

Electra

> None other than myself must be the subject
> of your ill-omened words, sir.

Orestes

> O, alas!
>
> For your life without husband or happiness!

Electra

> Why do you look at me so, sir? Why lament?

Orestes

> How little then I knew of my own sorrows!

Electra

> In what of all that was said did you find this out?

Orestes

So great, so sore, I see your sufferings.

Electra

It's little of my suffering that you see.

Orestes

How can there be things worse than those I see?

Electra

Because I live with those that murdered him.   1190

Orestes

Murderers? And whose? Where is the guilt you hint at?

Electra

My father's murderers. I am their slave perforce.

Orestes

Who is it that forces you to such subjection?

Electra

She is called my mother—but like a mother in nothing.

Orestes

How does she force you? Hardship or violence?

Electra

With violence and hardship and all ills.

Orestes

You have none to help you or to hinder her?

Electra

No. There was one. You have shown me his dust.

Orestes

Poor girl! When I look at you, how I pity you.

Electra

Then you are the only one that ever pitied me.   1200

Orestes

Yes. I alone came here and felt your pain.

Electra

You haven't come as, in some way, our kinsman?

Orestes

I will tell—if (*pointing to the Chorus*) I may speak here among friends.

Electra

Yes, friends indeed. You may speak quite freely.

Orestes

Give up this urn then, and you shall know all.

Electra

Don't take it from me, stranger—by the Gods!

Orestes

Do what I bid you. You will not be wrong.

Electra

By your beard! Do not rob me of what I love most!

Orestes

I will not let you have it.

Electra

O Orestes!

Alas, if I may not even give you burial!   1210

Orestes

No words of ill omen! You have no right to mourn.

Electra

Have I no right to mourn for my dead brother?

Orestes

You have no right to call him by that name.

Electra

Am I then so dishonored in his sight?

Orestes

No one dishonors you. Mourning is not for you.

Electra

It is—if I hold Orestes' body here.

Orestes

No body of Orestes—except in fiction.

Electra

Where is the poor boy buried then?

Orestes

Nowhere.

There is no grave for living men.

Electra

How, boy,

What do you mean?

Orestes

Nothing that is untrue.   1220

Electra

Is he alive then?

Orestes

Yes, if I am living.

Electra

And are you he?

Orestes

Look at this signet ring
that was our father's, and know if I speak true.

Electra

O happiest light!

Orestes

Happiest I say, too.

Electra

Voice, have you come?

Orestes

Hear it from no other voice.

Electra

Do my arms hold you?

Orestes

Never again to part.

Electra (to the Chorus)
> Dearest of women, fellow citizens,
> here is Orestes, that was dead in craft,
> and now by craft restored to life again.

Chorus
> We see, my child, and at your happy fortune   1230
> a tear of gladness trickles from our eyes.

Electra
> Child of the body that I loved the best,
> at last you have come,
> you have come, you have found, you have known those you
> yearned for.

Orestes
> Yes, I have come.
> But bide your time in silence.

Electra
> Why?

Orestes
> Silence is better, that none inside may hear.

Electra
> No, by Artemis, ever virgin.
> *That* I will never stoop to fear—
> the women inside there,   1240
> always a vain burden on the earth.

Orestes
> Yes, but consider that in women too
> there lives a warlike spirit. You have proof of it.

Electra
> Alas, indeed.
> You have awakened my sorrow no cloud can dim,
> no expiation wash away,
> no forgetfulness overcome,
> no measure can fit,
> in all its frightfulness.

1250

Orestes

> I know that too. But when you may speak freely,
> then is the time to remember what was done.

Electra

> Every moment, every moment of all time
> would fit justly for my complaints.
> For hardly now are my lips free of restraint.

Orestes

> And I agree. Therefore, hold fast your freedom.

Electra

> By doing what?

Orestes

> Where there is no occasion,
> do not choose to talk too much.

Electra

> Who could find a fit bargain   1260
> of words for that silence,
> now you have appeared?
> Past hope, past calculation,
> I see you.

Orestes

> You see me when the Gods moved me to come.

Electra

> You tell me then of a grace surpassing
> what I knew before, if in very truth
> the Gods have given you to this house.
> This I count an action divine.   1270

Orestes

> Indeed, I hesitate to check your joy;
> only I fear your pleasure may be too great.

Electra

> Orestes, you have come at last,
> have made the journey worth all the world to me,

have come before me at last.
Now that I see you
after so much sorrow,
do not, I beg you—

Orestes

What should I not do?

Electra

               Do not deprive me
of the joy of seeing your face.

Orestes

I would be angry if I saw another
trying to take me from you.

Electra

             You agree?

Orestes

                 Yes.   1280

Electra

My dear one, I have heard you speaking,
the voice I never hoped to hear.
Till now I have held my rage speechless;
I did not cry out when I heard bad news.
But now I have you. You have come,
your darling face before me
that even in suffering I never forgot.

Orestes

Spare me all superfluity of speech.
Tell me not how my mother is villainous,
nor how Aegisthus drains my father's wealth   1290
by luxury or waste. Words about this
will shorten time and opportunity.
But tell me what we need for the present moment,
how openly or hidden we may make
this coming of ours a check for mocking foes.
Take care, you, that our mother may not discover you
by your radiant face, when we two go inside.

Groan as for my destruction, emptily
described in words. For when we have reached success,
then you may freely show your joy, and laugh.   1300

Electra

Brother, your pleasure shall be mine. These joys
I have from you. They are not mine to own.
To grieve you, though it were ever so little,
I would not buy a great good for myself.
If I did so, I would not properly
be servant to the Genius who attends us.
You know the situation. You have heard
Aegisthus is not at home, our mother is.
Do not be afraid that she will see my face
radiant with smiles. Our hatred is too old.   1310
I am too steeped in it. And since I have seen you,
my tears of joy will still run readily.
How can they cease when on the selfsame day
I have seen you dead and then again alive?
For me your coming is a miracle,
so that if my father should come back to life
I would think it no wonder but believe
I saw him. Since your coming is such for me,
lead as you will. Had I been all alone,
I would not have failed to win one of two things,   1320
a good deliverance or a good death for me.

Orestes

Hush, hush! I hear one of the people within
coming out.

Electra (still loudly to the servants of Orestes)
                    In with you, friends and guests,
more so, since what you are carrying in is that
which no one will reject there—nor be glad,
once he has got it.

Paedagogus (coming from inside)
                    Fools and madmen! No
concern for your own lives at all! No sense

to realize that you are not merely near
the deadliest danger, but in its very midst.   1330
If I had not, this while past, stood sentry here
at the door, your plans would now be in the house
before your bodies. I and I only
took the precautions. Have done once and for all
with your long speeches, your insatiate
cries of delight! And in with you at once.
As we are now, delay is ruinous.
It is high time to have done with our task.

Orestes

How shall I find everything inside?

Paedagogus

Well. There is no chance of your recognition.   1340

Orestes

You have announced my death, I understand.

Paedagogus

You are dead and gone—for all your being here.

Orestes

Were they glad of it? Or what did they say?

Paedagogus

I will tell you at the end. As things are now,
all on their side is well—even what is not so.

Electra

Brother, who is this man? I beg you, tell me.

Orestes

Do you not know him?

Electra

                              I cannot even guess.

Orestes

Do you not know him to whose hands you gave me?

Electra

What, this man?

Orestes

By his hands and by your forethought
I was conveyed away to Phocian country.   1350

Electra

Is this the man, alone among so many,
whom I found loyal when my father was murdered?

Orestes

This is he. There is no need for further questions.

Electra

O light most loved! O only rescuer
of Agamemnon's house, in what a shape
you come again! Are you indeed that other
who saved me and Orestes from many sorrows?
O most loved hands, service of feet most kind!
To think you have stood beside me for so long,
I not to know you, you to give no sign!
You killed me with your words while you had for me
most sweet reality. Bless you, my father,   1360
for in you I think I see my father. Bless you!
Within the selfsame day, of all mankind
I have most hated and loved you most.

Paedagogus

Enough, I think. As for the story
of the happenings in between, there are many days
and nights, as time comes round, to tell you all
clearly, Electra. But as you two stand here
I say to you: now is your chance to act.
Clytemnestra is alone. No man is there.
If you stop now, you will have others to fight   1370
more clever and more numerous than these.

Orestes

Pylades, we have time no longer for lengthy speeches.
We must get inside as quick as ever we can,
only first worshiping the ancestral Gods
whose statues stand beside the forecourt here.

(Exit Orestes.)

Electra (praying to the statue of Apollo)
    Apollo, Lord, give gracious ear to them
    and to me, too, that often made you offerings,
    out of such store as I had, with hand enriching.
    Lycean One, Apollo, now I pray,
    adore, entreat you on my knees, with all   1380
    the resources that I have, be kind to us,
    help us in the fulfilment of our plans
    and prove to all mankind the punishment
    the Gods exact for wickedness.

Chorus
    See how the War God approaches,
    breathing bloody vengeance, invincible.
    They have gone under the rooftree now,
    the pursuers of villainy,
    the hounds that none may escape.
    So that the dream that hung hauntingly   1390
    in my mind shall not lack fulfilment.
    Stealthy, stealthy, into the house,
    he goes, the champion of dead men,
    to his father's palace, rich from of old,
    with his hands on the tool of blood, new-whetted.
    Hermes, the child of Maia, conducts
    the crafty deed to its end, and delays not.

Electra
  Dear ladies, now is the moment that the men
  are finishing their work. Wait in silence.

Chorus
  What do you mean? What are they doing?

Electra
                           She is preparing   1400
  the urn for burial, and they stand beside her.

Chorus
  Why have you hurried out here?

Electra
>   To watch
> That Aegisthus does not come on them unawares.

Clytemnestra (*cries from within the house*)
> House, O house
> deserted by friends, full of killers!

Electra
> Someone cries out, inside. Do you hear?

Chorus
>   What I hear is a terror to the ear.
>   I shudder at it.

Clytemnestra (*cries again*)
> Oh! Oh!
> Aegisthus, where are you?

Electra
> Again, that cry!

Clytemnestra
> My son, my son,   1410
> pity your mother!

Electra
> You had none for him,
> nor for his father that begot him.

Chorus
>   City,
>   and miserable generation, now
>   the day-to-day pursuing fate is dying.

Clytemnestra
> Oh! I am struck!

Electra
>   If you have strength—again!

Clytemnestra
> Once more! Oh!

Electra
>   Would Aegisthus were with you!

Chorus

> The courses are being fulfilled;
> those under the earth are alive;
> men long dead draw from their killers
> blood to answer blood.   1420

> And here they come. The red hand reeks
> with War God's sacrifice. I cannot blame them.

Electra

> Orestes, how have you fared?

Orestes

>   In the house, all
> is well, if well Apollo prophesied.

Electra

> Is the wretch dead?

Orestes

>   You need fear no more
> that your proud mother will dishonor you.

Chorus

> Stop! I can see Aegisthus clearly
> coming this way.

Electra

> Boys, back to the house!   1430

Orestes

> He is in our power!

Electra

> He walks from the suburb full of joy.

Chorus

> Back to the vestibule, quick as you can.
> You have done one part well. Here is the other.

Orestes

> Do not be concerned, we will do it.

Electra

Go

where you will, then.

Orestes

See, I am gone (*hiding himself*).

Electra

Leave what is here to me.

Chorus

A few words spoken softly in his ear
would be good, that unawares
he may rush to his fight where Justice   1440
will be his adversary.

Aegisthus

Which of you knows where the Phocians are?
I am told they are come here with news for me
that Orestes met his end in a chariot wreck.
You there, yes, I mean you, you, you—
you have been bold enough before, and I should think
it is you these news concern most and therefore
you will know best to tell me.

Electra

I know. Of course. Were it not so, I would
be outcast from what concerns my best beloved.

Aegisthus

Where are the strangers then? Tell me that.   1450

Electra

Inside. They have found their hostess very kind.

Aegisthus

And do they genuinely report his death?

Electra

Better than that. They have brought himself, not news.

Aegisthus

Can I then see the body in plain sight?

Electra

You can indeed. It is an ugly sight.

Aegisthus

What you say delights me—an unusual thing!

Electra

You may delight, if you can find it here.

Aegisthus

Silence now! (*to the servants*) I command you, open the doors
for Mycenaeans, Argives all, to see
that if there be a man whom empty hope   1460
has still puffed up, he may look on the dead
and so accept my bitting, so may shun
a forcible encounter with myself
and punishment to make him grow some sense.

Electra

I have done everything on my side. At long last
I have learned some sense, agreement with the stronger.

Aegisthus (*looking at the shrouded corpse*)

O Zeus, I see an image of what happened
not without envy of Gods. If that is something
I should not say, because of Nemesis,
I take it back. Draw all the covers from
his face that kinship at least may have due mourning.

Orestes

Touch it yourself. This body is not mine,   1470
it is only yours—to see and greet with love.

Aegisthus

True. I accept that. Will you call out
Clytemnestra if she is at home?

Orestes

                          She is near you.
You need not look elsewhere.

Aegisthus (as the face of Clytemnestra confronts him)
                    What do I see?

Orestes

Something you fear? Do you not know the face?

Aegisthus

Who are you that have driven us into the net
in which this victim fell?

Orestes

                    Did you take so long
to find that your names are all astray
and those you call the dead are living?

Aegisthus

                              Ah!
I understand. And you who speak to me   1480
can only be Orestes.

Orestes

Were you, so good a prophet, so long misled?

Aegisthus

This is my end then. Let me say one word.

Electra

Not one, not one word more,
I beg you, brother. Do not draw out the talking.
When men are in the middle of trouble, when one
is on the point of death, how can time matter?
Kill him as quickly as you can. And killing
throw him out to find such burial as suit him
out of our sights. This is the only thing
that can bring me redemption from
all my past sufferings.   1490

Orestes (to Aegisthus)

In with you, then. It is not words that now
are the issue, but your life.

Aegisthus

Why to the house?
Why do you need the dark if what you do
is fair? Why is your hand not ready to kill me?

Orestes

You are not to give orders. In where you killed him,
my father, so you may die in the same place!

Aegisthus

Must this house, by absolute necessity,
see the evils of the Pelopidae, now and to come?

Orestes

Yours it shall see, at least.
At least yours. There I am an excellent prophet.

Aegisthus

Your father did not have the skill you boast of.   1500

Orestes

Too many words! You are slow to take your road.
Go now.

Aegisthus

You lead the way.

Orestes

No, you go first.

Aegisthus

Afraid that I'll escape you?

Orestes

No, but you shall not
die as you choose. I must take care that death
is bitter for you. Justice shall be taken
directly on all who act above the law—
justice by killing. So we would have less villains.

Chorus

O race of Atreus, how many sufferings
were yours before you came at last so hardly
to freedom, perfected by this day's deed.   1510

PHILOCTETES

Translated and with an Introduction by

DAVID GRENE

INTRODUCTION TO
PHILOCTETES

The *Philoctetes* is the second-last play that Sophocles wrote. It probably came out in 409 B.C., and the last play, the *Oedipus at Colonus*, in 404, the year of Sophocles' death. Aristotle in the *Poetics* criticizes the *Philoctetes* for its happy ending, and many commentators since have been annoyed, or puzzled, or both by the solution of the play, which involves the God from the machine. Latterly, however, it has been more appreciated. There have been performances on the radio, and a surprising amount has been written about it, including a very interesting essay by Edmund Wilson in the *Wound and the Bow*. It is perhaps the most modern in feeling of all Sophocles' tragedies, and Sophocles is the most modern, the nearest to us, of the three Greek tragedians.

We may see the play simply as a duel between Philoctetes and Odysseus, with Neoptolemus as a pawn in the contest. But this play has a theme and a pattern which become deeper and more complicated, if we realize that in many of its aspects the story is the same as that of the *Oedipus at Colonus*. Each play, seen in the light of the other, makes more comprehensible Sophocles' tragic vision. Out of what personal suffering or vicarious experience he wrote this story twice in his last years, we shall never know. It is not only a preoccupation with the end of his life. With certain important differences the *Ajax*, written more than thirty years earlier than the *Philoctetes*, shows him thinking in the same way. Of course, each of these plays is individual in tone and character. What I mean is that, in both, the story is of a man offensive to his own society and banished by it, who, at last, must be reinstated and who becomes again miraculously potent, both alive and dead. And this story is the same in both plays in all its significant aspects.

Philoctetes is afflicted by some divine power without having committed a crime or being guilty of anything which the words "conscious guilt" mean, either to the fifth-century Greek or to ourselves.

He had unconsciously stumbled into a precinct or shrine of a God. Such shrines must not be thought of in the light of the Christian associations with the word. This was probably an unmarked and unfenced place, similar to the grove of the Eumenides in the *Oedipus at Colonus*. A snake—very often in Greece a symbol of a God's power —bit him in the foot and left him crippled. It is worth noting that Philoctetes' offense against the Gods is left at this. We are not allowed by the dramatist to speculate on any symbolic significance of his act of guilt or to construe it in any way as peculiar to Philoctetes. It is, in fact, an accident. He thus becomes burdened with the mark of God's resentment without any explanation for it humanly cogent either for himself or for others. The smell of his wound and his cries of agony render him so offensive to his comrades that he is marooned on a desert island for ten years, at the end of which time the Gods intervene to rescue him as mysteriously as they had injured him at the first. A glance at the Oedipus figure later and that of the Ajax in the earlier play shows a similar emphasis on the hero's innocence. It is true that Ajax is driven mad in the commission of an attempted murder against his generals, but Sophocles never tries to emphasize the matter of the murder afterward; it is only the performance of his act of frustration and misery by Ajax that we are likely to concern ourselves with.

Philoctetes is now an outcast from human sympathy but also the future conqueror of Troy. In both destruction and triumph, his lot does not make sense for ordinary men. This troubles them very little. They discarded him out of disgust at his affliction, when it looked as though God's hatred of him made that a safe course as well as a convenient one for themselves. Now that, with similar incomprehensibility, the divine purpose insists on the value of his bow and himself for the capture of Troy, they are prepared to restore him again to their society, particularly as the God has also arranged for his healing. In the *Philoctetes* Sophocles expresses what it feels like to be a man so isolated, so impersonally, so instrumentally used by his fellows.

The moment chosen is when the restoration to potency is near. Characteristically, Odysseus, who had marooned him originally and had taken advantage of Philoctetes when off his guard, plans to recapture him by similar strategic means. Neither time is he concerned to establish any human contact with the strange magical monster, so tormented and so honored by the non-human forces of the world. In this, Odysseus is blood-brother of Creon, who, in the *Oedipus at Colonus*, plays a similar role with the terrifying old beggar, Oedipus. In neither play does this cynical inhumanity have success. But neither are Philoctetes' brooding hatred and resentment allowed to have their way entirely. Here is where the role of Neoptolemus is important.

By trying to obey Odysseus, this boy comes to realize what cruelty is being inflicted on Philoctetes. So he undoes his offense and gives back the bow. However, when the deception is over and when the opportunity of healing and renown are offered Philoctetes again, by Neoptolemus this time, and as equal to equal, Philoctetes still refuses. The issue is clearly joined. Philoctetes' final refusal is the refusal of a man so wounded as to be unwilling to resume normal life itself because, with that life, will come new and unpredictable suffering. Better the old known pain, with the old known remedies, than the new hurt as unforeseeable as the future itself:

> It is not the sting of wrongs past,
> but what I must look for in wrongs to come.

This is all understandable, and, more than understandable, it claims our sympathy. But it is also irreconcilable with the vital principle which in anyone's life involves change and risk. It is easy for young Neoptolemus to face the future confidently. He has not yet been hurt enough to know what it feels like. Philoctetes' refusal is a great tragic human truth.

So Heracles is invoked not as an ordinary God from the machine but as the influence of a hero and old comrade, similarly injured, similarly restored, whose example must force Philoctetes to a step which will bring him healing and renown—but also more suffering. It is not that, as Aeschylus says, "out of suffering comes learning," but that only at the cost of suffering does life itself exist. As Philoctetes' final refusal is the mark of the play's truth to humanity, so is his final acquiescence in Heracles' order the mark of a truth to a universal principle, more imperative than humanity. But it is not the Philoctetes of the island, whom we have come to know so well, who goes to Troy with Odysseus and Neoptolemus. The significant part of that Philoctetes died, persisting to the end not to surrender his resentment and to risk new wrongs. This tragedy ends with his renewed refusal of Neoptolemus. What follows is what might well happen in the world as in the theater—the surrender of the individual life to the universal demands of life itself. As Hamlet must die and Fortinbras succeed, the new Philoctetes succeeds the old; but with the other Philoctetes of the island are buried all the years of wrong and of suffering and also the meaning that they had rendered to his agony.

CHARACTERS

Odysseus

Chorus of Sailors under the Command of Neoptolemus

The Spy Disguised as a Trader

Neoptolemus, Prince of Scyrus and Son of Achilles

Philoctetes

Heracles

PHILOCTETES

Scene: *A lonely spot on the island of Lemnos. Enter Odysseus and Neoptolemus.*

Odysseus
    This is it; this Lemnos and its beach
    down to the sea that quite surrounds it; desolate,
    no one sets foot on it; there are no houses.
    This is where I marooned him long ago,
    the son of Poias, the Melian, his foot
    diseased and eaten away with running ulcers.

    Son of our greatest hero,
    son of Achilles, Neoptolemus,
    I tell you I had orders for what I did:
    my masters, the princes, bade me do it.

    We had no peace with him: at the holy festivals,
    we dared not touch the wine and meat; he screamed
    and groaned so, and those terrible cries of his
    brought ill luck on our celebrations; all
    the camp was haunted by him.   10

    Now is no time to talk to you of this,
    now is no time for long speeches.
    I am afraid that he may hear of my coming
    and ruin all my plans to take him.

    It is you who must help me with the rest. Look about
    and see where there might be a cave with two mouths.
    There are two niches to rest in, one in the sun
    when it is cold, the other a tunneled passage
    through which the breezes blow in summertime.

A man can sleep there and be cool. To the left,   20
a little, you may see a spring to drink at—
if it is still unchoked—go this way quietly,
see if he's there or somewhere else and signal.
Then I can tell you the rest. Listen:
I shall tell you. We will both do this thing.

Neoptolemus

What you speak of is near at hand, Odysseus.
I think I see such a cave.

Odysseus

Above or below? I cannot see it myself.

Neoptolemus

Above here, and no trace of a footpath.

Odysseus

See if he is housed within, asleep.   30

Neoptolemus

I see an empty hut, with no one there.

Odysseus

And nothing to keep house with?

Neoptolemus

A pallet bed, stuffed with leaves, to sleep on, for someone.

Odysseus

And nothing else? Nothing inside the house?

Neoptolemus

A cup, made of a single block, a poor
workman's contrivance. And some kindling, too.

Odysseus

It is his treasure house that you describe.

Neoptolemus

And look, some rags are drying in the sun
full of the oozing matter from a sore.

Odysseus

    Yes, certainly he lives here, even now   40
    is somewhere not far off. He cannot go far,
    sick as he is, lame cripple for so long.
    It's likely he has gone to search for food
    or somewhere that he knows there is a herb
    to ease his pain. Send your man here to watch,
    that he may not come upon me without warning.
    For he would rather take me than all the Greeks.

Neoptolemus

    Very well, then, the path will be watched.
    Go on with your story; tell me what you want.

Odysseus

    Son of Achilles,   50
    our coming here has a purpose; to it be loyal
    with more than with your body. If you should hear
    some strange new thing, unlike what you have heard
    before, still serve us; it was to serve you came here.

Neoptolemus

    What would you have me do?

Odysseus

                         Ensnare
    the soul of Philoctetes with your words.
    When he asks who you are and whence you came,
    say you are Achilles' son; you need not lie.
    Say you are sailing home, leaving the Greeks
    and all their fleet, in bitter hatred. Say
    that they had prayed you, urged you from your home,   60
    and swore that only with your help
    could Troy be taken. Yet when you came and asked,
    as by your right, to have your father's arms,
    Achilles' arms, they did not think you worthy
    but gave them to Odysseus. Say what you will
    against me; do not spare me anything.

Nothing of this will hurt me; if you will not
do this, you will bring sorrow on all the Greeks.
If this man's bow shall not be taken by us,
you cannot sack the town of Troy.

Perhaps you wonder why you can safely meet him,   70
why he would trust you and not me. Let me explain.
You have come here unforced, unpledged by oaths,
made no part of our earlier expedition.
The opposite is true in my own case;
at no point can I deny his charge.
If, when he sees me, Philoctetes
still has his bow, there is an end of me,
and you too, for my company would damn you.
For this you must sharpen your wits, to become a thief
of the arms no man has conquered.

I know, young man, it is not your natural bent
to say such things nor to contrive such mischief.   80
But the prize of victory is pleasant to win.
Bear up: another time we shall prove honest.
For one brief shameless portion of a day
give me yourself, and then for all the rest
you may be called most scrupulous of men.

Neoptolemus
Son of Laertes, what I dislike to hear
I hate to put in execution.
I have a natural antipathy
to get my ends by tricks and stratagems.
So, too, they say, my father was. Philoctetes
I will gladly fight and capture, bring him with us,   90
but not by treachery. Surely a one-legged man
cannot prevail against so many of us!
I recognize that I was sent with you
to follow your instructions. I am loath
to have you call me traitor. Still, my lord,

I would prefer even to fail with honor
than win by cheating.

Odysseus
> You are a good man's son.
> I was young, too, once, and then I had a tongue
> very inactive and a doing hand.
> Now as I go forth to the test, I see
> that everywhere among the race of men
> it is the tongue that wins and not the deed.

Neoptolemus
> What do you bid me do, but to tell lies? 100

Odysseus
> By craft I bid you take him, Philoctetes.

Neoptolemus
> And why by craft rather than by persuasion?

Odysseus
> He will not be persuaded; force will fail.

Neoptolemus
> Has he such strength to give him confidence?

Odysseus
> The arrows none may avoid, that carry death.

Neoptolemus
> Then even to encounter him is not safe?

Odysseus
> Not if you do not take him by craft, as I told you.

Neoptolemus
> Do you not find it vile yourself, this lying?

Osysseus
> Not if the lying brings our rescue with it.

Neoptolemus
> How can a man not blush to say such things? 110

Odysseus

When one does something for gain, one need not blush.

Neoptolemus

What gain for me that he should come to Troy?

Odysseus

His weapons alone are destined to take Troy.

Neoptolemus

Then I shall not be, as was said, its conqueror?

Odysseus

Not you apart from them nor they from you.

Neoptolemus

They must be my quarry then, if this is so.

Odysseus

You will win a double prize if you do this.

Neoptolemus

What? If I know, I will do what you say.

Odysseus

You shall be called a wise man and a good.

Neoptolemus

Well, then I will do it, casting aside all shame.   120

Odysseus

You clearly recollect all I have told you?

Neoptolemus

Yes, now that I have understood it.

Odysseus

                                    Stay
and wait his coming here; I will go
that he may not spy my presence.
I will take with me to the ship this guard.
If you are too slow, I will send him back again,
disguise him as a sailor; Philoctetes
will never know him.
Whatever clever story he give you, then   130

fall in with it and use it as you need.
Now I will go to the ship and leave you in charge.
May Hermes, God of Craft, the Guide, for us
be guide indeed, and Victory and Athene,
the City Goddess, who preserves me ever.

(*Exit Odysseus.*)

Chorus

Sir, we are strangers, and this land is strange;
what shall we say and what conceal from this suspicious man?
Tell us.
For cunning that passes another's cunning
and a pre-eminent judgment lie with the prince,
in whose sovereign keeping is Zeus's holy scepter.   140
To you, young lord, all this has come,
all the power of your forefathers. Tell us now
what we must do to serve you.

Neoptolemus

Now—if you wish to see where he sleeps
on his crag at the edge—look, be not afraid.
But when the terrible wanderer returns,
be gone from the hut, but come to my beckoning.
Take your cues from me. Help when you can.

Chorus

Sir, this we have always done,   150
have kept a watchful eye over your safety.
But now
tell us what places he inhabits
and where he rests. It would not be amiss
for us to know this,
lest he attack us unawares.
Where does he live? Where does he rest?
What footpath does he follow? Is he in the house or not?

Neoptolemus

This, that you see, is his two-fronted house,
and he sleeps inside on the rock.   160

Chorus

   Where is he gone, unhappy creature?

Neoptolemus

                        I am sure
   he has gone to find food somewhere near here;
   stumbling, lame, dragging along the path,
   he is trying to shoot birds to prolong his miserable life.
   This indeed, they say, is how he lives.
   And no one comes near to cure him.

Chorus

   Yes, for my part I pity him:
   how unhappy, how utterly alone, always   170
   he suffers the savagery of his illness
   with no one to care for him,
   with no friendly face near him,
   but bewildered and distraught at each need as it comes.
   God pity him, how has he kept a grip on life?

   Woe to the contrivances of death-bound men,
   woe to the unhappy generations of death-bound men
   whose lives have known extremes!

   Perhaps this man is as well born as any,   180
   second to no son of an ancient house.
   Yet now his life lacks everything,
   and he makes his bed without neighbors
   or with spotted shaggy beasts for neighbors.
   His thoughts are set continually on pain and hunger.
   He cries out in his wretchedness;
   there is only a blabbering echo,
   that comes from the distance speeding
   from his bitter crying.   190

Neoptolemus

   I am not surprised at any of this:
   this is a God's doing, if I have any understanding.

These afflictions that have come upon him
are the work of Chryse, bitter of heart.
As for his present loneliness and suffering,
this, too, no doubt is part of the God's plan
that he may not bend against Troy
the divine invincible bow
until the time shall be fulfilled, at which it is decreed,
that Troy, as they say, shall fall to that bow.   200

Chorus
  Hush.

Neoptolemus
        What is it?

Chorus
              Hush! I hear a footfall,
  footfall of a man that walks painfully.
  Is it here?   Is it here?
  I hear a voice, now I can hear it clearly,
  voice of a man, crawling along the path,
  hard put to it to move. It's far away,
  but I can hear it; I can hear the sound well
  the voice of a man wounded; it is quite clear now.

  No more now, my son.   210

Neoptolemus
              No more of what?

Chorus
  Your plots and plans. He is here, almost with us.
  His is no cheerful marching to the pipe
  like a shepherd with his flock.
  No, a bitter cry.
  He must have stumbled far down on the path,
  and his moaning carried all the way here.
  Or perhaps he stopped to look at the empty harbor,
  for it was a bitter cry.

Philoctetes

    Men, who are you that have put in, rowing   220
    to a shore without houses or anchorage?
    What countrymen may I call you without offense?
    What is your people? Greeks, indeed, you seem
    in fashion of your clothing, dear to me.
    May I hear your voice? Do not be afraid
    or shrink from such as I am, grown a savage.
    I have been alone and very wretched,
    without friend or comrade, suffering a great deal.
    Take pity on me; speak to me; speak,
    speak if you come as friends.
                          No—answer me.   230
    If this is all
    that we can have from one another, speech,
    this, at least, we should have.

Neoptolemus

    Sir, for your questions, since you wish to know,
    know we are Greeks.

Philoctetes

                       Friendliest of tongues!
    That I should hear it spoken once again
    by such a man in such a place! My boy,
    who are you? Who has sent you here? What brought you?
    What impulse? What friendliest of winds?
    Tell me all this, that I know who you are.

Neoptolemus

    I am of Scyrus that the sea surrounds;
    I am sailing home. My name is Neoptolemus,   240
    Achilles' son. Now you know everything.

Philoctetes

    Son of a father—that I loved so dearly—
    and of a country that I loved, you that were reared
    by that old man Lycomedes, what kind of venture
    can have brought you to port here? Where did you sail from?

Neoptolemus

At present bound from Troy.

Philoctetes

From Troy? From Troy!
You did not sail with us to Troy at first.

Neoptolemus

You, then, are one that also had a share
in all that trouble?

Philoctetes

Is it possible
you do not know me, boy, me whom you see here?

Neoptolemus

I never saw you before. How could I know you?   250

Philoctetes

You never heard my name then? Never a rumor
of all the wrongs I suffered, even to death?

Neoptolemus

I never knew a word of what you ask me.

Philoctetes

Surely I must be vile! God must have hated me
that never a word of me, of how I live here,
should have come home through all the land of Greece.
Yet they that outraged God casting me away
can hold their tongues and laugh! While my disease
always increases and grows worse. My boy,
you are Achilles' son. I that stand here   260
am one you may have heard of, as the master
of Heracles' arms. I am Philoctetes
the son of Poias. Those two generals
and Prince Odysseus of the Cephallenians
cast me ashore here to their shame, as lonely
as you can see me now, wasting with my sickness
as cruel as it is, caused by the murderous bite
of a viper mortally dangerous.

I was already bitten when we put in here
on my way from sea-encircled Chryse.   270
I tell you, boy, those men cast me away here
and ran and left me helpless. They were happy
when they saw that I had fallen asleep on the shore
in a rocky cave, after a rough passage.
They went away and left me with such rags—
and few enough of them—as one might give
an unfortunate beggar and a handful of food.
May God give them the like!
Think, boy, of that awakening when I awoke
and found them gone; think of the useless tears
and curses on myself when I saw the ships—
my ships, which I had once commanded—gone,
all gone, and not a man left on the island,   280
not one to help me or to lend a hand
when I was seized with my sickness, not a man!
In all I saw before me nothing but pain;
but of that a great abundance, boy.

Time came and went for me. In my tiny shelter
I must alone do everything for myself.
This bow of mine I used to shoot the birds
that filled my belly. I must drag my foot,
my cursed foot, to where the bolt
sped by the bow's thong had struck down a bird.   290
If I must drink, and it was winter time—
the water was frozen—I must break up firewood.
Again I crawled and miserably contrived
to do the work. Whenever I had no fire,
rubbing stone on stone I would at last produce
the spark that kept me still in life.
A roof for shelter, if only I have fire,
gives me everything but release from pain.

Boy, let me tell you of this island.   300
No sailor by his choice comes near it.

There is no anchorage, nor anywhere
that one can land, sell goods, be entertained.
Sensible men make no voyages here.
Yet now and then someone puts in. A stretch
of time as long as this allows much to happen.
When they have come here, boy, they pity me—
at least they say they do—and in their pity
they have given me scraps of food and cast-off clothes;
that other thing, when I dare mention it,   310
none of them will—bringing me home again.

It is nine years now that I have spent dying,
with hunger and pain feeding my insatiable
disease. That, boy, is what they have done to me,
the two Atridae, and that mighty Prince
Odysseus. May the Gods that live in heaven
grant that they pay, agony for my agony.

Chorus

In this, I too resemble your other visitors.
I pity you, son of Poias.

Neoptolemus

            I am a witness,
I also, of the truth of what you say.   320
I know it is true. I have dealt with those villains,
the two Atridae and the prince Odysseus.

Philoctetes

Are you, as well as I, a sufferer
and angry? Have you grounds against the Atridae?

Neoptolemus

Give me the chance to gratify my anger
with my hand some day!
Then will Mycenae know and Sparta know
that Scyrus, too, breeds soldiers.

Philoctetes

                  Well said, boy!
You come to me with a great hate against them.
Because of what?

Neoptolemus

              I will tell you, Philoctetes—
for all that it hurts to tell it—
of how I came to Troy and what dishonor   330
they put upon me.
When fatefully Achilles came to die. . . .

Philoctetes

O stop! tell me no more. Let me understand
this first. Is he dead, Achilles, dead?

Neoptolemus

Yes, he is dead; no man his conqueror
but bested by a god, Phoebus the archer.

Philoctetes

Noble was he that killed and he that died.
Boy, I am at a loss which to do first,
ask for your story or to mourn for him.

Neoptolemus

God help you, I would think that your own sufferings
were quite enough without mourning for those of others.   340

Philoctetes

Yes, that is true. Again, tell me your story
of how they have insulted you.

Neoptolemus

                  They came
for me, did great Odysseus and the man
that was my father's tutor, with a ship
wonderfully decked with ribbons. They had a story—
be it truth or lie—that it was God's decree
since he, my father, was dead, I and I only
should take Troy town.

This was their story. Sir, you can imagine
it did not take much time, when they had told it,   350
for me to embark with them.
Chiefly, you know, I was prompted by love of him,
the dead man. I had hope of seeing him
while still unburied. Alive I never had.
We had a favoring wind; on the second day
we touched Sigeion. As I disembarked,
all of the soldiers swarmed around me, blessed me,
swore that they saw Achilles alive again,
now gone from them forever. But he still lay
unburied. I, his mourning son, wept for him;   360
then, in a while, came to the two Atridae,
my friends, as it seemed right to do, and asked them
for my father's arms and all that he had else.
They needed brazen faces for their answer:
"Son of Achilles, all that your father had.
all else, is yours to take, but not his arms.
Another man now owns them, Laertes' son."
I burst into tears, jumped up, enraged,
cried out in my pain, "You scoundrels, did you dare
to give those arms that were mine to someone else   370
before I knew of it?" Then Odysseus
spoke—he was standing near me—"Yes, and rightly,"
he said, "they gave them, boy. For it was I
who rescued them and him, their former owner."
My anger got the better of me; I cursed him outright
with every insult that I knew, sparing none,
if he should take my arms away from me.
He is no way given to quarreling, but at this
he was stung by what I said. He answered:
"You were not where we were. You were at home,
out of the reach of duty. Since, besides,
you have so bold a tongue in your head, never   380
will you possess them to bring home to Scyrus."

There it was, abuse on both sides. But I lost
what should be mine and so sailed home. Odysseus,
that filthy son of filthy parents, robbed me.
Yet I do not blame him even so much as the princes.
All of a city is in the hand of the prince,
all of an army; unruly men become so
by the instruction of their betters.
This is the whole tale. May he that hates the Atridae
be as dear in the Gods' sight as he is in mine.   390

Chorus

Earth, Mountain Mother, in whom we find sustenance,
Mother of Zeus himself,
Dweller in great golden Pactolus,
Mother that I dread:
on that other day, too, I called on thee, Thou Blessed One,
Thou that rides on the Bull-killing Lions,
when all the insolence of the Atridae assaulted our Prince,
when they gave his arms, that wonder of the world,   400
    to the son of Laertes.

Philoctetes

You have sailed here, as it seems, with a clear tally;
your half of sorrow matches that of mine.
What you tell me rings in harmony. I recognize
the doings of the Atridae and Odysseus.
I know Odysseus would employ his tongue
on every ill tale, every rascality,
that could be brought to issue in injustice.
This is not at all my wonder, but that Ajax   410
the Elder should stand by, see and allow it.

Neoptolemus

He is no longer living, sir; never, indeed,
if he were, would they have robbed me of the arms.

Philoctetes

What! Is he, too, dead and gone?

Neoptolemus

    Yes, dead and gone. As such now think of him.

Philoctetes

    But not the son of Tydeus nor Odysseus
    whom Sisyphus once sold to Laertes,
    they will not die; for they should not be living.

Neoptolemus

    Of course, they are not dead; you may be sure
    that they are in their glory among the Greeks.   420

Philoctetes

    What of an old and honest man, my friend,
    Nestor of Pylos? Is he alive? He used
    to check their mischief by his wise advice.

Neoptolemus

    Things have gone badly for him. He has lost
    his son Antilochus, who once stood by him.

Philoctetes

    Ah!
    You have told me the two deaths that most could hurt me.
    Alas, what should I look for
    when Ajax and Antilochus are dead,
    and still Odysseus lives, that in their stead
    ought to be counted among the dead?   430

Neoptolemus

    A cunning wrestler; still, Philoctetes,
    even the cunning are sometimes tripped up.

Philoctetes

    Tell me, by the Gods, where was Patroclus,
    who was your father's dearest friend?

Neoptolemus

                        Dead, too.
    In one short sentence I can tell you this.
    War never takes a bad man but by chance,
    the good man always.

Philoctetes

You have said the truth.

So I will ask you of one quite unworthy
but dexterous and clever with his tongue. 440

Neoptolemus

Whom can you mean except Odysseus?

Philoctetes

It is not he: there was a man, Thersites,
who never was content to speak once only,
though no one was for letting him speak at all.
Do you know if he is still alive?

Neoptolemus

I did not know him,
but I have heard that he is still alive.

Philoctetes

He would be; nothing evil has yet perished.
The Gods somehow give them most excellent care.
They find their pleasure in turning back from Death
the rogues and tricksters, but the just and good
they are always sending out of the world. 450
How can I reckon the score, how can I praise,
when praising Heaven I find the Gods are bad?

Neoptolemus

For my own part, Philoctetes of Oeta,
from now on I shall take precautions.
I shall look at Troy and the Atridae both
from very far off. I shall never abide
the company of those where the worse man
has more power than the better, where the good
are always on the wane and cowards rule.
For the future, rocky Scyrus will content me
to take my pleasure at home. 460
Now I will be going to my ship. Philoctetes,
on you God's blessing and goodbye. May the Gods

recover you of your sickness, as you would have it!
Let us go, men, that when God grants us sailing
we may be ready to sail.

Philoctetes

                 Boy, are you going,
going now?

Neoptolemus

           Yes, the weather favors.
We must look to sail almost at once.

Philoctetes

My dear—I beg you in your father's name,
and in your mother's, in the name of all
that you have loved at home, do not leave me here   470
alone, living in sufferings you have seen
and others I have told you of.
I am not your main concern; give me a passing thought.
I know that there is horrible discomfort
in having me on board. Put up with it.
To such as you and your nobility,
meanness is shameful, decency honorable.
If you leave me here, it is an ugly story.
If you take me, men will say their best of you,
if I shall live to see Oetean land.
Come! One day, hardly one whole day's space   480
that I shall trouble you. Endure this much.
Take me and put me where you will,
in the hold, in the prow or poop, anywhere
where I shall least offend those that I sail with.
By Zeus himself, God of the Suppliants,
I beg you, boy, say "Yes," say you will do it.
Here I am on my knees to you, poor cripple,
for all my lameness. Do not cast me away
so utterly alone, where no one even walks by.
Either take me and set me safe in your own home,
or take me to Chalcedon in Euboea.

From there it will be no great journey for me   490
to Oeta or to ridgy Trachis or
to quick-flowing Spercheius,
and so you show me to my loving father.
For many a day I have feared that he is dead.
With those who came to my island I sent messages,
and many of them, begging him to come
and bring me home himself. Either he's dead,
or, as I rather think, my messengers
made little of what I asked them and hurried home.
Now in you I have found both escort and messenger;   500
bring me safe home. Take pity on me.
Look how men live, always precariously
balanced between good and bad fortune.
If you are out of trouble, watch for danger.
And when you live well, then consider the most
your life, lest ruin take it unawares.

Chorus
Have pity on him, prince.
He has has told us of a most desperate course run.
God forbid such things should overtake friends of mine.
And, prince, if you hate the abdominable Atridae   510
I would set their ill treatment of him
to his gain and would carry him
in your quick, well-fitted ship
to his home and so avoid offense before the face of God.

Neoptolemus
Take care that your assent is not too ready,
and that, when you have enough of his diseased company,   520
you are no longer constant to what you have said.

Chorus
No. You will never be able in this
to reproach me with justice.

Neoptolemus

                I should be ashamed
to be less ready than you to render a stranger service.
Well, if you will then, let us sail. Let him
get ready quickly. My ship will carry him.

May God give us a safe clearance from this land
and a safe journey where we choose to go.

Philoctetes

God bless this day!   530
Man, dear to my very heart,
and you, dear friends, how shall I prove to you
how you have bound me to your friendship!
Let us go, boy. But let us first kiss the earth,
reverently, in my homeless home of a cave.
I would have you know what I have lived from,
how tough the spirit that did not break. I think
the sight itself would have been enough for anyone
except myself. Necessity has taught me,
little by little, to suffer and be patient.

Chorus

Wait! Let us see. Two men are coming.
One of them is of our crew, the other a foreigner.   540
Let us hear from them and then go in.

                      (Enter the Sailor disguised as a Trader.)

Trader

Son of Achilles, I told my fellow traveler here—
he with two others were guarding your ship—
to tell me where you were. I happened on you.
I had no intentions this way. Just by accident
I came to anchor at this island.
I am sailing in command of a ship outward bound
from Ilium, with no great company, for Peparethus—
a good country, that, for wine. When I heard
that all those sailors were the crew of your ship,   550

I thought I should not hold my tongue and sail on
until I spoke with you—and got my reward,
a fair one, doubtless. Apparently you do not know
much of your own affairs, nor what new plans
the Greeks have for you. Indeed, not only plans,
actions in train already and not slowly.

Neoptolemus

Thank you for your consideration, sir.
I will remain obliged to your kindness
unless I prove unworthy. Please tell me
what you have spoken of. I would like to know
what are these new plans of the Greeks.   560

Trader

Old Phoenix and the two sons of Theseus are gone,
pursuing you with a squadron.

Neoptolemus

                                  Do they intend
to bring me back with violence or persuade me?

Trader

I do not know. I tell you what I heard.

Neoptolemus

Are Phoenix and his friends in such a hurry
to do the bidding of the two Atridae?

Trader

It is being done.
There is no delay about it. That you should know.

Neoptolemus

How is it that Odysseus was not ready
to sail as his own messenger on such
an errand? It cannot be he was afraid?

Trader

When I weighed anchor, he and Tydeus' son   570
were in pursuit of still another man.

Neoptolemus

Who was this other man that Odysseus himself should seek him?

Trader

There was a man—perhaps you will tell me first
who this is; and say softly what you say.

Neoptolemus

This, sir, is the famous Philoctetes.

Trader

                              Do not
ask me any further questions. Get yourself out,
as quickly as you can, out of this island.

Philoctetes

What does he say, boy? Why in dark whispers
does he bargain with you about me, this sailor?

Neoptolemus

I do not know yet what he says, but he must say it,   580
openly, whatever it is, to you and me and these.

Trader

Son of Achilles, do not slander me,
speaking of me to the army as a tattler.
There's many a thing I do for them and in return
get something from them, as a poor man may.

Neoptolemus

I am the enemy of the Atridae. This
is my greatest friend because he hates the Atridae.
You have come to me as a friend, and so you must
hide from me nothing that you heard.

Trader

Well, watch what you are doing, sir.

Neoptolemus

                              I have.

Trader

I put the whole responsibility
squarely upon yourself.

Neoptolemus

                  Do so; but speak.   590

Trader

    Well, then. The two I have spoken of,
    the son of Tydeus and the Prince Odysseus,
    are in pursuit of Philoctetes.
    They have sworn, so help them God, to bring him with them
    either by persuasion or by brute force.
    And this all the Greeks heard clearly announced
    by Prince Odysseus; for he was much surer
    of success than was the other.

Neoptolemus

                  What can have made
    the Atridae care about him after so long—
    one whom they, years and years since, cast away?   600
    What yearning for him came over them? Was it the Gods
    who punish evil doings that now have driven them
    to retribution for injustice?

Trader

    I will explain all that. Perhaps you haven't heard.
    There was a prophet of very good family,
    a son of Priam indeed, called Helenus.
    He was captured one night in an expedition
    undertaken singlehanded by Odysseus,
    of whom all base and shameful things are spoken,
    captured by stratagem. Odysseus brought
    his prisoner before the Greeks, a splendid prize.
    Helenus prophesied everything to them   610
    and, in particular, touching the fortress of Troy,
    that they could never take it till they persuaded
    Philoctetes to come with them and leave his island.
    As soon as Odysseus heard the prophet say this,
    he promised at once to bring the man before them,
    for all to see—he thought, as a willing prisoner,
    but, if not that, against his will. If he failed,

"any of them might have his head," he declared. My boy,
that is the whole story; that is why I urge you   620
and him and any that you care for to make haste.

Philoctetes

Ah!
Did he indeed swear that he would persuade me
to sail with him, did he so, that utter devil?
As soon shall I be persuaded, when I am dead,
to rise from Death's house, come to the light again,
as his own father did.

Trader

I do not know about that. Well, I will be going now
to my ship. May God prosper you both!

(Exit Trader.)

Philoctetes

Is it not terrible, boy, that this Odysseus
should think that there are words soft enough to win me,
to let him put me in his boat, exhibit me
in front of all the Greeks?   630
No! I would rather listen to my worst enemy,
the snake that bit me, made me into this cripple.
But he can say anything, he can dare anything.
Now I know that he will come here.
Boy, let us go, that a great sea may sever
us from Odysseus' ship.
Let us go. For look, haste in due season shown
brings rest and peace when once the work is done.

Neoptolemus

When the wind at our prow falls, we can sail, no sooner.
Now it is dead against us.   640

Philoctetes

It is always fair sailing, when you escape evil.

Neoptolemus

Yes, but the wind is against them, too.

Philoctetes
                              For pirates
   when they can thieve and plunder, no wind is contrary.

Neoptolemus
   If you will, then, let us go. Take from your cave
   what you need most and love most.

Philoctetes
   There are some things I need, but no great choice.

Neoptolemus
   What is there that you will not find on board?

Philoctetes
   A herb I have, the chief means to soothe my wound,
   to lull the pain to sleep.   650

Neoptolemus
                        Bring it out then.
   What else is there that you would have?

Philoctetes
   Any arrow
   I may have dropped and missed. For none of them
   must I leave for another to pick up.

Neoptolemus
   Is this, in your hands, the famous bow?

Philoctetes
                                     Yes, this,
   this in my hands.

Neoptolemus
                     May I see it closer,
   touch and adore it like a god?

Philoctetes
                           You may have it
   and anything else of mine that is for your good.

Neoptolemus
   I long for it, yet only with such longing   660

that if it is lawful, I may have it, else
let it be.

Philoctetes

      Your words are holy, boy. It is lawful.
for you have given me, and you alone,
the sight of the sun shining above us here,
the sight of my Oeta, of my old father, my friends.
You have raised me up above my enemies,
when I was under their feet. You may be confident.
You may indeed touch my bow, give it again
to me that gave it you, proclaim that alone
of all the world you touched it, in return
for the good deed you did. It was for that,
for friendly help, I myself won it first.   670

Neoptolemus

I am glad to see you and take you as a friend.
For one who knows how to show and to accept kindness
will be a friend better than any possession.
Go in.

Philoctetes

      I will bring you with me. The sickness in me
seeks to have you beside me.

Chorus

In story I have heard, but my eyes have not seen
him that once would have drawn near to Zeus's bed.
I have heard how he caught him, bound him on a running wheel,
Zeus, son of Kronos, invincible.
But I know of no other,   680
by hearsay, much less by sight, of all mankind
whose destiny was more his enemy when he met it
than Philoctetes', who wronged no one, nor killed
but lived, just among the just,
and fell in trouble past his deserts.
There is wonder, indeed, in my heart
how, how in his loneliness,

listening to the waves beating on the shore,
how he kept hold at all
on a life so full of tears.   690

He was lame, and no one came near him.
He suffered, and there were no neighbors for his sorrow
with whom his cries would find answer,
with whom he could lament the bloody plague
that ate him up.
No one who would gather
fallen leaves from the ground
to quiet the raging, bleeding sore,
running, in his maggot-rotten foot.   700
Here and there he crawled
writhing always—
suffering like a child
without the nurse he loves—
to what source of ease he could find
when the heart-devouring suffering gave over.

No grain sown in holy earth was his, nor other food
of all enjoyed by us, men who live by labor,
save when with the feathered arrows shot by the quick bow   710
he got him fodder for his belly.
Alas, poor soul,
that never in ten years' length
enjoyed a drink of wine
but looked always for the standing pools
and approached them.
But now he will end fortunate. He has fallen in
with the son of good men. He will be great, after it all.   720
Our prince in his seaworthy craft will carry him
after the fulness of many months, to his father's home
in the country of the Malian nymphs,
by the banks of the Spercheius,

where the hero of the bronze shield ascended
to all the Gods, ablaze in holy fire
above the ridges of Oeta.

Neoptolemus
    Come if you will, then. Why have you nothing to say?   730
    Why do you stand, in silence transfixed?

Philoctetes
    Oh! Oh!

Neoptolemus
    What is it?

Philoctetes
                Nothing to be afraid of. Come on, boy.

Neoptolemus
    Is it the pain of your inveterate sickness?

Philoctetes
    No, no, indeed not. Just now I think I feel better.
    O Gods!

Neoptolemus
    Why do you call on the Gods with cries of distress?

Philoctetes
    That they may come as healers, come with gentleness.
    Oh! Oh!

Neoptolemus
    What ails you? Tell me; do not keep silence.   740
    You are clearly in some pain.

Philoctetes
    I am lost, boy.
    I will not be able to hide it from you longer.
    Oh! Oh!
    It goes through me, right through me!
    Miserable, miserable!
    I am lost, boy. I am being eaten up. Oh!

By God, if you have a sword, ready to hand, use it!
Strike the end of my foot. Strike it off, I tell you, now.
Do not spare my life. Quick, boy, quick.   750

(*A long silence.*)

Neoptolemus

What is this thing that comes upon you suddenly,
that makes you cry and moan so?

Philoctetes

Do you know, boy?

Neoptolemus
What is it?

Philoctetes

Do you know, boy?

Neoptolemus

What do you mean?

I do not know.

Philoctetes

Surely you know. Oh! Oh!

Neoptolemus
The terrible burden of your sickness.

Philoctetes
Terrible it is, beyond words' reach. But pity me.

Neoptolemus
What shall I do?

Philoctetes

Do not be afraid and leave me.
She comes from time to time, perhaps when she has had
her fill of wandering in other places.

Neoptolemus
You most unhappy man,
you that have endured all agonies, lived through them,   760
shall I take hold of you? Shall I touch you?

Philoctetes

    Not that, above everything. But take this bow,
    as you asked to do just now, until the pain,
    the pain of my sickness, that is now upon me, grows less.
    Keep the bow, guard it safely. Sleep comes upon me
    when the attack is waning. The pain will not end till then.
    But you must let me sleep quietly.
    If they should come in the time when I sleep,
    by the Gods I beg you do not give up my bow   770
    willingly or unwillingly to anyone.
    And let no one trick you out of it, lest you prove
    a murderer—your own and mine that kneeled to you.

Neoptolemus

    I shall take care; be easy about that. It shall not pass
    except to your hands and to mine. Give it to me now,
    and may good luck go with it!

Philoctetes

                  Here,
    take it, boy. Bow in prayer to the Gods' envy
    that the bow may not be to you a sorrow
    nor as it was to me and its former master.

Neoptolemus

    You Gods, grant us both this and grant us
    a journey speedy with a prosperous wind   780
    to where God sends us and our voyage holds.

Philoctetes

    An empty prayer, I am afraid, boy:
    the blood is trickling, dripping murderously
    from its deep spring. I look for something new.
    It is coming now, coming. Ah!
    You have the bow. Do not go away from me.
        Ah!
    O man of Cephallenia, would it were you,
    Would it were your breast that the pains transfix.
        Ah!   790

Agamemnon and Menelaus, my two generals,
would it were your two bodies that had fed
this sickness for as long as mine has. Ah!

Death, death, how is it that I can call on you,
always, day in, day out, and you cannot come to me?
Boy, my good boy, take up this body of mine
and burn it on what they call the Lemnian fire.   800
I had the resolution once to do this for another,
the son of Zeus, and so obtained the arms
that you now hold. What do you say?
What do you say? Nothing? Where are you, boy?

Neoptolemus
  I have been in pain for you; I have been
  in sorrow for your pain.

Philoctetes
  No, boy, keep up your heart. She is quick in coming
  and quick to go. Only I entreat you, do not
  leave me alone.

Neoptolemus
  Do not be afraid. We shall stay.   810

Philoctetes
  You will?

Neoptolemus
  You may be sure of it.

Philoctetes
  Your oath,
  I do not think it fit to put you to your oath.

Neoptolemus
  I *may* not go without you, Philoctetes.

Philoctetes
  Give me your hand upon it.

Neoptolemus
　Here I give it you,
　to remain.

Philoctetes
　Now—take me away from here—

Neoptolemus
　　　　　　　　What do you mean?

Philoctetes
　　　　　　　　　　　　　　　Up, up.

Neoptolemus
　What madness is upon you? Why do you look
　on the sky above us?

Philoctetes
　　　　　　Let me go, let me go.

Neoptolemus
　Where?

Philoctetes
　　　　Oh, let me go.

Neoptolemus
　　　　Not I.

Philoctetes
　You will kill me if you touch me.

Neoptolemus
　Now I shall let you go, now you are calmer.

Philoctetes
　Earth, take my body, dying as I am.
　The pain no longer lets me stand.　　　　　　　　　　　820

Neoptolemus
　In a little while, I think,
　sleep will come on this man. His head is nodding.
　The sweat is soaking all his body over,
　and a black flux of blood and matter has broken
　out of his foot. Let us leave him quiet, friends,
　until he falls asleep.

Chorus

Sleep that knows not pain nor suffering
kindly upon us, Lord,
kindly, kindly come.
Spread your enveloping radiance,   830
as now, over his eyes.
Come, come, Lord Healer.

Boy, look to your standing,
look to your going, look to your plans
for the future. Do you see? He sleeps.
What is it we are waiting to do?
Ripeness that holds decision over all things
wins many a victory suddenly.

Neoptolemus

Yes, it is true he hears nothing, but I see we have hunted in vain,
vainly have captured our quarry the bow, if we sail without him.   840
His is the crown of victory, him the God said we must bring.
Shame shall be ours if we boast and our lies still leave victory
    unwon.

Chorus

Boy, to all of this the God shall look.
Answer me gently;
low, low, whisper,
whisper, boy.
The sleep of a sick man has keen eyes.
It is a sleep unsleeping.

But to the limits of what you can,
look to this, look to this secretly,   850
how you may do it.
You know of whom I speak.
If your mind holds the same purpose touching this man,
the wise can see trouble and no way to cure it.
It is a fair wind, boy, a fair wind:
the man is eyeless and helpless,

outstretched under night's blanket—
asleep in the sun is good—
neither of foot nor of hand nor of anything is he master,   860
but is even as one that lies in Death's house.
Look to it, look if what you say
is seasonable. As far as my mind,
boy, can grasp it, best is the trouble taken
that causes the least fear.

Neoptolemus

Quiet, I tell you! Are you mad? He is stirring,
his eyes are stirring; he is raising his head.

Philoctetes

Blessed the light that comes after my sleep,
blessed the watching of friends.
I never would have hoped this,
that you would have the pity of heart to support   870
my afflictions, that you should stand by me and help.
The Atridae, those brave generals, were not so,
they could not so easily put up with me.
You have a noble nature, Neoptolemus,
and noble were your parents. You have made light
of all of this—the offense of my cries and the smell.
And now, since it would seem I can forget
my sickness for a while and rest, raise me yourself,
raise me up, boy, and set me on my feet,
that when my weariness releases me,
we can go to the ship and sail without delay.   880

Neoptolemus

I am glad to see you unexpectedly,
eyes open, free of pain, still with the breath of life.
With suffering like yours, all the signs pointed
to your being dead. Now, lift yourself up.
If you would rather, these men will lift you. They
will spare no trouble, since you and I are agreed.

Philoctetes
    Thanks, boy. Lift me yourself, as you thought of it.
    Do not trouble them, let them not be disquieted   890
    before they need by the foul smell of me; living
    on board with me will try their patience enough.

Neoptolemus
    Very well, then; stand on your feet; take hold yourself.

Philoctetes
    Do not be afraid; old habit will help me up.

Neoptolemus
    Now is the moment. What shall I do from now on?

Philoctetes
    What is it, boy? Where are your words straying?

Neoptolemus
    I do not know what to say. I am at a loss.

Philoctetes
    Why are you at a loss? Do not say so, boy.

Neoptolemus
    It is indeed my case.

Philoctetes
    Is it disgust at my sickness? Is it this   900
    that makes you shrink from taking me?

Neoptolemus
    All is disgust when one leaves his own nature
    and does things that misfit it.

Philoctetes
    It is not unlike your father, either in word
    or in act, to help a good man.

Neoptolemus
    I shall be shown to be dishonorable:
    I am afraid of that.

Philoctetes

    Not in your present actions. Your words make me hesitate.

Neoptolemus

    Zeus, what must I do? Twice be proved base,
    hiding what I should not, saying what is most foul?

Philoctetes

    Unless I am wrong, here is a man who will   910
    betray me, leave me—so it seems—and sail away.

Neoptolemus

    Not I; I will not leave you. To your bitterness,
    I shall send you on a journey—and I dread this.

Philoctetes

    What are you saying, boy? I do not understand.

Neoptolemus

    I will not hide anything. You must sail to Troy
    to the Achaeans, join the army of the Atridae.

Philoctetes

    What! What can you mean?

Neoptolemus

               Do not cry yet
    until you learn.

Philoctetes

    Learn what? What would you do with me?

Neoptolemus

    First save you from this torture, then with you
    go and lay waste the land of Troy.   920

Philoctetes

              You would?
    This is, in truth, what you intend?

Neoptolemus

            Necessity,
    a great necessity compels it. Do not be angry.

Philoctetes

    Then I am lost. I am betrayed. Why, stranger,
    have you done this to me? Give me back my bow.

Neoptolemus

    That I cannot. Justice and interest
    make me obedient to those in authority.

Philoctetes

    You fire, you every horror, most hateful engine
    of ruthless mischief, what have you done to me,
    what treachery! Have you no shame to see me
    that kneeled to you, entreated you, hard of heart?   930

    You robbed me of my livelihood, taking my bow.
    Give it back, I beg you, give it back, I pray, my boy!
    By your father's Gods, do not take my livelihood.
    He does not say a word,
    but turns away his eyes. He will not give it up.

    Caverns and headlands, dens of wild creatures,
    you jutting broken crags, to you I raise my cry—
    there is no one else that I can speak to—
    and you have always been there, have always heard me,
    Let me tell you what he has done to me, this boy,   940
    Achilles' son. He swore to bring me home;
    he brings me to Troy. He gave me his right hand,
    then took and keeps my sacred bow,
    the bow of Heracles, the son of Zeus,
    and means to show it to the Argives,
    as though in me he had conquered a strong man,
    as though he led me captive to his power.
    He does not know he is killing one that is dead,
    a kind of vaporous shadow, a mere wraith.
    Had I had my strength, he had not conquered me,
    for, even as I am, it was craft that did it.
    I have been deceived and am lost.
    What can I do?

Give it back. Be your true self again. Will you not? 950
No word. Then I am nothing.

Two doors cut in the rock, to you again,
again I come, enter again, unarmed,
no means to feed myself! Here in this passage
I shall shrivel to death alone. I shall kill no more,
neither winged bird nor wild thing of the hills
with this my bow. I shall myself in death
be a feast for those that fed me. Those that I hunted
shall be my hunters now.
Life for the life I took, I shall repay
at the hands of this man that seemed to know no harm. 960

My curse upon your life!—but not yet still
until I know if you will change again;
if you will not, may an evil death be yours!

Chorus

What shall we do? Shall we sail? Shall we do as he asks?
Prince, it is you must decide.

Neoptolemus

A kind of compassion,
a terrible compassion, has come upon me
for him. I have felt for him all the time.

Philoctetes

Pity me, boy, by the Gods; do not bring on yourself
men's blame for your crafty victory over me.

Neoptolemus

What shall I do? I would I had never left
Scyrus, so hateful is what I face now. 970

Philoctetes

You are not bad yourself; by bad men's teaching
you came to practice your foul lesson. Leave it to others
such as it suits, and sail away. Give me my arms.

Neoptolemus

What shall we do, men?

(*Odysseus appears.*)

Odysseus

Scoundrel, what are you doing? Give me those arms.

Philoctetes

Who is this? Is that Odysseus' voice?

Odysseus

It is.

Odysseus certainly; you can see him here.

Philoctetes

Then I have been sold indeed; I am lost. It was he
who took me prisoner, robbed me of my arms.

Odysseus

Yes, I, I and no other. I admit that.   980

Philoctetes

Boy, give me back my bow, give it back to me.

Odysseus

That he will never
be able to do now, even if he wishes it.
And you must come with the bow, or these will
bring you.

Philoctetes

Your wickedness and impudence are without limit.
Will these men bring me, then, against my will?

Odysseus

Yes, if you do not come with a good grace.

Philoctetes

O land of Lemnos and all mastering brightness,
Hephaestus-fashioned, must I indeed bear this,
that he, Odysseus, drags me from you with violence?

Odysseus

It is Zeus, I would have you know, Zeus this land's ruler,
who has determined. I am only his servant.   990

Philoctetes

    Hateful creature,
    what things you can invent! You plead the Gods
    to screen your actions and make the Gods out liars.

Odysseus

    They speak the truth. The road must be traveled.

Philoctetes

    I say No.

Odysseus

             I say Yes. You must listen.

Philoctetes

    Are we slaves and not free? Is it as such
    our fathers have begotten us?

Odysseus

             No, but as equals
    of the best, with whom it is destined you must take Troy,
    dig her down stone by stone.

Philoctetes

    Never, I would rather suffer anything than this.
    There is still my steep and rugged precipice here.   1000

Odysseus

    What do you mean to do?

Philoctetes

             Throw myself down,
    shatter my head upon the rock below.

Odysseus

    Hold him. Take this solution out of his power.

Philoctetes

    Hands of mine, quarry of Odysseus' hunting,
    now suffer in your lack of the loved bowstring!

    You who have never had a healthy thought
    nor noble, you Odysseus, how you have hunted me,
    how you have stolen upon me with this boy

as your shield, because I did not know him, one
that is no mate for you but worthy of me,
who knows nothing but to do what he was bidden,   1010
and now, you see, is suffering bitterly
for his own faults and what he brought on me.
Your shabby, slit-eyed soul taught him step by step
to be clever in mischief against his nature and will.
Now it is my turn, now to my sorrow you have me
bound hand and foot, intend to take me away,
away from this shore on which you cast me once
without friends or comrades or city, a dead man among the living.

My curse on you! I have often cursed you before,
but the Gods give me nothing that is sweet to me.   1020
You have joy to be alive, and I have sorrow
because my very life is linked to this pain,
laughed at by you and your two generals,
the sons of Atreus whom you serve in this.
And yet, when you sailed with them, it was by constraint
and trickery, while I came of my own free will
with seven ships, to my undoing, I
whom they dishonored and cast away—
you say it was they that did it and they you.

But now why are you taking me? For what?
I am nothing now. To you all I have long been dead.   1030
God-hated wretch, how is it that now I am not
lame and foul-smelling? How can you burn your sacrifice
to God if I sail with you? Pour your libations?
This was your excuse for casting me away.

May death in ugly form come on you! It will so come,
for you have wronged me, if the Gods care for justice.
And I know that they do care for it, for at present
you never would have sailed here for my sake
and my happiness, had not the goad of God,

a need of me, compelled you.
Land of my fathers, Gods that look on men's deeds, 1040
take vengeance on these men, in your own good time,
upon them all, if you have pity on me!
Wretchedly as I live, if I saw them
dead, I could dream that I was free of my sickness.

Chorus

He is a hard man, Odysseus, this stranger,
and hard his words: no yielding to suffering in them.

Odysseus

If I had the time, I have much I could say to him.
As it is, there is only one thing. As the occasion
demands, such a one am I.
When there is a competition of men just and good, 1050
you will find none more scrupulous than myself.
What I seek in everything is to win
except in your regard: I willingly yield to you now.

Let him go, men. Do not lay a finger on him.
Let him stay here. We have these arms of yours
and do not need you, Philoctetes.
Teucer is with us who has the skill and I,
who, I think, am no meaner master of them
and have as straight an aim. Why do we need you?
Farewell: pace Lemnos. Let us go. Perhaps 1060
your prize will bring me the honor you should have had.

Philoctetes

What shall I do? Will you appear
before the Argives in the glory of my arms?

Odysseus

Say nothing further to me. I am going.

Philoctetes

Your voice has no word for me, son of Achilles?
Will you go away in silence?

Odysseus
Come, Neoptolemus.
Do not look at him. Your generosity
may spoil our future.

Philoctetes
You, too, men, will you go   1070
and leave me alone? Do you, too, have no pity?

Chorus
This young man is our captain. What he says to you
we say as well.

Neoptolemus (to the Chorus)
Odysseus will tell me
that I am full of pity for him. Still
remain, if he will have it so, as long
as it takes the sailors to ready the tackle
and until we have made our prayer to the Gods.
Perhaps, in the meantime, he will have better thoughts
about us. Let us go, Odysseus.
You, when we call you, be quick to come.   1080
(*Exeunt Odysseus and Neoptolemus.*)

Philoctetes
Hollow in the rock, hollow cave, sun-warmed, ice cold,
I was not destined, after all, ever to leave you.
Still with me, you shall be witness to my dying.
Passageway, crowded with my cries of pain,
what shall be, now again, my daily life with you?
What hope shall I find of food to keep my wretched life alive?   1090
Above me, in the clouds, down the shrill winds
the birds; no strength in me to stop them.

Chorus
It was you who doomed yourself,
man of hard fortune. From no other,
from nothing stronger, came your mischance.
When you could have chosen wisdom,

with better opportunity before you,
you chose the worse.   1100

Philoctetes

Sorrow, sorrow is mine. Suffering has broken me,
who must live henceforth alone from all the world,
must live here and die here;
no longer bringing home food nor winning
it with strong hands. Unmarked, the crafty words   1110
of a treacherous heart stole on me. Would I might see him,
contriver of this trap,
for as long as I am, condemned to pain.

Chorus

It was the will of the Gods
that has subdued you, no craft
to which my hand was lent.   1120
Turn your hate, your ill-omened curses, elsewhere.
This indeed lies near my heart,
that you should not reject my friendship.

Philoctetes

By the shore of the gray sea he sits and laughs at me.
He brandishes in his hand the weapon which kept me alive,
which no one else had handled. Bow that I loved,
forged from the hands that loved you, if you could feel,
you would see me with pity, successor to Heracles,   1130
that used you and shall handle you no more.
You have found a new master, a man of craft, and shall be bent
    by him.
You shall see crooked deceits and the face of my hateful foe,
and a thousand ill things such as he contrived against me.

Chorus

A man should give careful heed to say what is just;   1140
and when he has said it, restrain his tongue from rancor and taunt.
Odysseus was one man, appointed by many,
by their command he has done this, a service to his friends.

Philoctetes

    Birds my victims, tribes of bright-eyed wild creatures,
    tenants of these hills, you need not flee from me or my house.
    No more the strength of my hands, of my bow, is mine.   1150
    Come! It is a good time
    to glut yourselves freely on my discolored flesh.
    For shortly I shall die here. How shall I find means of life?
    Who can live on air without any of all that life-giving earth sup-
        plies?   1160

Chorus

    In the name of the gods, if there is anything that you hold in re-
        spect,
    draw near to a friend that approaches you in all sincerity.
    Know what you are doing, know it well.
    It lies with you to avoid your doom.
    It is a destiny pitiable to feed
    with your body. It cannot learn how
    to endure the thousand burdens with which it is coupled.

Philoctetes

    Again, again you have touched my old hurt,   1170
    for all that you are the best of those that came here.
    Why did you afflict me? What have you done to me?

Chorus

    What do you mean by this?

Philoctetes

    Yes, you have hoped to bring me
    to the hateful land of Troy.

Chorus

    I judge that to be best.

Philoctetes

    Then leave me now at once.

Chorus

    Glad news, glad news.
    I am right willing to obey you.
    Let us go now to our places in the ship.   1180

Philoctetes

No, by the God that listens to curses, do not go,
I beseech you.

Chorus

Be calm!

Philoctetes

Friends, stay!
I beg you to stay.

Chorus

Why do you call on us?

Philoctetes

It is the God, the God. I am destroyed.
My foot, what shall I do with this foot of mine
in the life I shall live hereafter?
Friends, come to me again.   1190

Chorus

What to do that is different
from the tenor of your former bidding?

Philoctetes

It is no occasion for anger
when a man crazy with storms of sorrow
speaks against his better judgment.

Chorus

Unhappy man, come with us, as we say.

Philoctetes

Never, never! That is my fixed purpose.
Not though the Lord of the Lightning, bearing his fiery bolts,
come against me, burning me
with flame and glare.
Let Ilium go down and all that under its walls   1200
had the heart to cast me away, crippled!
Friends, grant me one prayer only.

Chorus

What is it you would seek?

Philoctetes
　A sword, if you have got one,
　or an ax or some weapon—give it me!

Chorus
　What would you do with it?

Philoctetes
　　　　　　　Head and foot,
　head and foot, all of me, I would cut with my own hand.
　My mind is set on death, on death, I tell you.

Chorus
　Why this?　　　　　　　　　　　　　　　　　　　　1210

Philoctetes
　　　　　I would go seek my father.

Chorus
　Where?

Philoctetes
　　　　In the house of death.
　He is no longer in the light.
　City of my fathers, would I could see you.
　I who left your holy streams,
　to go help the Greeks, my enemies,
　and now am nothing any more.

Chorus
　I should have been by now on my way to the ship,
　did I not see Odysseus coming here　　　　　　　　1220
　and with him Neoptolemus.

　　　(*Enter Odysseus and Neoptolemus in front of the cave, talking.*
　　　　　　　　　Philoctetes withdraws into the cave.)

Odysseus (to Neoptolemus)
　You have turned back, there is hurry in your step.
　Will you not tell me why?

Neoptolemus
　I go to undo the wrong that I have done.

Odysseus
  A strange thing to say! What wrong was that?

Neoptolemus
  I did wrong when I obeyed you and the Greeks.

Odysseus
  What did we make you do that was unworthy?

Neoptolemus
  I practiced craft and treachery with success.

Odysseus
  On whom? Would you do some rash thing now?

Neoptolemus
  Nothing rash. I am going to give something back.   1230

Odysseus
  What? I am afraid to hear what you will say.

Neoptolemus
  Back to the man I took it from, this bow.

Odysseus
  You cannot mean you are going to give it back.

Neoptolemus
  Just that. To my shame, unjustly, I obtained it.

Odysseus
  Can you mean this in earnest?

Neoptolemus
                              Yes, unless
  it is not in earnest to tell you the truth.

Odysseus
  What do you mean, Neoptolemus, what are you saying?

Neoptolemus
  Must I tell you the same story twice or thrice?

Odysseus
  I should prefer not to have heard it once.

Neoptolemus

You can rest easy. You have now heard everything. 1240

Odysseus

Then there is someone who will prevent its execution.

Neoptolemus

Who will that be?

Odysseus

The whole assembly
of the Greeks and among them I myself.

Neoptolemus

You are a clever man, Odysseus, but
this is not a clever saying.

Odysseus

In your own case
neither the words nor the acts are clever.

Neoptolemus

Still
if they are just, they are better than clever.

Odysseus

How can it be just to give to him again
what you won by my plans?

Neoptolemus

It was a sin,
a shameful sin, which I shall try to retrieve.

Odysseus

Have you no fear of the Greeks if you do this? 1250

Neoptolemus

I have no fear of anything you can do,
when I act with justice; nor shall I yield to force.

Odysseus

Then we shall fight
not with the Trojans but with you.

Neoptolemus
  Let that be as it will.

Odysseus
                  Do you see my hand,
  reaching for the sword?

Neoptolemus
                  You shall see me do as much
  and that at once.

Odysseus
                  I will let you alone;
  I shall go and tell this to the assembled Greeks,
  and they will punish you.

Neoptolemus
                  That is very prudent.
  If you are always as prudent as this,
  perhaps you will keep out of trouble.   1260

                              (*Exit Odysseus.*)

  I call on you, Philoctetes, son of Poias,
  come from your cave.

                  (*Philoctetes appears at the mouth of the cave.*)

Philoctetes
                  What cry is this at the door?
  Why do you call me forth, friends? What would you have?
  Ah! This is a bad thing. Can there be some fresh mischief
  you come to do, to top what you have done?

Neoptolemus
  Be easy. I would only have you listen.

Philoctetes
  I am afraid of that.
  I heard you before, and they were good words, too.
  But they destroyed me when I listened.

Neoptolemus
  Is there no place, then, for repentance?   1270

Philoctetes

You were just such a one in words when you stole my bow,
inspiring confidence, but sly and treacherous.

Neoptolemus

I am not such now. But I would hear from you
whether you are entirely determined
to remain here, or will you go with us?

Philoctetes

Oh, stop! You need not say another word.
All that you say will be wasted.

Neoptolemus

You are determined?

Philoctetes

            More than words can declare.

Neoptolemus

I wish that I could have persuaded you.
If I cannot speak to some purpose, I have done.

Philoctetes

You will say it all   1280
to no purpose, for you will never win my heart
to friendship with you, who have stolen my life
by treachery, and then came and preached to me,
bad son of a noble father. Cursed be you all,
first the two sons of Atreus, then Odysseus,
and then yourself!

Neoptolemus

            Do not curse me any more.
Take your bow. Here I give it to you.

Philoctetes

What can you mean? Is this another trick?

Neoptolemus

No. That I swear by the holy majesty
of Zeus on high!

Philoctetes

These are good words, 1290
if only they are honest.

Neoptolemus

The fact is plain.
Stretch out your hand; take your own bow again.

(Odysseus appears.)

Odysseus

I forbid it, as the Gods are my witnesses,
in the name of the Atridae and the Greeks.

Philoctetes

Whose voice is that, boy? Is it Odysseus?

Odysseus

Himself and near at hand.
And I shall bring you to the plains of Troy
in your despite, whether Achilles' son
will have it so or not.

Philoctetes

You will rue your word
if this arrow flies straight.

Neoptolemus

No, Philoctetes, no! 1300

Do not shoot.

Philoctetes

Let me go, let go my hand, dear boy.

Neoptolemus

I will not.

(Exit Odysseus.)

Philoctetes

Why did you prevent me killing my enemy,
with my bow, a man that hates me?

Neoptolemus

This is not to our glory, neither yours nor mine.

Philoctetes

> Well, know this much, that the princes of the army,
> the lying heralds of the Greeks, are cowards
> when they meet the spear, however keen in words.

Neoptolemus

> Let that be. You have your bow. There is no further cause
> for anger or reproach against me.

Philoctetes

> None.
>
> You have shown your nature and true breeding,   1310
> son of Achilles and not Sisyphus.
> Your father, when he still was with the living,
> was the most famous of them, as now he is of the dead.

Neoptolemus

> I am happy to hear you speak well of my father
> and of myself. Now listen to my request.
> The fortunes that the Gods give to us men
> we must bear under necessity.
> But men that cling wilfully to their sufferings
> as you do, no one may forgive nor pity.   1320
> Your anger has made a savage of you. You will not
> accept advice, although the friend advises
> in pure goodheartedness. You loathe him, think
> he is your enemy and hates you.
> Yet I will speak. May Zeus, the God of Oaths,
> be my witness! Mark it, Philoctetes, write it in your mind.
> You are sick and the pain of the sickness is of God's sending
> because you approached the Guardian of Chryse,
> the serpent that with secret watch protects
> her roofless shrine to keep it from violation.
> You will never know relief while the selfsame sun   1330
> rises before you here, sets there again,
> until you come of your own will to Troy,
> and meet among us the Asclepiadae,

who will relieve your sickness; then with the bow
and by my side, you will become Troy's conqueror.

I will tell you how I know that this is so.
There was a man of Troy who was taken prisoner,
Helenus, a good prophet. He told us clearly
how it should be and said, besides, that all Troy   1340
must fall this summer. He said, "If I prove wrong
you may kill me."
Now since you know this, yield and be gracious.
It is a glorious heightening of gain.
First, to come into hands that can heal you,
and then be judged pre-eminent among the Greeks,
winning the highest renown among them, taking
Troy that has cost infinity of tears.

Philoctetes

Hateful life, why should I still be alive and seeing?
Why not be gone to the dark?
What shall I do? How can I distrust   1350
his words who in friendship has counseled me?
Shall I then yield? If I do so, how come
before the eyes of men so miserable?
Who will say word of greeting to me?
Eyes of mine, that have seen all, can you endure
to see me living with my murderers,
the sons of Atreus? With cursed Odysseus?
It is not the sting of wrongs past
but what I must look for in wrongs to come.
Men whose wit has been mother of villainy once   1360
have learned from it to be evil in all things.
I must indeed wonder at yourself in this.
You should not yourself be going to Troy
but rather hold me back. They have done you wrong
and robbed you of your father's arms. Will you go and help them
fight and compel me to the like?
No, boy, no; take me home as you promised.

Remain in Scyrus yourself; let these bad men
die in their own bad fashion. We shall both thank you,   1370
I and your father. You will not then, by helping
the wicked, seem to be like them.

Neoptolemus

What you say
is reasonable; yet I wish that you would trust
the Gods, my word, and, with me as friend, fare forth.

Philoctetes

What, to the plains of Troy, to the cursed sons
of Atreus with this suffering foot of mine?

Neoptolemus

To those that shall give you redress,
that shall save you and your rotting foot from its disease.

Philoctetes

Giver of dread advice, what have you said!   1380

Neoptolemus

What I see fulfilled will be best for you and me.

Philoctetes

And saying it, do you not blush before God?

Neoptolemus

Why should one feel ashamed to do good to another?

Philoctetes

Is the good for the Atridae or for me?

Neoptolemus

I am your friend, and the word I speak is friendly.

Philoctetes

How, then, do you wish to betray me to my enemies?

Neoptolemus

Sir, learn not to be defiant in misfortune.

Philoctetes

You will ruin me, I know it by your words.

Neoptolemus
Not I. You do not understand, I think.

Philoctetes
Do I not know the Atridae cast me away?   1390

Neoptolemus
They cast you away; will, now again, restore you.

Philoctetes
Never, if of my will I must see Troy.

Neoptolemus
What shall we do, since I cannot convince you
of anything I say? It is easiest for me
to leave my argument, and you to live,
as you are living, with no hope of cure.

Philoctetes
Let me suffer what I must suffer.
But what you promised to me and touched my hand,
to bring me home, fulfil it for me, boy.
Do not delay, do not speak again of Troy   1400
I have had enough of sorrow and lamentation.

Neoptolemus
If you will then, let us go.

Philoctetes
Noble is the word you spoke.

Neoptolemus
Brace yourself, stand firm on your feet.

Philoctetes
To the limit of my strength.

Neoptolemus
How shall I avoid the blame of the Greeks?

Philoctetes
Give it no thought.

Neoptolemus
    What if they come and harry my country?

Philoctetes
    I shall be there.

Neoptolemus
    What help will you be able to give me?

Philoctetes
    With the bow of Heracles.

Neoptolemus
    Will you?

Philoctetes
    I shall drive them from it.

Neoptolemus
    If you will do what you say,
    come now; kiss this ground farewell, and come with me.

      (*Heracles appears standing on the rocks above the cave of Philoctetes.*)

Heracles
    Not yet, not until you have heard
    my words, son of Poias.
    I am the voice of Heracles in your ears;   1410
    I am the shape of Heracles before you.
    It is to serve you I come and leave my home among the dead.
    I come
    to tell you of the plans of Zeus for you,
    to turn you back from the road you go upon.
    Hearken to my words.

    Let me reveal to you my own story first,
    let me show the tasks and sufferings that were mine,
    and, at the last, the winning of deathless merit.   1420
    All this you can see in me now.
    All this must be your suffering too,
    the winning of a life to an end in glory,
    out of this suffering. Go with this man to Troy.

First, you shall find there the cure of your cruel sickness,
and then be adjudged best warrior among the Greeks.
Paris, the cause of all this evil, you shall kill
with the bow that was mine. Troy you shall take.
You shall win the prize of valor from the army
and shall send the spoils to your home,
to your father Poias, and the land of your fathers, Oeta.   1430
From the spoils of the campaign you must dedicate
some, on my pyre, in memory of my bow.

Son of Achilles, I have the same words for you.
You shall not have the strength to capture Troy
without this man, nor he without you,
but, like twin lions hunting together,
he shall guard you, you him. I shall send Asclepius
to Ilium to heal his sickness. Twice
must Ilium fall to my bow. But this remember,   1440
when you shall come to sack that town, keep holy in the sight of
    God.
All else our father Zeus thinks of less moment.
Holiness does not die with the men that die.
Whether they die or live, it cannot perish.

Philoctetes
    Voice that stirs my yearning when I hear,
    form lost for so long,
    I shall not disobey.

Neoptolemus
    Nor I.

Heracles
    Do not tarry then.
    Season and the tide are hastening you on your way.   1450

Philoctetes
    Lemnos, I call upon you:
    Farewell, cave that shared my watches,
    nymphs of the meadow and the stream,

the deep male growl of the sea-lashed headland
where often, in my niche within the rock,
my head was wet with fine spray,
where many a time in answer to my crying
in the storm of my sorrow the Hermes mountain sent its echo! 1460
Now springs and Lycian well, I am leaving you,
leaving you.
I had never hoped for this.
Farewell Lemnos, sea-encircled,
blame me not but send me on my way
with a fair voyage to where a great destiny
carries me, and the judgment of friends and the all-conquering
Spirit who has brought this to pass.

Chorus

Let us go all
when we have prayed to the nymphs of the sea 1470
to bring us safe to our homes. 1471